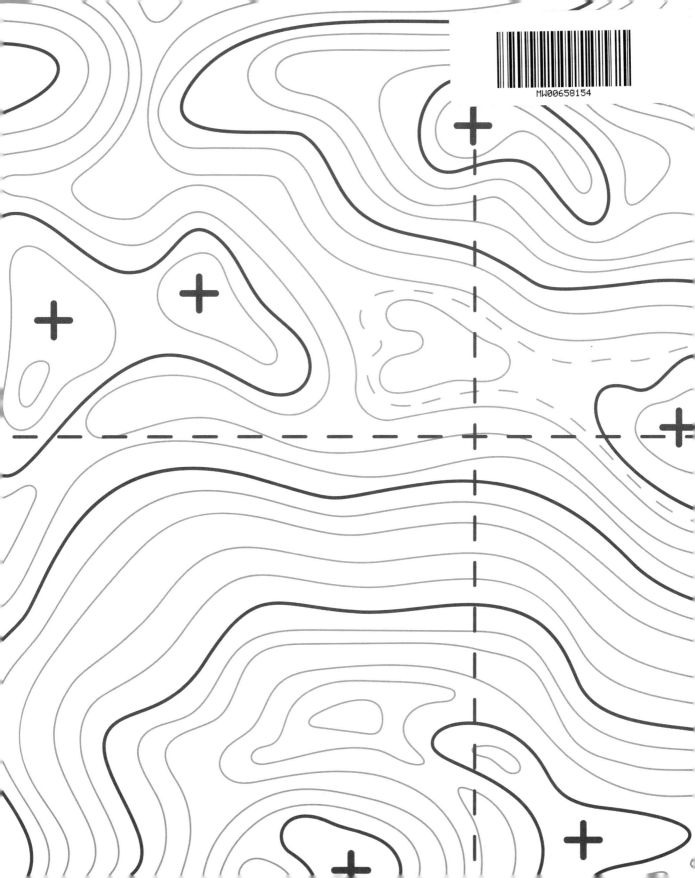

THRUHIKERS
A GUIDE TO LIFE ON THE TRAIL

RENEE MILLER & TIM BEISSINGER

THRUHIKERS

A GUIDE TO LIFE ON THE TRAIL

Publisher Mike Sanders
Art & Design Director William Thomas
Editorial Director Ann Barton
Senior Editor Olivia Peluso
Assistant Director of Art & Design Rebecca Batchelor
Photographer Nader Khouri
Illustrator Kendra "Skunkbear" Allenby
Food Stylist Jillian Knox
Recipe Tester Patricia Sebben Malone
Copyeditor Christy Wagner
Proofreader Georgette Beatty
Indexer Johnna VanHoose Dinse

First American Edition, 2024
Published in the United States by DK Publishing
1745 Broadway, 20th Floor, New York, NY 10019

The authorized representative in the EEA is Dorling Kindersley Verlag GmbH. Arnulfstr. 124, 80636 Munich, Germany

24 25 26 27 10 9 8 7 6 5 4 3 2 1
001–339919–Aug/2024

A catalog record for this book is available from the Library of Congress.
ISBN 978-0-74409-488-6

Printed and bound in China

www.dk.com

DEDICATION

This book is dedicated to long-distance trails, wilderness areas, and the people who build, maintain, protect, and preserve them.

CONTENTS

INTRODUCTION

Hi. We're Renee and Tim, two long-distance adventurers who love spending as much time outside as possible! Renee grew up in Wisconsin as an athlete, swimming and running from a young age. Tim grew up in Illinois, camping, fishing, and going on occasional group backpacking and canoeing trips with the Boy Scouts. We met at a football game at the University of Wisconsin–Madison and soon combined our hobbies. We spent our early relationship being athletic outside together, biking, swimming, and running as well as camping and hiking whenever we got the chance. We also volunteered with the Wisconsin Department of Natural Resources to help count wolves in the state.

As our relationship grew, the nature of our adventures did, too. We started going on longer backpacking trips and participating in endurance sports, including marathons and long-distance triathlons. We took what we learned about nutrition for endurance sports and built it into our approach to backpacking food. We began dehydrating our own meals and refined our recipes to ensure that each was filling and nutritious with a balance of carbohydrates, protein, vegetables, and flavor. With a bit of practice, we learned how to make dehydrated meals that are lighter weight, more nutritious, and less expensive than store-bought versions. And they taste much better, too!

Eventually, our careers took us to California, where we fell in love with the Pacific Crest Trail (PCT), which runs for 2,650 miles along the western edge of the United States, from Mexico, through the desert and high mountains of California, Oregon, and Washington and into Canada. Hiking the PCT became a dream, but we had no idea how we'd fit it into our busy lives and advancing careers. (Renee is a mechanical engineer, and Tim is a scientist who works on the genetics of plants.) We were able to find time to hike a two-week section of the PCT, starting just south of Yosemite National Park and continuing south about 200 miles. Experiencing the trail's remote beauty and wildlife, while being totally free for two whole weeks, was amazing. All we had to do every day was eat, drink, walk, and sleep. We loved it! But Renee, in particular, needed more. Two weeks just wasn't enough: She wanted to thruhike the whole trail, from start to finish.

As our careers progressed, we moved to Missouri, where we continued to squeeze in as many wilderness trips as possible. But we still craved a longer experience. After a few years, we decided it was foolish to put off until retirement something we wanted so badly. We had enough savings for the 4.5-month trip, so we decided to go for it and quit our jobs. Soon, we were back out on the PCT, and this time, we were hiking the whole way, from Mexico to Canada. Talk about a life-changing experience! Each day on the PCT felt like the best day of our lives. When we sent photos of our adventure to our families, they said they had never seen our smiles so big. Every morning we woke up not knowing where we'd camp that night, but we were carrying plenty of food and knew that there were enough water sources along the way for us to make it as far as our bodies would carry us. That connection to simple and basic human needs is difficult to replicate in off-trail life.

After completing the PCT, we realized that we didn't want it to be a once-in-a-lifetime experience. We needed to thruhike another trail! We moved again for our jobs, this time to Germany. (Renee was an engineer working on international building design and construction, and Tim worked as a professor and chair of plant breeding.) In Germany, we hiked more than 1,000 miles on long-distance trails. To bring the long-distance experience to more of Germany, we worked with a fellow hiker we had met on the PCT, Jonas "Parmesan" Traut, to develop and release a mapping app and guide for multiple German trails.

A few years later, we hiked the 3,100-mile Continental Divide Trail (CDT), which runs from Mexico to Canada across New Mexico, Colorado, Wyoming, Idaho, and Montana. We are among no more than a handful of people who have completed the CDT without deviating from the officially designated path. For our next challenge, we created our own route, the Pacific Northwest Circuit, which involved 1,500 miles of hiking in the Pacific Northwest followed by 1,200 miles of canoeing. We started at the Pacific Ocean, headed east along the Pacific Northwest Trail, and then walked north into Canada to the headwaters of the Columbia River. We then headed back west to the ocean by canoeing the entire length of the Columbia River. As of this writing, we have well over 10,000 miles of hiking and canoeing under our belts, with lots more to come!

Despite spending so much time outside, we've managed to maintain our careers. We've been lucky to have employers willing to let us work part-time and take leave for our several-months-long trips. We've also been willing to take risks by quitting our jobs, trusting that we'd find comparable or better positions after each adventure. And we've discovered a new facet of our careers: Since our time on the CDT, we have produced surprisingly popular short videos about our outdoor experiences, sharing them on social media. When we started filming, we had no idea that so many people would find the topic entertaining. Now, we are known as @thruhikers across social media platforms, where millions of people subscribe to our outdoor content, and we share additional information on our website, thruhikers.co. We are grateful that we have a platform to share what we've learned from our time in the outdoors and motivate others to get outside and enjoy everything it has to offer.

Our videos are almost entirely short-form (60 seconds or less), which leaves little time to go into the entire process of a topic or the finer details of preparing for, and enjoying, trips outside. All of our time in the outdoors has provided us with valuable tips, tricks, advice, and techniques that make the experience more enjoyable and more achievable. With this book, we want to share what we've learned, to help others have the best possible time when they head out. This means having trips that are simpler, less prone to mishaps, and more fun all around. The trips we go on are of every length and duration, from 1-mile hikes on local trails to multiple-month thruhikes covering thousands of miles.

This book is for anybody who wants to explore the outdoors. Whether you're gearing up for a day hike, preparing for your first night in a tent, or even if you're a seasoned pro with thousands of miles under your belt, we hope you'll find the information in this book useful to enhance your outdoor experience. In these pages, we walk you through the timeline of a trip: before the trail, on the trail, and after the trail. Before you get out on the trail, we'll take you through topics like how to plan your trip and the gear you'll need, and then we'll explore life on the trail, including camping, hygiene, interacting with animals, and Leave No Trace principles. The final part of the book provides recipes and guidance for dehydrating your own meals for outdoor adventures. We've found that planning and preparing meals ahead of time not only helps us get in the trip mindset, but also results in food that tastes great and fuels our bodies better. Throughout the book, we'll share some stories from our experience out on the trail that can help you plan your own adventures.

Let's get out there!

PART

1

BEFORE THE TRAIL

1

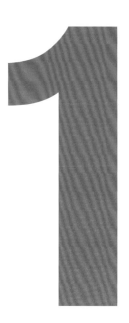

CHOOSING A TRIP

So you want to spend some time immersed in the outdoors. Wonderful! Whether your trip is short, medium, or long, we find that being outside is almost always more fun and exciting than being cooped up in a house or office. Before you pack your bags and head out, you first need to decide what kind of trip you want to go on, when you will go, and where you are going. Simply choosing a trip can be challenging—there are so many options to pick from! In this chapter, we describe different types of trips, potential regions for a trip, the way different agencies manage land, the positives and negatives that come with every season, and the benefit of going on practice trips if you're getting ready for bigger adventures.

TYPES OF TRIPS

There are many ways to get out and enjoy the outdoors, including day hiking, car camping, backpacking, and thruhiking. If you are curious about the outdoors but haven't spent much time outside, consider starting with a day hike. If you are interested in backpacking but have never slept outside before, consider trying a car camping trip first. If you love day hiking and car camping, consider an overnight backpacking trip. If you want to go on a thruhiking trip, like the Pacific Crest Trail (PCT) or Appalachian Trail (2,200 miles of trail through the Appalachian Mountains), consider trying a weeklong backpacking trip first. Let's review each type of trip so you can best determine which is right for you.

DAY HIKE: Day hiking is when you go out hiking, usually on a marked trail, and return home at night. The hike could be for an hour or the whole day. Little gear is required, other than hiking shoes, some water and snacks, and potentially extra clothing layers, depending on the weather. Day hiking can also be a nice option if you have only a few hours, if you prefer the comforts of a bed, or if you are passing through a new area and want to explore.

CAR CAMPING: Car camping involves loading all of the food and gear you require for one or more nights into your car, driving to a destination, and camping near your car. This could be at a designated campsite or campground, or it could be dispersed camping.

CAMPGROUND: Campgrounds usually have amenities, which could include water, toilets, trash service, picnic tables, fire rings, and power. Always check before you head out to determine what amenities your campground has. If the campground does not provide water, be sure to bring enough for your entire trip. If it doesn't provide trash service, bring all of your trash home with you.

DISPERSED CAMPING: Dispersed camping is camping outside of designated campgrounds and away from other campers. It usually offers no amenities, so you must be self-reliant. Be sure to bring enough water for your entire trip, and bring all of your trash home with you. Dispersed camping is usually done on public land, which is especially abundant in the western United States. Check the regulations and know the rules before you head out.

BACKPACKING: Backpacking involves loading all of the food and gear you require for one or more nights into a backpack and heading out. Backpacking trips can last for any number of days. Here are some types of routes to think about when planning a trip.

OUT AND BACK: Out-and-back routes involve backpacking out on a trail and then turning around and heading back in the opposite direction. The nice thing about an out-and-back trip is that if you aren't sure how many miles you'll be able to cover each day, you don't have to guess. Once you decide how long you want your trip to be, you can hike out for half of the total time and then hike back for the other half.

LOOP: Hikers often try to avoid hiking the same trail twice on a trip, as is done on an out-and-back trail. A loop trail starts and ends at the same place, forming a loop.

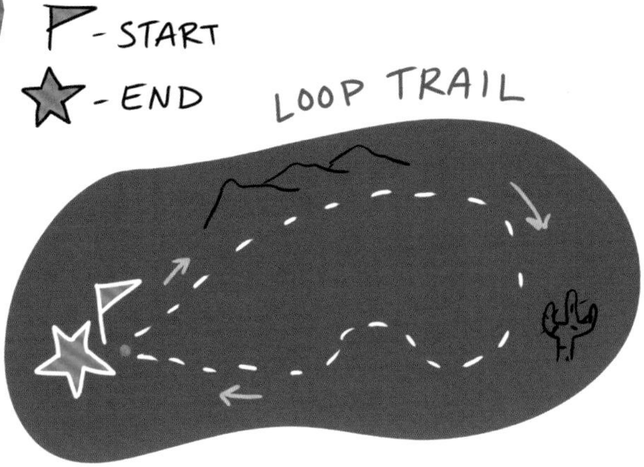

POINT TO POINT: This is when you backpack from one point to a different point (i.e., from where the trail crosses one road to where the trail crosses another road). This method requires a shuttle, car shuffle (parking a second car at your planned finish point), or hitchhiking.

LOLLIPOP: Sometimes, it's possible to combine an out-and-back hike with a loop to form a "lollipop" route. These take you out on a single trail and then have a loop that brings you back to the same trail.

BASE CAMP: This is when you backpack to a nice spot, set up a base camp, and then do one or more day hikes out from and back to your base camp. This can be nice because you don't need to carry all of your gear and food with you on your day hikes—you can leave it behind at camp. Be sure to store your food properly so animals don't get it. (See page 130 for more information on animal-proofing your campsite.)

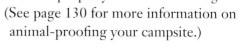

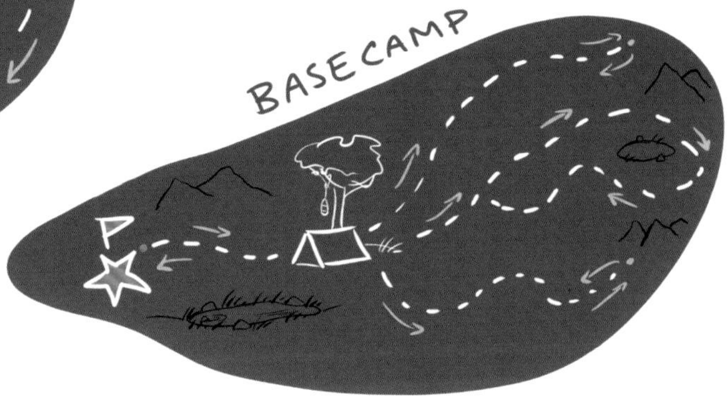

THRUHIKING: Thruhiking is when you backpack "through" an entire trail from beginning to end. Usually, thruhiking is associated with long-distance trails of 100 miles or more, but there is no strict distance minimum or maximum. Many famous thruhiking trails like the PCT take you from point A to point B, but some, such as the Tahoe Rim Trail (170 miles around the Lake Tahoe Basin) and Wonderland Trail (93 miles around Washington's Mount Rainier), are loops.

SECTION HIKING: Section hiking breaks a thruhike into more manageable parts and lets you tackle the trail one chunk at a time. It doesn't matter if you are doing day hikes, overnight trips, or a multiple-month segment of a longer trail. As long as you are considering your hike to be a section of a longer trail, it counts as a section hike.

Before going on a backpacking trip of any distance, it's a good idea to do some day hiking and a few nights of car camping to be sure you're comfortable sleeping outside with only a sleeping bag and tent around you. The outdoors has bugs, animals, noises, wind, and weather conditions that can take some getting used to. The nice thing about testing the waters with car camping is that you can bring as much stuff as you think you could possibly need, and if you don't enjoy the experience, you can simply drive home.

Assuming your car camping test runs go well and you're ready to give backpacking a try, it's time to choose a trip! For your first time backpacking, try not to be too ambitious. Backpackers of all skill levels (including us) often overestimate how many miles they can comfortably cover each day, and venturing out with a goal that's physically difficult to achieve can be frustrating and demoralizing. For your first few trips, it's a good idea to find relatively easy terrain and aim for no more than 5 to 8 miles per day. Keep your early trips short—weekend trips are a good way to start. As you gain experience, your body will become more accustomed to time on the trail, and you'll be able to increase your daily mileage and trip length accordingly. You may find that you love being outside on short trips but have no desire to travel farther or for longer. If so, that's fine! Or you may find that you want to spend more time heading deeper and deeper into the wilderness.

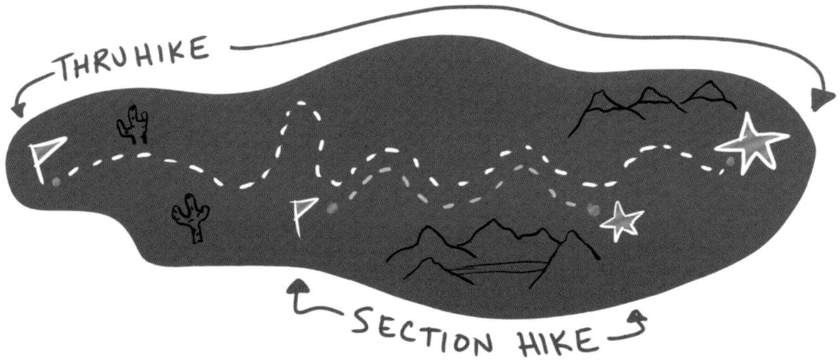

LOCATION & REGION

The location of a trip and the season in which you travel will dictate the experience you'll have, and some locations and seasons are definitely easier than others. Going on a trip near where you live means you'll be most familiar with the weather and animals you are likely to encounter, but traveling for an epic adventure is tons of fun, too. The different regions of the United States each have their own unique aspects to consider.

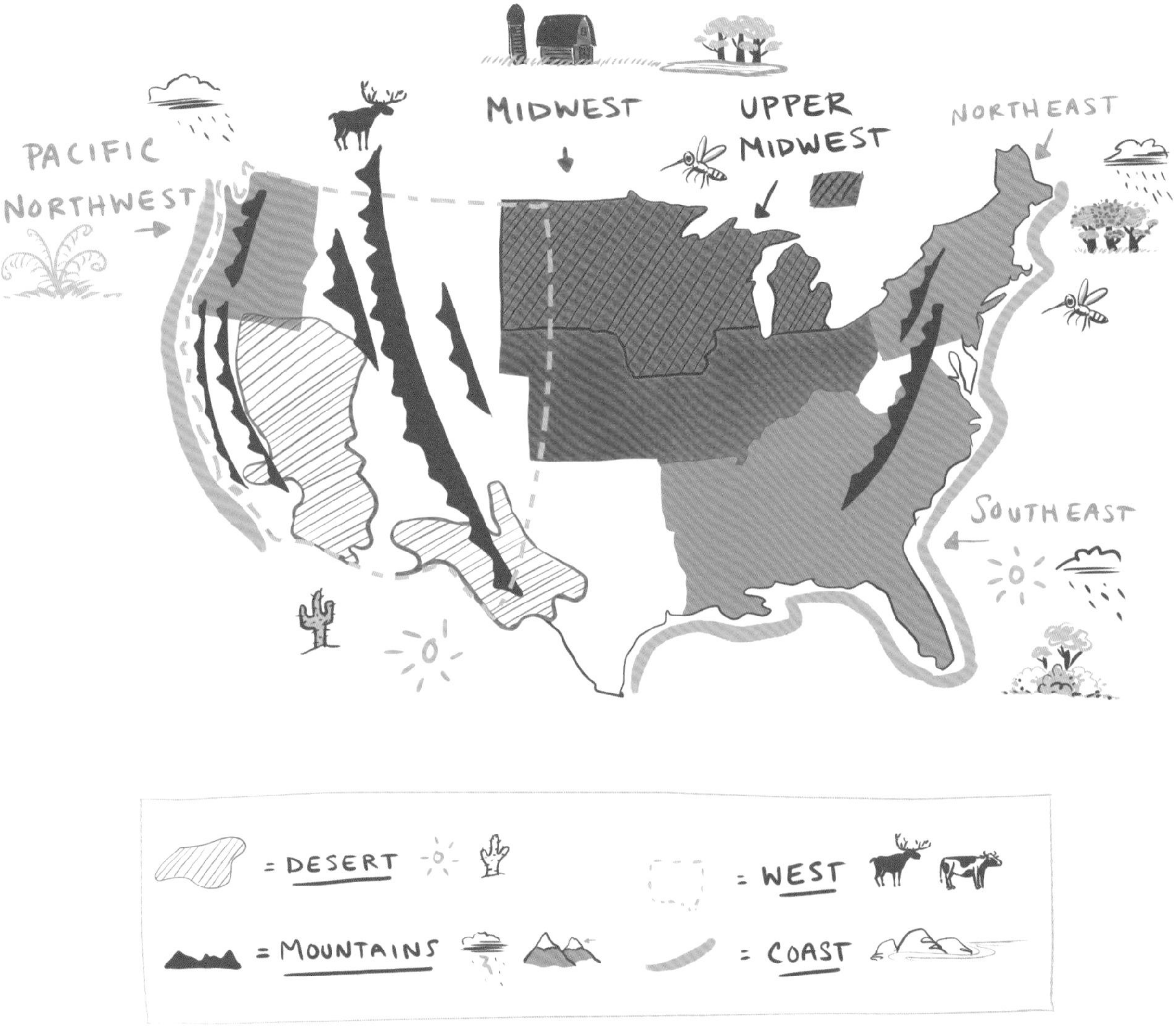

DESERT: The desert has a reputation for being harsh and difficult for backpacking trips. The heat and sparse water can be challenging, but the desert also offers unique facets that can make it an ideal place to backpack. Deserts have little rain (for much of the year) and fewer annoying insects like mosquitoes than most of the rest of the country. When it gets on your body and gear, the rocky and sandy desert soil is easier to deal with than the moist black dirt you might find in a dense forest. In the winter, mild temperatures in the desert can be much easier to deal with than the frigid cold elsewhere.

MOUNTAIN WEST: Backpacking is often associated with the mountains more than any other location. There are few things better than reaching the top of a mountain peak to look out in all directions at a vast mountain landscape. But mountain hiking isn't easy. Challenges include difficult terrain, snow that lingers even late into the summer, stream crossings, unexpected storms, and being far from civilization. If you venture into the mountains, you should be experienced, know your route well, and carry backup gear just in case conditions are worse than expected.

WEST: The western United States is unique due to its lack of precipitation and abundance of public land. Much of this region is characterized by wide open spaces and a lack of dense urban development. You can camp almost anywhere that is flat enough to set up a tent (see pages 25 and 128 for information about camping on public land). It is not uncommon to share the land with roaming cattle or, when you're lucky, wild mammals such as deer, coyotes, bison, and elk.

COAST: Remote coastal areas are exciting places to backpack. Being able to explore tide pools and observe sea life is unique to coastal hikes. Sandy beaches can provide an alternative to trails, but if you are walking on sand, expect to cover fewer miles per day because you'll walk slower on sand than on most other surfaces. Pay attention to the tides because certain routes may be passable only at low tide.

PACIFIC NORTHWEST: The beauty of the Pacific Northwest is hard to match. Green vegetation is everywhere, and snow-capped peaks dot the landscape in almost every direction. Water is abundant, but so is rain. If you're hiking in the Pacific Northwest outside of the short summer dry period, expect to be rained on constantly. When backpacking or dispersed camping in the Pacific Northwest, it can be hard to find a clearing in the vegetation upon which to set up camp.

NORTHEAST: The Northeast is known for its forests, mountains, and fall colors. Despite lower elevations than the mountains out west, the Northeast has many high mountain peaks that tower above their surroundings. Challenges here include thick forests, frequent rain, and a high likelihood of encountering frustrating mosquitoes.

SOUTHEAST: The Southeast has plentiful parks and forests that are excellent for backpacking trips, and the dense green vegetation adds to the region's beauty. Water is abundant, but storms are not uncommon. The most challenging aspects of backpacking in the Southeast in the summer are heat, humidity, and bugs.

MIDWEST: The unending prairies of the Midwest have mostly been replaced by farms, but plenty of parks and forests preserve the region's beauty. Rivers and lakes are abundant, often with preserved hiking routes on their banks. Public land suitable for hiking is less common here than in other regions, such as the West. Summer heat, thunderstorms, and mosquitoes add to the challenge of hiking through this region.

UPPER MIDWEST: Dense forests abound in the Upper Midwest, and many of them have trails maintained for hiking. Summer temperatures are less extreme than in much of the country, but winter cold and snow make off-season hiking a challenge. Lakes are more common here than in most other regions, and like the Northeast, the Upper Midwest's fall colors are bright and glorious.

OUTSIDE THE UNITED STATES: Camping and hiking are by no means restricted to the United States, but it would take several books for us to cover all of the wonderful places the world has to offer. For example, it was only after moving to Germany that we learned about the strong hiking culture there and discovered numerous long-distance trails through the German forests and fields. For trips anywhere in the world, research the terrain and climate before heading out. Many of the regions of the United States are similar to those elsewhere in the world, so comparable rewards and challenges may apply.

TYPES OF US PUBLIC LAND

Most backpacking trips in the United States take place on public land. But not all public land is the same. Depending on the part of the country you're in and the ownership of the land you're hiking on, restrictions dictate what you can and can't do. Before you head out, always look up maps that show the ownership and regulations for the land you're planning to travel through. On federally owned public lands, camping is allowed by default, unless it is prohibited or regulated. This means that if your trail goes through federal land and there are no camping regulations in place, camping is allowed. However, in popular recreation areas, there are often regulations in place. Here are some general guidelines for different types of land, but always double-check the rules before you head out.

STATE PARKS AND STATE LANDS: Individual states have their own policies regarding management of outdoor areas. Permits are often required for backpacking through state parks, and many state parks only allow backpackers to camp in designated campsites, if at all. Although state parks aren't usually as well known as national parks, it's always worth checking to see if there is a state park in an area you want to visit because they often have networks of maintained trails that can be perfect for exploring.

NOTE

The land comprising the United States is home to Indigenous people and communities today, as it has been for thousands of years. During the expansion of the United States, millions of acres of ancestral lands were stolen or immorally acquired by the government and private ownership, but that does not erase the rich history that Indigenous people have with these lands. During our thruhikes, we have been lucky to experience some of this history: We have dipped our toes in the ocean in Chinook and Quileute ancestral lands. We have walked across lava flows on the Zuni-Acoma Trail through Zuni and Pueblo ancestral lands. We have sought shelter from dangerously high winds on the shore of the Columbia River, on Yakima ancestral lands. And on and on. Still, we only have a small glimpse into the history and impact of this land and the many ways that Indigenous people care for their communities through lands that they originally inhabited and currently inhabit today. We want to acknowledge here and pay respects to Indigenous people and the long-standing relationships they have with the lands featured in this book.

NATIONAL PARKS: National parks operate with a mission to preserve natural and cultural resources for human enjoyment, especially recreation. This means that the National Park Service has two (sometimes opposing) goals: preservation and human use. The National Park Service manages this by implementing permit systems in popular areas that limit the number of people who can use specific trails or regions. Likewise, several national parks only allow camping in designated sites, so be sure to look up the regulations for each park you want to visit. National parks encompass some of the most majestic regions of the country, but compared to less heavily managed regions, they are often quite populated. As you gain experience in the outdoors, don't be afraid to go beyond the confines of national parks to find additional areas to explore.

NATIONAL FORESTS: Whereas national parks focus on preservation for enjoyment, national forests have the mission to preserve forests and grasslands for human needs. Such needs include recreation as well as logging, livestock, mining, and more. There's more than twice as much national forest land in the United States as national park land, and much of it is ideal for hiking, backpacking, and adventuring. Many of the most remote areas of the United States are national forest lands, and they tend to have many fewer permit and camping restrictions than national and state parks.

BUREAU OF LAND MANAGEMENT (BLM) LAND: There is even more land managed by the BLM than there are national forests. The mission of the BLM is similar to that of the National Forest System: to manage land for all uses. Like national forests, permit requirements and camping restrictions on BLM land are much less common than they are for national and state parks.

WILDERNESS AREAS: Hiking through large wilderness areas tends to be our favorite way to backpack. Since the mid-1960s, the US government has set aside tracts of land to preserve as wilderness areas. According to the Wilderness Act of 1964, wilderness is "an area where the earth and its community of life are untrammeled by man, where man himself is a visitor who does not remain."[1] Wilderness areas are designated within national parks, state parks, national forests, BLM land, and more, but they're always managed in the same unique way. Mechanized travel, including cars and bicycles, is prohibited in wilderness areas, as are extractive practices, such as logging and mining. Some livestock grazing is permitted, but it's rare.

OTHER: We've reviewed the most common types of places for outdoor adventures, but this is by no means an exhaustive list. Trails can also be found in county parks, in wildlife areas, on private land owned by foundations, and more. Wherever you are headed, be sure you research what is allowed so you don't run into trouble when you just want to be enjoying your time outside.

1 US Congress. *United States Code: National Wilderness Preservation System*, 16 U.S.C. §§–1131-1136. 1964. https://www.loc.gov/item/uscode1964-004016023.

SEASONS

Plan your trips to take place in seasons for which you have the appropriate gear and experience. In much of the United States, the most popular season for backpacking trips is summer, when the weather is warm and the rain is minimal. Be aware that in very hot and dry climates, the peak of summer may not be the ideal time for a trip due to heat and lack of water. In these areas, hiking in fall and spring can be best, with the caveat that deserts and the mountains of the West sometimes have even less water in the fall than they do in the summer.

If you intend to head out during shoulder seasons (fall or spring) when rain is more likely, be sure to check the forecast and, if necessary, carry adequate rain gear, such as a raincoat and potentially rain pants and gloves. Ensure that your tent is waterproof enough to repel a downpour. (See pages 56, 57, 79, 80, 157, and 159 for more information on rain equipment.)

If you are up for a challenge, winter camping can be exciting and fulfilling. Snow makes everything quiet and beautiful, but it also makes camping more difficult. Winter camping requires warm layers, a warm sleeping bag, a heavy-duty tent, and potentially an extra sleeping pad. (See pages 59 to 67 for more information on winter equipment.) Canister stoves work poorly in the cold, so you'll want to consider using a different cooking system than you would for warm-weather camping (see page 66). Snowshoe and ski camping can be lots of fun if you have the experience and gear, but know that hiking through snow is much slower than hiking on solid ground, so expect to do vastly fewer miles per day.

PRACTICE TRIPS

Practice makes perfect. And when it comes to outdoor adventures, practice also can be fun! If you are getting ready for your first major backpacking trip, go on a few shorter practice trips near home to dial in your camping system and ensure you can cover your intended miles per day. If you get a new piece of gear that you're planning to take on a major trip, see if you can find time for a shorter trip to test it out, or at least test it out at home. The more time you spend practicing, the less likely it is that something unexpected, like gear that doesn't fit or malfunctions, will come up while you are in the midst of a major trip and can't take care of it easily. Don't think of these practice trips as chores—who doesn't need an excuse to spend more time outside?

THRUHIKERS' TIPS

CHOOSING A TRIP

- Based on your interests and previous experience, day hiking, car camping, backpacking, and thruhiking are all great options to get outside and enjoy the outdoors.
- There are beautiful and rewarding places to enjoy the outdoors everywhere in the United States—and all over the world.
- Research your anticipated hiking location to determine the best times of year to hike and the terrain you'll encounter.
- There are several different types of public land with unique approaches to regulating and permitting trips. Check out the type of land you want to visit before you head out so you don't run afoul of the rules.

2

PLANNING A ROUTE

Now that you've chosen your trip, it's time to plan a route. When planning your route, it's important to figure out your distance, which maps you'll be using, what permits you might need, and, for longer trips, where and how to resupply.

RESOURCES

Tons of online, print, and other resources are dedicated to helping with trip and route planning. If you are headed to a popular area, such as a national park, start on the park's website, where you can peruse maps and descriptions. Consider also searching online for trip reports from others who have been to the same area. Park rangers are also extremely helpful; they can describe specific trails and conditions in more detail than the website. We have been amazed at how helpful park rangers are when we call and ask about the trails in a specific park—after all, their job is to know the park better than anybody else!

For more remote trips, the USDA Forest Service (FS) and US Geological Survey (USGS) have interactive and static maps online that can give you a good sense of an area. If you intend to design your own route, CalTopo (caltopo.com) provides an amazing tool that shows topographic maps and trails that you can use to lay out a route. If you're headed to Forest Service or BLM land, a phone call to the corresponding district office often puts you in touch with somebody very knowledgeable about an area or trail.

For short trips, apps such as Strava and AllTrails provide user-uploaded routes that have been hiked before. Sometimes these routes are great, but be careful because the data are not professionally curated and can sometimes lead you astray.

Always check the website of the park or forest you are headed to for hiking and camping regulations, and for a general overview of how to best practice Leave No Trace on any trail, check out lnt.org, the website of the not-for-profit Leave No Trace organization (see chapter 11).

DISTANCE

Planning daily mileage is not easy. Variables such as fitness, elevation change, surface type, gear weight, and weather impact mileage dramatically. Having a realistic mileage goal is much more fun than an overly optimistic goal, especially if there is no way to shorten your trip on the fly. Pushing too hard takes the fun out of a trip, and in the worst case, it can lead to injury. For beginner hikers, plan to cover no more than 5 to 8 miles per day in easy terrain and less than that if the terrain is difficult. Ninety-nine percent of people who go backpacking do it to be outside, not to see how many miles they can cover, so keep this in mind and remind yourself that you have nothing to prove by hiking more miles. After you have a trip or two under your belt, assess how comfortable you were each day of your trip and adjust your mileage up or down accordingly for future hikes. Despite knowing we can hike more than 30 miles per day, we start every one of our thruhikes with a limit of 15 miles per day for the first week. This gives our bodies a chance to get used to the rigors of daily hiking even if our brains are full of adrenaline and just want to GO-GO-GO. For every hiker, factors that impact daily mileage can include the following.

FITNESS: As with any endurance sport, the more physically fit you are, the faster you'll be able to hike and the longer you'll be able to maintain that speed. If you are just getting into hiking, your body will need some time to build the muscles required for long and far days on the trail.

ELEVATION CHANGE: Hiking up and down mountains is harder than hiking on a flat surface. A hiker who may do 3 miles or more per hour on flat, easy terrain could find their speed reduced to 1 or 2 miles per hour through difficult mountains and may need to take more breaks as they go. Even in terrain that looks mild, double-check a topographical map or elevation profile to assess whether there are steep climbs. Frequent short and steep climbs can take even longer to hike than longer stretches of trail with steady but gradual changes in elevation.

PACK WEIGHT: Hikers move more slowly with heavy packs than with light ones. Reducing pack weight usually leads to higher-mileage days.

SURFACE TYPE: Sand, snow, and rocks are slower to travel on than gravel and hard dirt.

TRAIL CONDITION: Wide, well-built, and well-maintained trails are usually faster and easier to walk on than sparsely used trails. This has a lot to do with how much time you spend looking at your feet and the mental effort required to do so. When you are watching out for obstacles in your way and climbing over trees across the path, you'll tend to move slower. Likewise, off-trail travel is much slower than on-trail travel. When hiking through thick vegetation with no trail at all, we have sometimes found our speed reduced to only ½ mile per hour.

WEATHER: When the weather turns sour, expect to reduce your miles per day. Part of this has to do with the difficulty of setting up and breaking down camp, which cuts into hiking time. Speed in bad weather is also reduced due to wet ground and the need to avoid puddles and take breaks to put on rain gear.

DAYLIGHT: This seems like a no-brainer, but it's easy to forget that in wintertime, there is much less daylight than there is during the summer. This almost always translates to less time spent on the trail and more time spent at camp or in your tent. Account for this by reducing your expected mileage to match the daylight. For example, if you tend to cover 15 miles in 15 hours of summer daylight, you'll probably only cover 8 miles in 8 hours of winter daylight, excluding the other factors that can slow you down further, such as weather and ground surface.

LESSONS LEARNED: GROUP BACKPACKING IN ISLE ROYALE NATIONAL PARK

Since the day we met, Tim and I have loved adventuring together. Those adventures have gotten longer and more extreme over the years, but they started with biking around the lakes of Madison, Wisconsin, and going on car camping trips. After college, we started backpacking together. Tim had backpacked before with the Boy Scouts, but I was newer to backpacking and immediately fell in love with it. One year, Tim's family wanted to plan a summer vacation, so we suggested a backpacking trip at Isle Royale National Park, a 45-mile by 9-mile island in Lake Superior that requires a boat ride to get there. We had tons of fun planning our food and route for the trip, and we were required to reserve backcountry camping spots ahead of time. We thought 8 miles per day seemed more than reasonable for everyone coming. In total, there were nine of us on the trip, including Tim's mom, all of his siblings, and some significant others. We had a wide range of skills—some of us had backpacked before, but for others, it was their first time backpacking. We quickly learned that 8 miles per day was far too ambitious for such a large group with such a wide range of skill levels. To make matters worse, Tim's younger brother got quite sick with strep throat. We had to shorten our daily mileage substantially and even took a day off to relax and recover at camp. Luckily, even though we hadn't reserved the camp spots for the extra day, the people who did were happy to share with us.

—Renee

MAPS

Maps, and knowing how to use them, are two of the most important parts of backpacking. Without a good map, you may get lost or have trouble finding water. Let's go through the different types of maps and the benefits and pitfalls of each.

TOPOGRAPHICAL MAPS

It can be helpful to have a large-scale overview map of the area you are hiking in, but detailed topographical maps (aka topo maps) are a must for backpacking. Topo maps have contour lines that help you visualize three-dimensional features on a two-dimensional piece of paper or device screen. This is extremely helpful for both navigation and knowing what to expect: Are you headed up a steep slope to a mountain pass? Will you be walking in a flat valley? Topo maps show you exactly what the terrain looks like. If you're hiking off-trail, a topo map is essential. Knowing the landmarks, such as mountain peaks, that surround you is extremely useful for understanding where you are. It is important to practice reading topo maps before you head out into the backcountry. (See page 108 for more information on how to read topo maps.)

PHONE MAPS

The large color screens on modern smartphones display maps beautifully. They also offer a feature completely unavailable with traditional paper maps: They know where you are. The little blue locator dot on a smartphone map is one of the greatest benefits of navigating with a phone. Many mapping apps are available for backpacking, including Gaia GPS, Avenza Maps, CalTopo, and FarOut for longer trails and Strava, AllTrails, Outdooractive, and komoot for shorter trails, just to name a few. Most apps show your current location using your phone's GPS. PDF maps downloaded to your phone are also an option, but most won't show your current location (unless they are "geo-referenced" and you're using them with an app capable of reading them). Any good smartphone app can calculate the distance along the trail from where you are to a specified point. This is extremely useful and much easier than approximating the distance along a curvy trail using the scale on a paper map.

Be sure whatever map or app you put on your phone has all of the information you need: Look for topo maps with high resolution that show trails and water sources and cover the entire area you will be hiking in, including a buffer around the area in case you need to find an alternate route. Be sure you download offline maps BEFORE you head out because there's a good chance you won't have cell service on the trail. To conserve battery power while you're out, keep your phone in airplane mode, turn the battery saver on, and set your screen to dim. (Note: Putting your phone in airplane mode will turn off cellular data, but most hiking apps still work in airplane mode if you have location turned on.) Bring a power bank with enough power for your trip and the correct cable to charge your phone, and be

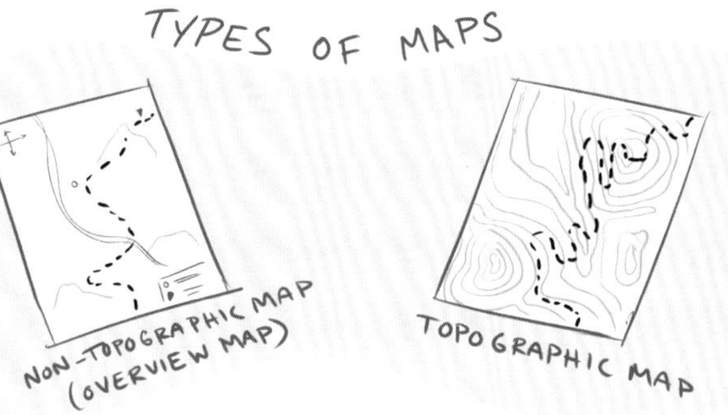

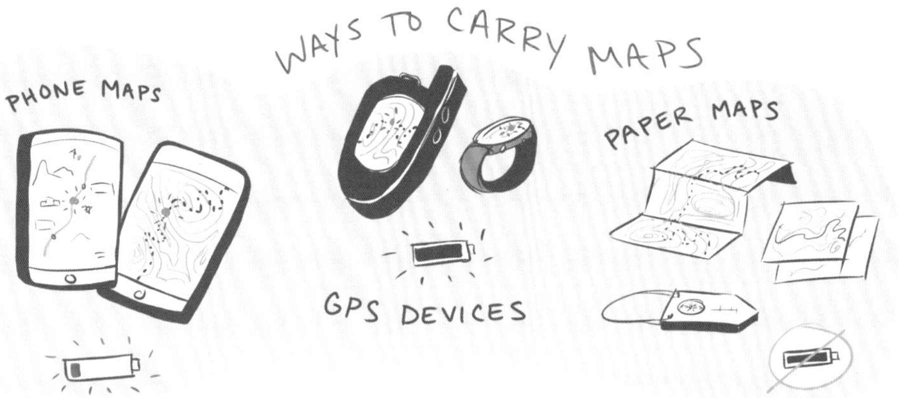

sure your phone and power bank are completely charged before you head out.

When using phone maps, it's also a good idea to bring a backup map in case your phone breaks or the battery dies. Your backup could be a paper map or just a friend with a map on their phone as well. Phones are our preferred method for mapping on most of our hikes.

GPS DEVICES

Another navigational tool to consider is a dedicated GPS device. GPS devices can be expensive, and the screens are rarely as useful as those on a phone. For these reasons, they have become less commonly used for backpacking and other adventures, but they are far from obsolete. Many GPS devices on the market have built-in mapping capabilities, produced by companies like Garmin. They can be handhelds or watches. Several older models do not come with preloaded maps, so be sure you know how to load maps onto the device and do so before heading out. Choose a detailed topo map that covers the entire area you are headed to and then some, in case you need to find an alternate route. Modern high-end GPS devices often come with an entire continent's maps preloaded in memory, which eliminates the need to download a dedicated map before your trip. Still, you may want to plan and load your specific route ahead of time.

DEVELOPING THE WANDERFREUND APP

After thruhiking the Pacific Crest Trail (PCT)—142 days and 2,650 miles from Mexico to Canada—we moved to Germany. On the PCT, we had met a fellow thruhiker who went by the trail name "Parmesan," and we learned that he lived not too far from our new home in Germany. As soon as the weather was nice enough, the three of us planned a short thruhike of the Harzer-Hexen-Stieg (the Harz Witches' Trail): 4 days and 100 kilometers in Northern Germany's Harz Mountains. As we researched our trip, we learned that there are many named and marked mid-distance trails in Germany, but there were no good phone-mapping options for people wanting to thruhike them. On the PCT, we all had used the FarOut app (then called Guthook), which had great information for thruhikers, so we were inspired to make our own mapping app for Germany's long trails. We named it Wanderfreund, which means "hiking friend" in German. Tim and I learned to code Android and iOS apps, Parmesan did the design (and as a native German speaker, helped with the language because Tim and I knew no German before we moved), and the three of us hiked all over Germany together, collecting data on different long trails. It was a great way to explore our new country, we made an amazing lifelong friend, and the app is still available for download from the iPhone and Android app stores.

—Renee

One clear advantage of a GPS device over a cell phone is its ability to communicate with satellites for longer without draining the battery as much. Cell phones are multifunction devices that spend battery power on many features, like taking photos, even while in airplane mode. Therefore, when using a phone for navigating, the default setting is for the phone to save power by shutting off the GPS when the screen is dim (and if you change this to let the GPS run continuously, your phone battery will die quickly). GPS devices, on the other hand, only spend their power communicating with satellites, which usually means the battery lasts longer. A high-quality GPS device will be useful not only for mapping, but also for tracking your route continuously as you travel, creating a set of digital breadcrumbs that can be interesting to look at later. Although we usually opt for phone maps to navigate, we also wear GPS watches with long-lasting batteries to track our trips so we can have fun analyzing the data afterward. Experiment with your device to become familiar with its rate of power consumption and recharging method and speed before heading out.

PAPER MAPS

They're not always the easiest or most convenient tool, yet paper maps do still work as well as they always have, and they don't require you to be reliant on a battery. Look for high-resolution topo maps that show trails and water sources. A good paper map will show all of the trails in the area, not just the one you are hiking—it can be very confusing to arrive at a junction with a trail that isn't labeled on your map! Another feature to look for on a map is detail. If the map squeezes much more than 10 miles of trail onto a single page, it probably isn't detailed enough to use for hiking.

For many trails, especially short routes in popular areas, paper maps may be available at the trailhead. These can be helpful for short day hikes, but don't count on trailhead maps for backpacking trips! The USGS and *National Geographic* have great topo maps available to download for free and print. Outdoor recreation stores also sell paper maps of trails in the area and usually have some water-resistant options. Paper maps require a bit more expertise than phone maps because you need to know how to figure out where you are on the map. To use paper maps, you should bring a compass (and know how to use it) or a watch or phone with a compass. As a backup, it is possible to ascertain the direction you are headed based on the sun or other aspects of the landscape.

CARRYING 17 DAYS OF FOOD

In 2015, when we headed out into the High Sierras with 17 days of food on our backs, we had never heard the term *resupply* before. It was our longest backpacking trip to date. Before the trip, we spent a few weeks dehydrating meals, buying the perfect number of snacks, and rationing each day's food into gallon-size ziplock plastic bags. We even weighed our food; it was about 1 pound per person per day, which was pretty light, but it meant that we each set out on the trail that first day with 17 pounds of food! As we bumped into folks along the trail and got to chatting with them, we learned that they were taking side trails out of the mountains and hitchhiking into towns to pick up more food along the way. Our route even took us right past a general store, with cheeseburgers and groceries for sale, which we foolishly hadn't planned to stop at. The weight on our backs during this trip taught us the power of resupplying!

—Renee

RESUPPLYING FOR LONGER TRIPS

Resupplying means stopping along the trail to pick up more supplies, especially food and gear. Food is heavy, so on trips longer than 5 to 7 days, stopping to resupply along the way can be a great strategy to keep your backpack weight more manageable. For longer trails, like a thruhike of the Appalachian or Pacific Crest Trails, which take 4 to 6 months to complete, resupplying along the way is a necessary part of the adventure. For these long-distance hikes, it is impossible to carry all of the food you will consume along the way, but gear changes become essential, too. Certain pieces of gear, such as shoes, won't last the duration of a long-distance hike and need to be replaced along the way. Other items, especially clothing and layers, may need to be swapped as seasons change.

WHERE TO RESUPPLY

Grocery stores, outdoors stores, and even convenience stores are good places to pick up food (like dehydrated meals, energy bars, oatmeal, ramen, and instant potatoes or rice) or supplies (like travel-size toothpaste). Sometimes trails take you right through a town or past a store, but often a detour off trail is required for resupplying. Sometimes trails cross a road. At other times, you need to take a side trail to get to a road. From the road, you can walk or hitchhike into a town. It's important to plan your resupply stops (or, at a minimum, your first resupply stop) before you head out on trail so you know how much food to bring when you set out. Check the map of your route to look for potential resupply spots near the trail, and be sure you know the store's opening hours. For popular trails, the internet is full of blogs and spreadsheets of potential resupply spots, posted by previous hikers describing what worked or didn't work for them. It also can be a good idea to plan backup resupply spots in case you don't make it as far as intended and need to resupply earlier than expected.

MAILING FOOD AND GEAR

Mailing food is another option for resupplying on trail. It's a great way to resupply gear, too. For specialty items such as shoes, clothing layers, and even replacement equipment like a new tent, having items delivered to a post office, hotel, or other business along the trail can be much more effective than trying to get to a shop that has the items you need in stock. The US Postal Service (USPS) has a great option for shipping food called "General Delivery." Most post offices hold mail shipped to General Delivery for 30 days. For shorter trips, you can mail boxes of food to yourself ahead of time, but for longer trips, like a 4- to 6-month thruhike, you will need to ask a friend or family member to mail your boxes periodically as you hike. For gear shipments, just place your order along the way. Most post offices also allow you to call and forward your packages to another post office or other location free of charge if your plans change. Remember to check the hours for each post office along your route—post offices are closed on Sundays, and those in smaller towns may have limited hours any (or every) day of the week.

How to label boxes for USPS General Delivery:

Your Name
℅ General Delivery
Address of Post Office

Is it better to mail or shop for food along a trail?

MAILING FOOD: Mailing food can be a great option if you have dietary restrictions. If you are preparing and mailing food ahead of time, be sure you send yourself a variety of meals so you don't get sick of eating the same thing every day.

SHOPPING FOR FOOD: Shopping for food requires less planning ahead of time, and you won't need to worry about the limited hours of post offices.

HYBRID METHOD: We like to prepare, dehydrate, and ship dinners to ourselves ahead of time when we're hiking long trails and then pick up our breakfasts, lunches, and snacks in stores along the way. This hybrid method ensures we have a well-balanced meal full of carbohydrates, protein, vegetables, and flavor to eat every night. It also allows us to buy other foods that we are craving while on trail, which can be hard to predict ahead of time.

PERMITS

Before heading out on trail, be sure to determine if you need a permit and when and where to get it. Some permits are available online; some are only available in person at a ranger station; some are available by self-registration at a ranger station or trailhead. Be aware that some permits, especially in more popular areas, are hard to get because the number allotted per day may be restricted by the managing agency (e.g., National Park Service or Forest Service). In these cases, you may need to get a permit many months in advance or enroll in a lottery, and you may not get a permit for your desired trip dates.

When required for hiking in national parks, permits are usually available from Recreation.gov, and typically some permits are held for day-of walk-up applications. When permits are required on state park, national forest, or BLM land, the application process varies, so look up the area you're headed to or call the park or district office.

Note that when hiking in an area that requires permits, it is important to get a permit for multiple reasons: Rangers check permits and can give you a ticket if you don't have one. Permits help search and rescue teams locate a missing person. They are also used to track how many people are using certain trails or areas; if lots of people are using a particular trail, permits can help that trail get funding.

THRUHIKERS' TIPS

PLANNING A ROUTE

- To ensure you have an enjoyable trip, be realistic about the number of miles you plan to cover per day, and take the terrain, your fitness level, trail conditions, and daylight hours into account.
- Carry high-resolution topographic maps on your phone, a GPS device, or paper, and have a backup.
- Download offline maps to your GPS device or phone BEFORE heading out on trail.
- Know if you need permits and where and how to get them.
- For trips longer than 5 to 7 days, it may make sense to stop and resupply with additional food and gear along the way.

3

PRINCIPLES FOR ASSEMBLING GEAR

All camping and backpacking trips are different and, therefore, require different gear. Plus, each person is unique and has their own preferences. If you ask five backpackers what their favorite tent is, you'll get 10 different answers. Still, a few guiding principles can be applied almost universally for a more enjoyable trip: For the best backpacking experience, you should minimize the weight of your pack, be sure your gear is as durable as possible, carry as little gear as you can, and consider gear brands and pricing before purchasing. In this chapter, we provide general guidance for choosing the right gear for a trip. Later, in chapter 4, we dive into specifics.

MINIMIZE WEIGHT

Backpacking involves strapping everything you need for days onto your back and lugging it along as you travel across some great distance by foot. This is hard! It's one thing to walk in circles around a gear shop while wearing a weighted backpack, but it's quite another to wear that pack with real gear, and wear it all day, climbing mountains and hopping over streams. A heavy pack (more than about 30 pounds without food and water) is not only exhausting and unpleasant to wear, but it also can cause falls, muscle fatigue, overuse injuries like stress fractures, and general soreness. However, there's no way out of wearing a backpack to go backpacking—it's in the name! The more that can be done to make wearing a pack more pleasant, the better. Sometimes there's a competitive attitude among backpackers: Whose pack is heaviest? Who can carry the most? Avoid this attitude as much as possible. It's likely that the winner of the weight competition will have the worst time on the trail. *For us, the best way to enjoy a trip more is to reduce our pack weights.*

Reducing weight doesn't mean that every hiker has to be an "ultra-lighter" with an 8-pound pack. What it means is that, on every trip, you make an intentional decision about the gear you decide to carry and factor the weight of each piece of gear into the decision-making process. This is a highly personal choice. For some people, carrying an extra pair of shoes along with a portable espresso maker is worth it. Others might carry virtually nothing and go so far as to saw off the end of their toothbrush.

CARRYING WAY TOO MUCH GEAR ON THE JOHN MUIR TRAIL

Our first relatively long-distance backpacking trip was a 180-mile section covering most of the John Muir Trail (JMT), which traverses the high Sierra Nevada mountain range in California. We packed like we always did for shorter trips (our longest trip before this was 6 days long), but we expected this trip to take 17 days, so there was just a lot more to bring—more clothing, more cooking equipment, and even a travel Scrabble set we never used! On top of that, because we were new to trips of this length, we hadn't yet learned about resupplying along the way, so we packed all 17 days of food into our enormous backpacks and thought this was normal. We set out on the trail under the weight of painfully heavy packs. Our section began with a steep climb of several thousand feet at elevation, which felt impossible to complete—we stopped to take a nap after only a few miles of climbing. We moved along slowly and painfully under the heavy burdens we were carrying.

We are both athletes, and shortly before this trip, we both completed a 140.6-mile Ironman race (2.4 miles of swimming followed by 110 miles of biking followed by 26.2 miles of running). But that didn't matter because it seemed like everybody else on the trail was flying past us. In conversations with other hikers, we learned that *everybody* was resupplying at least once, if not two times, during their treks along the JMT. (To this day, we have never met any other hikers foolish enough to carry 17 days of food like we did.) The real enlightening moments came when we saw how fast Pacific Crest Trail (PCT) thruhikers were flying down the trail and how small their packs were while they did it. The 2,650-mile PCT overlaps with much of the JMT, so we were excited and amazed when we saw *real, live thruhikers* in action for the first time. Even though their trips were so much longer than ours, the collection of gear they carried was tiny. *How could they survive with so little gear?*

We were equally impressed and inspired. Three years later, we had figured it out, and we were back on the JMT. But this time we were the ones with small packs, and the JMT was only a short segment of our trek along the entire PCT.

—Tim

zpacks

THRUHIKERS' TIPS

PRINCIPLES FOR ASSEMBLING GEAR

- Keeping your pack weight low (less than 20 pounds without food and water) will make hiking easier and probably lead to a more enjoyable trip.
- When choosing gear, take into account both durability and weight.
- Be intentional about all of the gear you bring on a backpacking trip.
- At first, try borrowing gear from a friend or renting it from a store to see if you like it before making a purchase.
- Consider purchasing gear from cottage companies; they make high-quality, durable, and lightweight backpacking gear, which is often not sold at retail stores.

4

GEAR

Backpacks, tents, sleeping bags, sleeping pads, water filters, camp kitchens, electronics, clothing, and more! It's time to dive into each piece of backpacking gear in depth. We also provide a sample packing list in this chapter to help you get started.

SAMPLE PACKING LIST

Although every trip requires a unique set of gear, there is a considerable amount of overlap from one adventure to the next. Here is a generic packing list that, with simple modifications, should apply for everything from a 5-mile overnight backpacking trip to a 4-month, 3,000-mile thruhike from Mexico to Canada.

NOTE

This is a generic packing list, applicable to many summer backpacking trips with cooler weather expected at night. Some areas or seasons may require additional gear. For example, snow gear, like microspikes and waterproof socks, may be necessary when hiking in the mountains, even in the summer. This packing list is meant for one person. If hiking with more than one person, some gear can be shared, if desired (e.g., tent, stove and pot, first-aid kit).

THE BIG STUFF

- ❒ Backpack
- ❒ Tent, including tent, rainfly, poles, and stakes as necessary
- ❒ Ground sheet
- ❒ Sleeping bag or quilt
- ❒ Sleeping pad

COOKING & EATING

- ❒ Stove
- ❒ Pot
- ❒ Spork
- ❒ Lighter
- ❒ Bandana, optional
- ❒ Food bag, bear-proof canister, or bear-proof bag (Check local requirements.)
- ❒ 40 feet of rope for hanging food in bear country, if necessary (Check local requirements.)
- ❒ Water filter
- ❒ Water bottles

ELECTRONICS

- ❒ Cell phone
- ❒ Power bank
- ❒ Rechargeable headlamp
- ❒ Wall plug, if applicable
- ❒ Charging cables for all electronics
- ❒ Emergency beacon, handheld GPS, and/or GPS watch, optional

TOILETRIES

- ❒ Hand sanitizer
- ❒ Poop shovel
- ❒ Toothbrush
- ❒ Toothpaste, travel-sized
- ❒ Lip balm, lotion, and/or Vaseline, if desired
- ❒ Toilet paper, wipes, and/or portable bidet, if desired
- ❒ Menstrual cup, if applicable; optional
- ❒ Pee cloth, if applicable; optional

MISCELLANEOUS

- ❒ Hiking poles
- ❒ Water-resistant bag (We use this to waterproof our extra layers and as a pillow.)
- ❒ Rain cover or waterproof liner (like a trash compactor or garbage bag) for pack, if pack is not waterproof
- ❒ Topo map, printed and/or downloaded to phone or GPS
- ❒ Permit, printed and/or saved on phone, if required
- ❒ ID, cash, credit card

CLOTHING (WORN CLOTHING AND CARRIED LAYERS)

- ❒ Trail running shoes, hiking shoes, or hiking boots
- ❒ Two or three pairs of wool or synthetic hiking socks
- ❒ Gaiters, if wearing trail running shoes or hiking shoes
- ❒ Two pairs of antimicrobial underwear
- ❒ Antimicrobial bra, if applicable
- ❒ Hiking pants or athletic shorts, synthetic or wool, not cotton
- ❒ T-shirt and/or long-sleeve shirt or sun hoodie, synthetic or wool, not cotton
- ❒ Base layer/pajamas, synthetic or wool, not cotton
- ❒ Raincoat
- ❒ Rain pants
- ❒ Rain mitts
- ❒ Puffy jacket
- ❒ Buff or beanie
- ❒ Gloves
- ❒ Sun or baseball hat
- ❒ Sunglasses

FIRST AID/GEAR-REPAIR KIT (A SMALL QUANTITY OF EACH ITEM)

- ❒ Prescription medicine, if applicable
- ❒ Painkillers
- ❒ Antihistamines
- ❒ Alcohol wipes
- ❒ First-aid ointment
- ❒ Bandages
- ❒ Gauze
- ❒ Leukotape P, for blisters
- ❒ Tweezers
- ❒ Nail clippers, for longer hikes
- ❒ Razor blade or knife
- ❒ Needle and thread
- ❒ Mini lighter, for backup
- ❒ Tenacious Tape and/or duct tape, for gear repair

CONSUMABLES

- ❒ Fuel for stove
- ❒ Sunscreen
- ❒ Bug spray
- ❒ Bear spray, if applicable
- ❒ Food and water

BACKPACKS

There are three types of backpacking backpacks: external-frame packs, internal-frame packs, and frameless packs. External-frame packs are large and heavy, and although they were popular decades ago, they are rarely seen on the trail anymore. Internal-frame packs are the most common. They have a support frame made of lightweight metal, plastic, or carbon fiber inside the pack that transfers much of the weight of the pack to your hips instead of your shoulders. Frameless packs have no frame at all, so they transfer much more of the weight to your shoulders. Frameless packs are only advisable for backpackers with extremely low gear and food weights (20 pounds total or less, including food and water).

FEATURES: Backpacks have a variable number of add-on features, from internal sleeves for water bladders to removable hip-belt pouches to futuristic-looking breathable padding systems. When shopping for a pack, keep in mind that extra features usually add weight, so sometimes simpler is better. But some features are worth the weight: We love our hip-belt pouches, which provide easy access to our cell phones and snacks for the day.

CAPACITY: Larger-capacity packs are heavier and more unwieldy to load and carry, so the smallest backpack that can reasonably carry all of your food, water, and gear is the best bet. When we were starting out, we bought packs that were 60 liters (Renee) and 85 liters (Tim). We never filled these completely, not even when we carried 17 days of food on the John Muir Trail (see page 45). Both of us now have 40-liter backpacks. Backpacks smaller than this make it difficult to fit a bear canister inside. For hikers with average gear who are just starting out, a pack in the 50- to 55-liter range is a good bet.

SIZE: Backpacks hug the space between your hips and shoulders, which is unique to every person. There is no single guideline to follow to determine pack size, so read the manufacturer's instructions closely to ensure you get the right size, and don't hesitate to exchange the pack if you think it is too small or too big.

WEIGHT: Consider the weight of the backpack itself. Some backpacks are surprisingly heavy—4 to 6 pounds for the backpack itself! Other backpacks weigh less than 1 pound.

WATERPROOFING: Rain happens, and when it does, it is great to have a system in place to keep your gear dry. Some backpacks are designed to be fully waterproof. For packs that are not waterproof, you can buy strap-on pack covers that you can wrap over a pack in the rain. Regardless of what the manufacturer claims about waterproofness and whether or not you have a pack cover, some water always finds a way inside, so it's important to have a second layer of internal waterproofing, which can either be an internal pack liner (trash compactor or garbage bags work well) or waterproof stuff sacks for gear you really don't want to get wet. Our method is to each carry a dry sack that we use for items we want to stay dry (clothing and our sleeping bag, especially) if it is raining. Bonus: Overnight, our dry sacks double as pillows.

TENTS & SHELTERS

A well-performing shelter can make the difference between an enjoyable trip and a cold, wet, or otherwise miserable one, particularly in buggy climates or during inclement weather. The primary function of a shelter is to provide protection from what's outside: This primarily includes water and insects and to a lesser extent cold and wind. Tents provide only minimal protection from animals; large or small mammals interested in food can easily chew or claw through tent fabric, but reptiles will likely be deterred by a fully zipped tent. In dry climates where bugs and condensation are not a major concern, we often use no tent at all, opting instead to "cowboy camp" under the stars if the weather is nice. Even then, we still carry a simple tarp to set up over ourselves if it is raining overnight.

When choosing a tent, waterproofing is absolutely essential. Whether you're car camping for a night or thruhiking thousands of miles, a single wet night can ruin a trip. Most tents produced by well-known manufacturers will be waterproof when used correctly, but cheap tents from non-outdoor stores like Walmart or Target might not be. Other key factors to consider are size and weight. Tents are rated for a specific number of people, and the rating always equates to a tight squeeze. It would be nearly impossible to fit three people in a two-person tent, but two people in a three-person tent is usually more comfortable than two people in a two-person tent. On backpacking trips, weight is always important, so it's a good idea to go with the smallest tent you're comfortable using. For car camping, it doesn't hurt to get something a little bit bigger so it is more pleasant to share.

TYPES OF SHELTERS

CAR CAMPING TENT: These tents are usually built to be spacious and robust. They have high ceilings and features like internal dividers to create separate "rooms." The idea behind these tents is that they should be fun to hang out in; they might be a good place for a card game on a rainy day. Car camping tents are always surprisingly heavy, often difficult to set up, and not always sufficiently waterproof. These tents can be perfect for car camping, but it is not advisable to try to carry one on a backpacking trip—the weight penalty is too great.

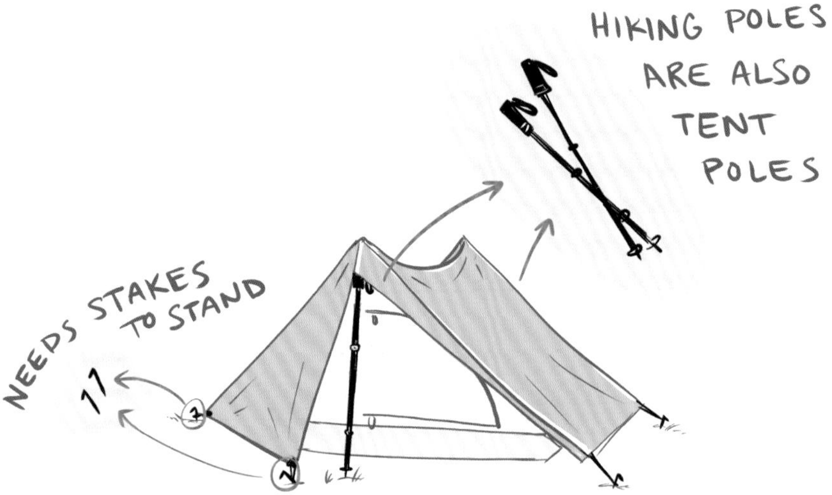

NON-FREESTANDING TENT

FREESTANDING BACKPACKING TENT: These tents have dedicated poles that hold the tent up. They are called “freestanding” because they stand freely even when they are not staked into the ground. The cost and durability of these tents is inversely proportional to their weight, which can be less than 2 pounds for a two-person tent.

ULTRALIGHT NON-FREESTANDING TENT: These tents are usually the lightest. They do not stand up on their own without being staked into the ground. They often do not include poles at all, but instead use hiking poles to prop up the tent—the idea is that the user will be carrying hiking poles either way, so eliminating dedicated tent poles is a way to minimize weight.

SINGLE-WALL VERSUS DOUBLE-WALL TENT: The most common type of modern tent has a main tent body containing lots of mesh covered by a separate rain fly that keeps out the rain. This is called a double-wall tent: The mesh is the first wall, and the rain fly is the second. On hot, dry days, the rain fly can be left off, which increases ventilation but still provides protection from insects. In single-wall tents, the body of the tent doubles as the rain fly. Single-wall tents are lighter, but the weight savings come at a price: They have worse ventilation and are hotter on hot days, and condensation can be a problem. Often, single-wall tent users carry a small cloth to wipe out condensation in the morning.

BIVY SACK: Bivy sacks, or bivvies, are essentially waterproof sleeping bags that cover their user through the night. They are like a cocoon that you lay out on the ground and put your sleeping bag and yourself right into. They are lightweight, and the bug and rain protection they provide is comparable to a tent, but they provide virtually no space to move around.

TARP: A tarp can be strung up between trees or on hiking poles with stakes to provide rain protection from above. In certain climates, such as deserts, mosquitoes and condensation are not a concern, so it can be pleasant to sleep under the stars and carry a lightweight tarp as a backup just in case rain does fall.

HAMMOCK: A hammock is also an option when backpacking in locations with adequate trees. A suspension system (ropes and carabiners) is needed, along with a tarp in case of rain. Underquilts and bug nets should also be considered when conditions warrant them.

ADDITIONAL SHELTER CONSIDERATIONS

STAKES: Stakes are little spears used to secure a shelter to the ground. Most tents come with stakes, but these are often heavier than necessary to serve their purpose. Swapping out steel stakes for lightweight aluminum or titanium stakes is a great way to save a bit of extra weight on a backpacking trip. Carbon-fiber stakes are a very light option, but beware that these can be fragile; we have broken several carbon-fiber stakes, especially in areas where the ground is not soft.

GROUND SHEETS: Most tent fabrics are not 100 percent waterproof. Although they keep raindrops from getting through, leakage may come up through the floor if a tent is set up on a sopping-wet surface. Ground sheets are a waterproof layer of fabric laid under the tent to prevent this. Some tent manufacturers sell or include custom-sized ground sheets that perfectly match a tent. Another commonly used moisture barrier is Tyvek, a waterproof, paperlike material used in home construction. Most hardware stores carry Tyvek, but it is often only sold in large rolls. If you find a store selling it by the foot, it should be no more than a few dollars to get enough to use as a ground sheet. Alternatively, you can order it precut online, although it will be slightly more expensive. Another use for a ground sheet is as a "floor" when sleeping under the stars. When conditions merit it, we like to unfold our Tyvek ground sheets, lay our sleeping pads on top, and sleep with no tent over our heads.

NOTHING BEATS TENT COFFEE ON A COLD, RAINY MORNING

On our long-distance hikes, we camp in a different spot every night. In the morning, we pack up all of our stuff and hit the trail. Repeating this for months at a time amounts to a very nomadic lifestyle, which leaves us with few things to call "home," at least for the duration of a trip. We've found that when conditions get tough, we do end up craving the comforts of home. But the home that we crave isn't our city life off trail; it's the security of being curled up and resting in our warm cozy tent after a full day of hiking.

One morning that stands out as an example of this feeling was when we were in Wyoming's Wind River Range on the Continental Divide Trail. We were in the middle of a long, 8-day stretch between towns, and every day we were dealing with rain. On top of this, wind storms the previous year had knocked down thousands of trees across the trail, which made the hiking much harder and slower than usual. We didn't have any extra food, so we were rationing every bite we ate. That morning, it was pouring when we woke up. We usually try to get going as early as possible, but with the downpour, neither of us had any desire to suit up and head out into the rain. We couldn't spend the time snacking because we didn't have extra food to spare, and because we hadn't planned to spend the morning hiding out in the tent, we didn't even have very much water on hand. Then Renee had a thought: We could collect rainwater from the side of the tent as it ran down the rain fly. We put our pot right under a heavily dripping spot, and in no time we had a pot full of water, which we used to make coffee right from our tent vestibule—the space under the rain fly but outside the tent. We repeated this a couple times as we waited out the storm, enjoying warm coffees from our dry and cozy tent. On a long-distance hike, when we aren't walking, we aren't making progress toward the finish, but miserable conditions can be a great excuse to slow down and savor the moment. Looking back, that morning was one of the highlights of the trip: We felt slow and stuck at the time, but we found a way to enjoy the moment.

—Tim

SLEEPING BAGS & QUILTS

Few things are worse than a miserable night spent shivering on the ground in the wrong sleeping bag. When the weather turns sour, having the right sleeping bag or quilt is a matter of safety. A good rule of thumb is to carry a bag rated to at least 10º below the minimum temperature you might reasonably encounter overnight. Overall, choosing a sleeping bag is a matter of balancing between weight, warmth, and cost. There are still a multitude of decisions to weigh in the decision process.

Rectangular sleeping bags are usually heavy and do not trap air effectively enough to provide warmth; therefore, they may be okay for car camping in the summertime, but they are ***not recommended*** for backpacking. Instead, consider a mummy-shaped sleeping bag or quilt.

MUMMY BAGS: These are tight-fitting sleeping bags that zip all the way from the legs to the head and fully encompass their user. When used properly, mummy bags trap warm air inside to keep you warm.

QUILT: These have no hood or zipper. Quilts are designed to only cover a person from above, which means they have the potential to allow more cold air to flow in than mummy bags. High-quality quilts are mummy-shaped and come with a strap meant to hold the quilt snugly to the body, which helps trap air if used correctly. Because they have less material, quilts can be lighter than bags.

TEMPERATURE RATING: There are mutliple temperature rating systems for sleeping bags and quilts, but most manufacturers specify a minimum temperature for comfortable sleep and another for extreme situations (where your bag's function is to keep you alive). Regardless, a bag's published rating won't match everybody's preference. Some backpackers notice that they "sleep hot," meaning they are comfortable with colder overnight temperatures than a bag is rated for, and others "sleep cold," meaning to be comfortable, they need a bag rated for much colder temperatures than they'll actually experience. The best way to learn which group you fall into is to spend some nights on the trail!

DOWN VERSUS SYNTHETIC: Natural goose down has long been the go-to material for sleeping bag insulation. It is warm, compresses to a tiny size to fit in a pack, and is very light. However, if the down gets wet, it loses all of its ability to provide insulation. Technology for synthetic insulation has been improving over time, and today it is a worthy competitor. It does not provide quite as much warmth as down per unit of weight, nor is it as compressible, but it is close. That said, synthetic materials are typically more affordable and still provide warmth when they get wet.

DOWN RATINGS: The quality of down is rated on a scale that indicates how much loft it provides per ounce of weight. Precisely speaking, the number shows how many cubic inches of volume a single ounce of down will fill. So down rated as 900 fill will occupy 900 cubic inches of volume per ounce, while 600-fill down occupies 600 cubic inches per ounce. This does not necessarily indicate warmth. A warmer sleeping bag will be filled with more cubic inches of down insulation, but the same amount of insulation can be achieved either by adding more ounces of low-quality down or fewer ounces of high-quality down. Down ratings indicate how heavy a bag is relative to its warmth, but on their own, they don't say much about warmth.

LENGTH: Whenever possible, a person's sleeping bag or quilt length should be only slightly longer (1 to 3 inches) than that person's height. Using a sleeping bag that is too short can be uncomfortable, and using

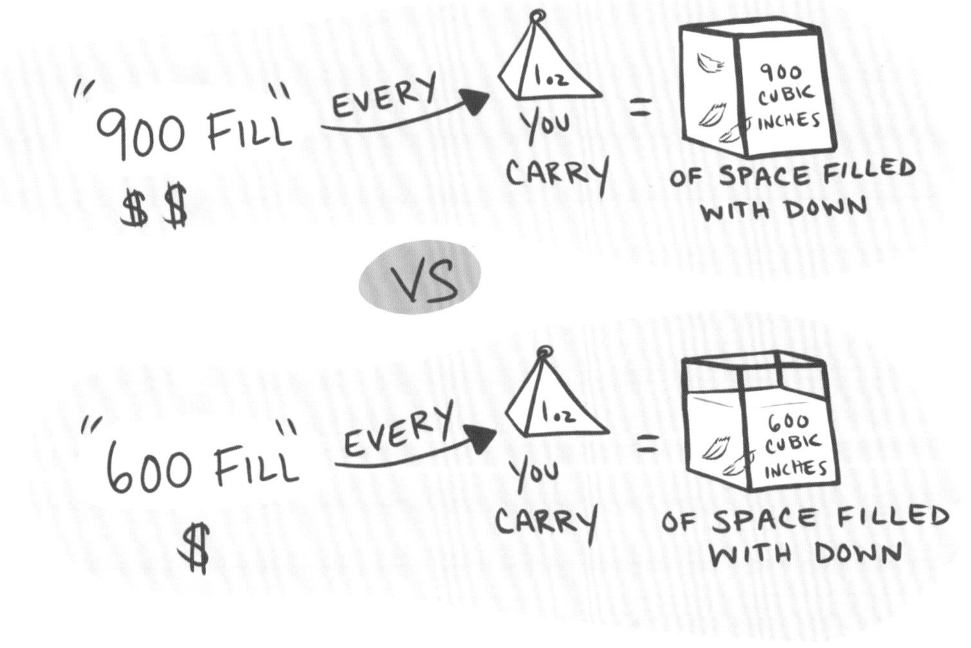

one that is too long can make it colder than its rating and heavier than necessary. This is because the extra space at the bottom provides a bigger space for your body to heat up, and there is extra material insulating that empty space. Many sleeping bag manufacturers only make sleeping bags in "regular" (6 feet) and "long" (6 feet, 6 inches) sizes. However, some manufacturers, especially cottage companies, sell bags in 3-inch increments down to 5 feet and even offer designs catered to female bodies. Some companies also make slim bags, wide bags, and/or kid-sized bags.

STORAGE: Between trips, down sleeping bags should be stored uncompressed. Some bags come with a large sack for long-term storage. If not, a large plastic lidded container works well. If a bag is stored in its stuff sack for months or years at a time, it will lose some of its loft and, as a result, its warmth. For more information about proper sleeping bag storage, see page 89.

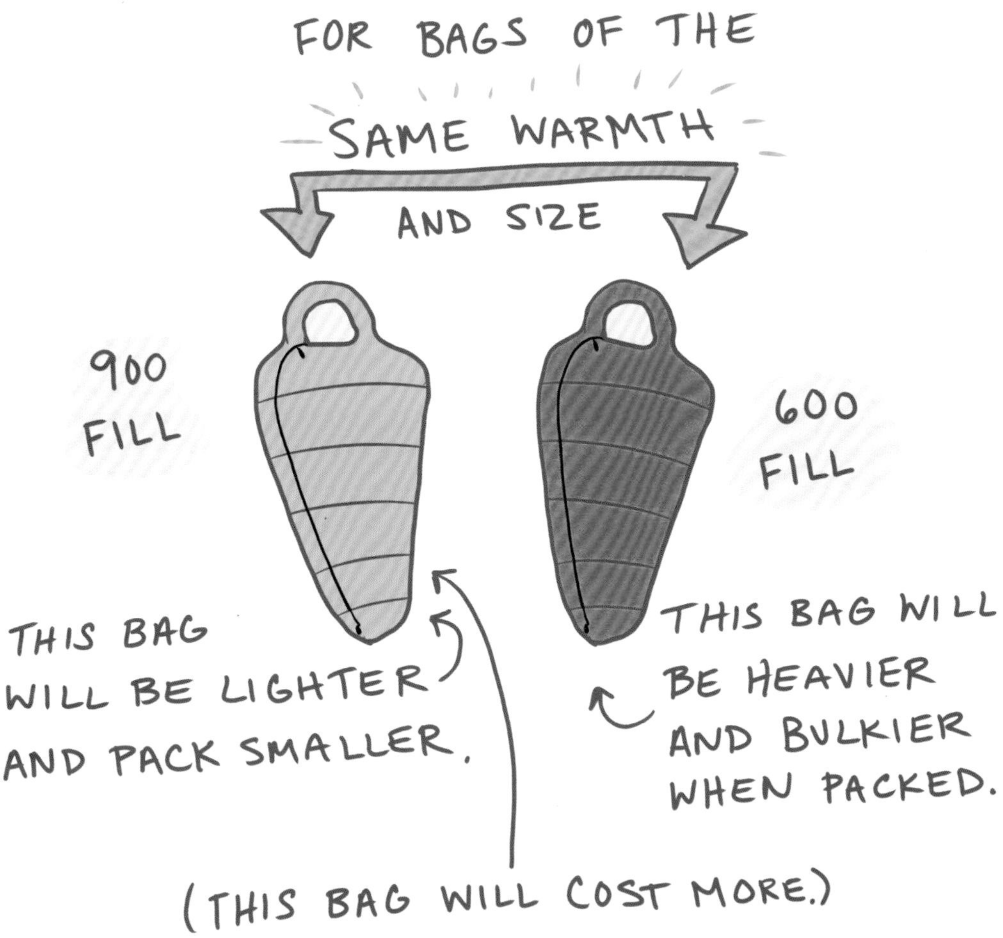
FOR BAGS OF THE
SAME WARMTH
AND SIZE
900 FILL
600 FILL
THIS BAG WILL BE LIGHTER AND PACK SMALLER.
THIS BAG WILL BE HEAVIER AND BULKIER WHEN PACKED.
(THIS BAG WILL COST MORE.)

STAYING WARM IN A SLEEPING BAG AS A SHORT PERSON

When camping on cold nights, I used to feel cold while Tim felt warm and cozy, even though we had the same sleeping bags. Before our first hike from Mexico to Canada on the Pacific Crest Trail, I did a lot of research on sleeping bags. I learned that some manufacturers make sleeping bags designed for short people and for women. I am only 5 feet, 2 inches tall. Because most sleeping bags are 6 feet long, my body was wasting energy trying to heat up lots of unused space. I switched to a 5-foot, 3-inch sleeping bag designed for women, and I've felt warm and cozy ever since!

—Renee

SLEEPING PADS

A sleeping pad is essential for overnight trips outdoors. The functions of any sleeping pad are twofold: They provide a comfortable sleeping surface on top of the hard ground, and they add a layer of insulation that keeps the user's body heat from dissipating into the cold ground. Comfort is nice, but it's the insulation that makes a sleeping pad an essential item for backpacking. Any sleeping bag or quilt, whether made of down feathers or synthetic fibers, loses most of its insulating properties when compressed. Therefore, quilts and sleeping bags provide protection from the cold air above, but not from the cold ground below. Sleeping pads do not compress completely when slept upon, which means they retain their ability to insulate.

TYPES OF SLEEPING PADS

CLOSED-CELL FOAM PADS: These sleeping pads are made out of partially compressible, non-inflatable foam. They are typically less than an inch thick and either roll up like a pastry or fold up like an accordion. Closed-cell foam pads are relatively bulky, and because they are thinner, many people find them less comfortable than other options. A frequent complaint is that closed-cell foam pads cause hip pain. They are unquestionably the most reliable type of sleeping pad available. Closed-cell foam pads cannot puncture or deflate and are among the lightest sleeping pads on the market. We keep our closed-cell foam pads buckled to the outside of our backpacks so we can quickly and easily unbuckle and throw them on the ground for use as sit pads during breaks or for impromptu lunchtime naps. (Tip: Renee has found that by stretching regularly, her hip pain experienced while using her closed-cell foam sleeping pad can be mediated or eliminated altogether. Her favorite stretch: "pigeon pose.")

INFLATABLE PADS: These sleeping pads are filled with air, either by blowing into a mouthpiece or by using a pump. They are approximately 3 inches thick and closely resemble plastic inflatable pool rafts. In addition to air, some inflatable pads are filled with an insulating material, such as down feathers, for added insulation. They compress to be much smaller than closed-cell foam pads and are almost always stowed inside hikers' backpacks. Despite their small size when packed, most inflatable pads are heavier than closed-cell foam pads, and they tend to be much more expensive. Although inflatable pads are excellent insulators and are considered by many to be the most comfortable type of sleeping pad, they are not without drawbacks. Some inflatable pads are noisy when their user is moving or rolling about. They also need to be inflated before use, which is a tedious task after a long day of hiking. They can pop or puncture and rapidly deflate. In desert areas where sharp thorns are abundant, inflatable sleeping pads often need to be patched to repair micropunctures. Sometimes leaks are not patchable, which can lead to extreme danger when pads go flat in cold temperatures; without the insulating layer of air, body heat is quickly lost to the cold ground.

SELF-INFLATING PADS: These sleeping pads are an attempt to achieve the comfort of an inflatable pad with the simplicity of a closed-cell foam pad. They are usually between 1 and 2 inches thick, and they have an inflatable chamber that is filled with expanding foam. When their valve is opened, the foam expands and sucks in air. Then, the valve can be closed to trap the air inside. After use, the user deflates the pad by rolling it like a nearly empty tube of toothpaste to force out all of the air. These are a great option for adventurers who want an air mattress but hate blowing it up. However, they are a compromise: They do not offer the insulation, comfort, or small size of inflatable pads, and they are not as light or reliable as closed-cell foam pads. Like an inflatable pad, self-inflating pads can pop or puncture and become useless.

A WINTER CAMPING TRIP IN FRIGID WISCONSIN

Relatively early in our love affair with the outdoors, Renee and I decided there would be no better adventure than an overnight snowshoeing trip in northern Wisconsin. We chose a weekend based on our schedules, not bothering to check the weather in advance. That was our first mistake. Before the trip, we had signed up to spend winter weekends volunteering as wolf trackers for the Wisconsin Department of Natural Resources. This involved looking for wolf prints in the snow to help count the number of wolves in the state. We had recently completed tracker training, and we couldn't wait for some hands-on experience. We envisioned frolicking along for miles in fresh, deep snow, counting wolf tracks while we went. Maybe we'd even get lucky and spot a wolf!

It was already afternoon when we set out snowshoeing into the wilderness, and in northern Wisconsin during the winter, days are short. Forward progress in the deep snow was slow. We had barely made it a mile in when we realized we should stop and set up camp; otherwise, we'd be pitching our tent in the dark. We thought we might have seen a set of wolf tracks, but we hadn't spotted any wolves. We built a fire and cooked dinner as the temperature started to plummet. Before we knew it, any traces of daylight were completely gone, and the temperature had dropped to 0°F. There wasn't much to do other than go to bed. It would be a long night ....

Shortly after getting into our sleeping bags, my inflatable sleeping pad began to soften. Soon, it was completely flat, and there was no insulation between me and the snow. I reinflated the pad, and it held for only minutes before it went flat again. We hadn't brought a patch kit for this short trip (not that the glue would have worked at these temperatures anyway), so the only possible solution, aside from heading back to the car through deep snow in the dark, was to keep reinflating the pad over and over again. Renee and I took turns trying to sleep on the punctured sleeping pad, but it was futile. Every time it deflated, whichever one of us who was using it became dangerously cold from being in contact with the cold ground below. At one point, we both put on our boots and coats and walked in circles around the tent to try to warm up.

Finally, after a mostly sleepless night, the sun came up and we seized the opportunity to move toward warmth. Our plan had been to spend the second day of the trip enjoying the outdoors and looking for more signs of wolves, but we were no longer interested in anything besides sitting in the car with the heat turned all the way up. When we finally we made it to our car, we climbed in and slowly started warming up. We survived!

We did not see any wolves or have the adventure we envisioned, but we learned an important lesson on this trip: Inflatable sleeping pads can and do pop, and a popped sleeping pad is useless. Because of the extremely cold temperature, our flat sleeping pad wasn't just a matter of discomfort; it was outright dangerous. Since that trip, we have never gone backpacking without bringing along our bulky but trusty closed-cell foam pads.

—Tim

COOKING & EATING

There are two general approaches to eating on a trip. The first is to cook on the trail, carrying all of the gear necessary to do that. The second is simply never to cook. By carrying a collection of bars, shakes, snacks, and cold-soakable meals, it is possible to eat a balanced diet on trail without cooking. We'll go over the pros and cons of each approach in part 3, but for now, let's dive into the gear requirements for each.

GEAR FOR COOKING ON THE TRAIL

The minimum essential gear for cooking on the trail is a stove, pot, lighter, fuel, and utensil. Optional items include a knife, a cup, a bandana (or napkin), and extras such as multiple pots and pans or additional utensils. This is an area where a lot of weight savings is possible; we have found that off-the-shelf cooking kits for camping or backpacking include far more gear than is necessary for a pleasant experience. If you buy or own a camp cooking set, look through it and consider which items you actually use.

STOVES AND FUEL

CANISTER STOVES: These are the most common type of stove for backpacking. They screw right onto the top of disposable fuel canisters. Canister stoves can be extremely light and are easy to use, but they do require special fuel, which is available from outdoor recreation shops, hardware stores, and even gas stations near areas with a lot of outdoor recreation. For cold-weather trips, canister stoves are not advised because the fuel canister can lose pressure and become unusable.

ALCOHOL STOVES: These stoves are lightweight and affordable. They are so simple that people often build their own alcohol stoves out of aluminum cans. Their fuel source is industrial alcohol, which is widely available as cleaning products, fuel additive for cars, and more. Most alcohol stoves cannot be shut off until they burn a complete load of fuel, which might take several minutes. This makes them a poor choice for dry areas that are at risk for forest fires. In much of the western United States, alcohol stoves are unsafe or prohibited because of forest fire risk.

LIQUID FUEL STOVES: These stoves have a refillable fuel canister that is separate from the stove apparatus. They also have a pump, allowing them to be pressurized at any temperature, even in the frigid cold. They run on a variety of fuels, often including regular gasoline you can pick up at any gas station. Despite their versatility when it comes to temperature and fuel, these stoves can be complicated to maintain and are by far the heaviest option.

CHOOSING A STOVE FOR WINTER CAMPING: On winter camping trips, stoves that work with canister fuel will not work well. Canister fuel comes pressurized from the store, and when the outside temperature is low, the pressure in the canister drops considerably. It is very frustrating to have a canister that you know is half full refuse to eject fuel because of a lack of pressure. (The same phenomenon will depressurize the fuel that powers a lighter. Fortunately, lighters are small enough that this can easily be prevented by keeping your lighter inside an inner pocket when it is cold out.) Liquid fuel stoves that include a manual pumping apparatus are ideal for cold weather because you can increase the pressure to match the changing temperature. Alcohol stoves also work in the winter.

POTS

There are lots of options for pots and pans to take on the trail. Some all-in-one sets include a pot or two, along with a lid that doubles as a pan. On backpacking trips, 99 percent of the cooking most people do is simply boiling water and mixing it with dehydrated food. (See part 3 for information on how to dehydrate food and recipes to make on trail with dehydrated ingredients.) For this type of cooking, all you'll need is a basic pot that's big enough to hold a meal's worth of food and water. We have found that a 1-liter (about 34-ounce) pot is the minimum size that works for us to cook meals for two people. We used to carry a much larger pot, but the added weight and bulk didn't bring any extra functionality. We also have found that by carrying a pot that is taller than it is wide, we can use it as a coffee cup in the morning, eliminating the need to carry a dedicated coffee cup.

MATERIAL: What a pot is made of has a significant impact on its weight, durability, and price. Steel pots are durable and cheap, but they are the heaviest option. Titanium pots are the lightest, but they are the least durable and most expensive. In the middle is aluminum, which is lighter than steel, is less expensive than titanium, and costs somewhere between the two.

HEAT SINKS: Also known as heat exchangers, heat sinks are an option on some, but not all, backpacking and camping pots. A pot with a heat sink has additional metal fins attached to the bottom to help transfer heat from the stove to the pot. These add weight, but they have the potential to save weight by reducing the amount of fuel required to cook a meal. Our own experiments suggest a heat sink reduces the amount of fuel required to boil water by about 33 percent. We use a pot with a heat sink, but this preference is not universal.

EATING UTENSILS

Because they're small and easy to carry, there's no universally best utensil for eating on the trail. Many outdoor enthusiasts use sporks because they combine two tools in one. Sporks are available in plastic, steel, aluminum, or titanium. We typically opt for a titanium spork for weight savings over the other metal options and increased durability compared to plastic. Some backpackers like to use a long-handled spoon. These make it easy to rehydrate store-bought meals right in the bag and then eat out of the bag without getting your hand dirty.

LIGHTERS

A disposable pocket lighter, like a BIC lighter, is an effective option for lighting your stove on trail.

BANDANAS

These can be useful to wipe out pots after use. A bandana also can double as a napkin.

KNIVES OR POCKETKNIVES

Knives are commonly carried by backpackers, either as part of their cook set or in their pocket for utility use. Our own preference is not to carry a knife at all; we realized that we rarely have a use for one. (Note: We do keep a tiny foldable razor blade in our first-aid kit just in case, and it's most frequently used to cut tape.)

GEAR FOR A STOVE-LESS SETUP

Some backpackers eat only bars and snacks on the trail, which requires no cooking gear at all. Another common approach is *cold soaking*, which involves soaking food in unheated water for an hour or two instead of cooking it. Some foods cold-soak well, including most dehydrated meals, but uncooked foods like pasta do not. (See part 3 for more information on cold soaking and recipes.) The only gear required for cold soaking is a sealable jar and an eating utensil. Talenti brand ice-cream jars are very commonly used by hikers for cold soaking. They are short and stout, which makes them easy to eat out of, but any sealable jar works. Peanut butter jars are another option. A sealable lid is important so you can start your cold soak while you're hiking so your food will be ready to eat when you arrive at camp. It would be no fun to get to camp and then have to wait an hour to eat while your food slowly rehydrates without heat!

GEAR FOR AN ANIMAL-PROOF CAMPSITE

A few additional pieces of gear are needed to protect a campsite from animals, particularly in areas frequented by bears and/or rodents. Always check local regulations because different public lands have different requirements for food storage. These regulations are usually set to match the habits of the animals in the region, so it is a good idea to follow them! (See pages 119 to 121 for more details about sharing the wilderness with animals.)

FOOD HANGING BAG: If you will be hanging your food, you'll need a dedicated food bag. The bag should be big enough to store all of your food and scented items like cooking equipment, toiletries, and bug spray. If you plan to counterbalance two bags of food, as is required in some areas, be sure to bring two bags, each large enough for half of your food. Look for bags that are light and water resistant. Carrying more weight than necessary should be avoided, but it is no fun to deal with soggy food after a rainstorm.

ROPE: Carry at least 40 feet of lightweight rope like parachute cord if you will be hanging food. Different rope materials generate different amounts of friction when strung over branches. Ropes with less friction are easier to use for hanging food.

BEAR-RESISTANT BAG: Ursack sells bear-resistant food bags that can be tied directly to the trunk of a tree. Bears are not able to bite through the bags, although they may chomp on them, crushing the food inside. These are simple to use, making them our favorite option wherever they are permitted. Not all public lands permit the use of these bags for food storage, so check regulations before you set out with these in your pack.

BEAR CANISTER: Several companies manufacture bear-proof canisters for backcountry food storage. These are rigid jars with tamper-proof lids that bears can't open. Many public lands require bear canisters, especially in areas with large black bear populations. Bear canisters are heavy and unwieldy to stuff in a backpack, but where they are required, they are the only option.

THE EVOLUTION OF OUR COOK SET

Over thousands of miles, we have whittled down our cook set. We started backpacking with an off-the-shelf camping cook set that included multiple pots and pans that fit together, two cups, two forks, two spoons, and two knives. We never actually used most of this equipment. When we set out on the 2,650-mile PCT, we ditched this setup and replaced it with one pot with a pan that doubled as a lid, two sporks, a titanium coffee cup, and two plastic cold-soak jars. The weight was one third as much as the original cook set, but it was still much more equipment than we needed. For the 3,000-mile CDT, we pared down even more: We started with only a single tall pot with a lid (that triples as a coffee cup and cold-soak container) and two sporks. We mailed one of the sporks home after about a week when we realized we weren't using it; our shared pot is small and narrow, so it's easy to pass it and the spork back and forth as we eat. Plus, this slows down our pace of eating. For hungry hikers, there's always the risk of scarfing down calories without remembering to enjoy them. This setup has been working for us for about 5,000 miles, but it took us our first 5,000 miles to figure it out! We don't necessarily recommend sharing a spork (or even a cook set), but we found that this works for us. It's always a good idea to evaluate and reevaluate what you're actually using and enjoying versus what is just wasting weight on your back.

—Renee and Tim

WATER, WATER FILTERS & WATER BOTTLES

It is extremely important that you stay hydrated on a hike and have enough water in your pack to cover the stretches between water sources. Our rule of thumb is to carry about 1 liter of water per person for every 5 miles of hiking and another liter for each meal. For example, a 15-mile dry stretch of trail that includes lunch would require that we carry 4 liters of water per person. On hot days you'll need more water, and on cold days you'll need less.

But water is heavy. Carrying a water filter allows you to collect water along the way from natural sources, such as streams, rivers, and lakes, to filter and drink. This lets you stay hydrated while minimizing the amount of water you need to carry on your back to only what is necessary to get from one water source to the next.

COMMERCIAL WATER FILTERS

Several different types of water filters are available. Different filters filter different things, so it's important to consider what is needed for the particular area you are hiking in. Following are some, but not all, of the more popular choices for backpackers that are safe to use while hiking in most of the United States. Most commercial water filters remove bacteria and protozoa (like the parasites that cause giardia) but not chemical pollutants. It is advisable not to drink from polluted water sources at all, no matter what kind of filter you have.

HOLLOW FIBER FILTERS: These rely on tiny tubes through which water is squeezed during the filtering process. Water can pass through the tubes, but pathogens cannot.

Hollow fiber filters are lightweight and easy to use, and they last a very long time. They should never be allowed to freeze; this will rupture the tubes and render the filter ineffective. We avoid freezing our filters by putting them inside our sleeping bags on cold nights. When they become clogged, hollow fiber filters can be "backflushed" to restore the flow rate. This involves running clean water backward through the filter. Due to their simplicity and reliability, hollow fiber filters are our favorite type of water purification device.

UV: These use ultraviolet (UV) light to kill any pathogens present in water. To use these purifiers, a UV light wand is stirred around in a water bottle for a minute or so until the pathogens have been killed. UV purifiers do not remove sediment, and they run on a rechargeable battery. If you opt for this type of purification system, be sure to have enough juice in your power bank to keep the battery charged.

HAND PUMPS: Until recently, hand pumps were the most common type of water filtration device seen on the trail. Hand pumping uses a pumping device that forces water through a filter made of ceramic, glass, or carbon. Hand pumps are effective, but they are heavier than other options and have to be maintained periodically. We stopped using hand pumps as soon as we discovered hollow fiber filters.

WATER PURIFICATION TABLETS

Water purification tablets are lighter and require less work than water filters. They use chemicals like iodine or chlorine dioxide to kill bacteria, protozoa, and viruses. You simply drop a tablet into your water bottle and wait about 30 minutes (or per the manufacturer's directions). The downsides are you have to wait, the tablets do not get rid of sediment, and some may make your water taste funny.

BOILING

Boiling water also kills bacteria, protozoa, and viruses. If you are already bringing along a pot, stove, and fuel for cooking, no extra gear is required. The downsides of boiling include that you have to wait and that boiling does not get rid of sediment. Boiling can be a good backup option when you aren't sure if your go-to water filter has been compromised (e.g., by freezing).

WATER BOTTLES

We've mentioned that it's essential to carry enough water while hiking; it's also important to ensure you have enough bottles and bottle capacity to carry that necessary water. Remember, you need about 1 liter of water per person for every 5 miles of hiking plus another liter for every meal.

DISPOSABLE BOTTLES: We usually reuse disposable plastic water bottles because they are extremely light and it's easy to adjust the quantity of bottles we're carrying; we can easily grab an extra bottle almost anywhere if we need more capacity or toss one in the recycling bin when we don't. Brands like Smartwater or LIFEWTR make surprisingly durable bottles. Experience has taught us that these "disposable" bottles will last for several months of constant use without failing. Plus, disposable water bottles have neck threading that matches many hollow fiber filters. A filter can be screwed directly onto the top of these water bottles in place of their cap.

WATER BLADDERS: Many hikers like to drink from a water bladder on the trail. These flexible plastic sacks can be filled with 2 or 3 liters of water and then slipped right into a backpack. They have a long straw you can strap over your shoulder and drink from while you walk. We have found it difficult to keep track of our water intake when the bladder is out of sight, which can cause us to run out of water sooner than we expected or drink less than we intended. That said, lots of hikers love the added convenience of bladders.

ELECTRONICS

Electronics have become very important for backpacking. Many people use their cell phone as their primary navigation tool instead of paper maps or a GPS device. A power bank is a great way to charge that cell phone and other small electronics like headlamps and emergency beacons. Following is an overview of these and other electronics commonly used on backpacking trips.

CELL PHONE: A cell phone can be used for maps and navigation (see page 35) as well as to take photos and videos.

POWER BANK: When choosing a power bank for backpacking or thruhiking, there are numerous factors to consider, including size in milliamp hours (mAh), weight, ports, and charging time.

Size: The required capacity of a power bank depends on phone usage, number of devices being charged, and trip length. We recommend starting with a 10,000-mAh power bank, which can fully charge most phones one or two times, with some additional power left over for charging a headlamp or other small device.

Charging time: Charging time is important for longer trips with resupply stops. Many companies market the time it takes for the power bank to charge a cell phone. The time it takes to charge the power bank itself actually can be more important for a hiker who wants their stops in town to be shorter. For short trips that don't require recharging a power bank along the way, this is not an important factor.

RECHARGEABLE HEADLAMP: If you are already carrying a power bank for your phone, a rechargeable headlamp is much more convenient than a battery-powered one. The amount of power needed to charge a headlamp is almost negligible compared to a cell phone. Weight and battery life also should be considered when choosing a headlamp.

WALL PLUG: A wall plug is necessary on longer trips with resupply stops. Whether you're spending the night at a hotel or just a few hours in town to resupply, even your wall plug can be optimized to charge your phone and power bank efficiently. A high-powered wall plug helps reduce charging times and can get you back out on the trail quicker. A dual-port wall plug allows you to charge your cell phone and power bank at the same time—and it can save weight compared to carrying two wall plugs.

CHARGING CABLES: Don't forget to bring the correct cables for your devices. This can be surprisingly challenging, considering all the options (USB-C, micro-USB, Lightning, etc.)! Minimize the number of cables you need to bring by choosing electronic devices with the same charging ports. If you plan to charge your cell phone and power bank at the same time during a resupply stop, don't forget to bring separate cables for each.

PLASTIC BAG: A simple ziplock plastic bag is an inexpensive and lightweight way to keep your power bank, headlamp, wall plug, and charging cables organized and dry.

EMERGENCY BEACON: An emergency satellite beacon can be used to send your location via satellite to rescue agencies. Cell phones do not always get service, so consider an emergency beacon, especially in remote locations or for solo hikers. A range of options are available to choose from. A personal locator beacon is only able to send an SOS signal. A satellite messenger can send an SOS signal as well as satellite-based text messages. When cell phone service is unavailable, satellite messaging can be nice for checking in with family and friends to let them know you are safe and to share your location. (See chapter 7 for more information on backcountry communication and emergency satellite beacons.)

A NOTE ABOUT SOLAR PANELS

A solar panel may sound like a great option to power a hike, but solar panels require strong, direct sunlight to work well. While hiking, especially in the forest and under clouds, it can be almost impossible to gain any power at all. Power banks are usually lighter and much more reliable than solar panels.

TOILETRIES

Hygiene is important out on the trail. However, depending on the type of trip, social expectations for cleanliness can vary, and likewise, the required toiletries can vary, too. Hygiene practices that preserve long-term health shouldn't be sacrificed, regardless of trip length. In other words: Always brush your teeth! But on the other hand, appearance and even odor-oriented practices become less important as a trip gets longer and more remote. Hygiene amounts to personal preference, so here are some of our own gear practices for toiletries and hygiene.

TOOTHBRUSH AND TOOTHPASTE: Tooth and gum maintenance is important for lifelong health and longevity. We bring toothbrushes and a travel-sized tube of toothpaste on every one of our camping trips, regardless of the length. We don't want to ignore our dental hygiene on a trip and pay the price later.

POOP SHOVEL: Everybody poops. On trips away from civilization, there are often no bathrooms or outhouses. On most (but not all) public lands, it is appropriate to dig a "cathole" for human waste. Holes should be 6 to 8 inches deep so that waste can be fully buried away from curious animals that might dig it up. For trips that involve digging catholes, it can be very helpful to bring along a lightweight trowel to help with digging. In some crowded areas or dry places where waste biodegrades slowly, it is not appropriate to use catholes at all, and instead all human waste should be carried out. You can get sealable human waste bags to carry out your waste. Check the regulations for wherever you are headed.

TOILET PAPER: If you expect to poop in the woods, it is important to have a plan for wiping. Some hikers carry toilet paper. In some areas, it's okay to bury toilet paper, but in others, regulations require (or recommend) packing it out. Many hikers choose to use natural products to wipe, including sticks, rocks, and water.

PORTABLE BIDET: A portable bidet is a small nozzle that can be screwed onto a disposable water bottle for cleaning your butt after going poop. An alternative is to just pour water from your bottle onto your butt, but the bidet adds pressure.

MENSTRUAL PRODUCTS: A menstrual cup is a lightweight, low-waste option for periods on trail. Tampons and/or pads are another option, but all waste needs to be packed out.

PEE CLOTH: An antimicrobial pee cloth, or even just a bandana, that can be clipped or tied onto the outside of your pack is an option for people who prefer to wipe after they pee on trail.

WIPES: Because real showers are so hard to come by on trail, many hikers carry small wipes to clean themselves at the end of a dirty day. These can be especially useful to maintain health and prevent infection in sensitive areas. Don't forget to pack out all waste! Wipes should not be buried.

LIP BALM, LOTION, AND/OR VASELINE: Dry skin and chapped lips are no fun. Consider carrying these items, especially in dry climates, to stay comfortable on the trail. Look for lip balm with sunscreen to avoid sunburned lips. Lotion can help relieve chafing, and Vaseline can help keep hot spots from turning into blisters. Experiment with what works for you.

DEODORANT: Although it sounds disgusting to skip deodorant, deodorant actually didn't exist for most of human history. We don't wear deodorant on our long-distance trips, and we skip it on short trips, too. Showers aren't usually possible while backpacking, and layering deodorant on top of deodorant isn't super effective.

SOAP AND SHAMPOO: When deciding whether or not to carry soap and shampoo on an outdoor trip, remember that these products are only useful when coupled with showers or baths. If you don't expect to take either in the wilderness, you probably won't have much use for soap or shampoo. Biodegradable soaps are available for camping, but whether they are actually harmless to the environment is hotly debated among outdoor enthusiasts. Plus, who wants to try to bathe in a cold stream, anyway? Most backpackers, including us, don't carry soap or shampoo on our camping trips, but on long trips we do use them when passing through a town where we are able to take a real shower at a hotel or campground.

HIKING POLES

Hiking poles are a modern form of walking stick. They are lightweight and can be used for extra power and balance. They are particularly useful on steep slopes, whether going uphill or down. They also reduce hand swelling because they keep your hands elevated, and gripping the poles promotes circulation, preventing blood from pooling in your hands. Some backpackers think hiking poles are a nerdy-looking piece of extraneous gear. Others consider them an essential part of their kit for comfort, speed, and balance. As mentioned earlier, hiking poles are sometimes needed for a surprising reason: Many models of ultralight tents shave weight by not including dedicated poles. Instead, they are propped up with hiking poles based on the assumption that the user will be carrying poles anyway.

A good set of hiking poles can easily last for thousands of miles. The best way to use hiking poles isn't always obvious on the first try; we recommend matching the speed of your hiking pole "steps" to your footsteps. There are a few points to consider when choosing a set of poles.

TYPE: Hiking poles are long and skinny—an awkward shape for travel! Non-collapsible poles are the hardest to travel with and have a fixed height, but they can be very strong and light. Foldable poles are the smallest for travel, but they are heavier than fixed poles and also have a fixed height. Telescoping poles are the heaviest variety, but they are relatively small when collapsed and their height is adjustable, making them a great option for beginners or for sharing.

WEIGHT: Lightweight hiking poles are much more pleasant to use than heavy poles. Poles are usually made from carbon fiber or aluminum. Carbon fiber poles are lighter than aluminum, but they usually cost substantially more.

CHANGEABLE TIPS: The point of contact between a hiking pole and the ground wears over time. A good set of poles will have removable tips that are easy to replace when needed. Pole tips do not wear out frequently, so even on long-distance trails, it is not necessary to carry a spare set of tips with you; just purchase new ones when needed.

SHOES

Shoes are an extremely important factor for backpacking enjoyment. Walking miles upon miles with a load on your back is hard enough; add blisters to the equation, and an enjoyable trip can turn miserable pretty quickly!

SIZE: We recommend backpacking shoes that are at least half a size bigger than your everyday shoes. Backpacking socks are usually thicker than everyday socks, and feet swell when you are walking all day. Shoes that are too small can lead to blisters.

TYPE: Hiking boots are the traditional backpacking shoe, but trail runners have become more popular recently, particularly for long-distance backpacking. As the name implies, trail runners are running shoes designed for trails. They are lighter and more breathable, and they dry faster than traditional hiking boots. Trail runners are the shoe of choice for 95 percent of long-distance hikers on trails like the PCT and CDT. Compared to trail runners, hiking boots are more durable and may provide more support, especially if you're carrying a heavier pack. Hiking shoes are also an option; they are a middle ground between hiking boots and trail runners. They are lighter than hiking boots but provide more support than trail runners.

We recommend trying out shoes to ensure they are comfortable before you head out on a backpacking trip. Going on a day hike with your loaded backpack is a great way to try out your shoes, but we recommend at least going for a walk in them around your neighborhood.

Note that shoes do not last forever! They should be replaced about every 500 miles (or per your shoe manufacturer's recommendation). On very long thruhikes, expect to go through several pairs of shoes and order replacements along the way.

GROWING FEET

I started our first long-distance hike on the PCT from Mexico to Canada in a size 7 trail running shoe, which was half a size bigger than my regular shoes. A few weeks into the hike, my feet were swollen from all of the walking in the desert heat, plus I had a few blisters. At mile 450, I switched to a size 7.5 shoe, and my feet were much happier for the remainder of the trail. I assumed my feet would eventually return to normal. But a few months after we completed the trail, my pre-trail shoes still did not fit. My feet were now a size 7.5 permanently—and also much wider than they had been before the trail.

On our second long-distance hike, on the CDT from Mexico to Canada, I started in my size 7.5 shoes. About 500 miles into the desert, both of my feet were covered in blisters. I had a blister on every single toe, on the insides and outsides of my heels, and on the pads of my feet, which were the most painful. At the end of every day, I could barely walk due to the pain. When I switched to a size 8 shoe, my feet were much happier.

Once again, my feet have not returned to their previous size. Over the course of 10,000 miles of hiking, my feet have grown from a size 6.5 to a size 8. Tim's feet also have grown due to hiking, from size 12 to size 13.

—Renee

CLOTHING

Clothing is a great place to save weight on a backpacking trip because clothes are heavy! Clothing is also important for both comfort and safety on trail. We recommend wearing the same outfit every day on backpacking trips. This may sound gross, but the trick is to choose materials that dry out quickly and don't absorb smells. Dirt is unavoidable; whether you change every day or not, you'll be filthy while backpacking. In this section, we highlight some of the tips, tricks, and lessons we've learned regarding clothing for outdoor adventures.

MATERIAL

Common backpacking materials include wool, polyester or other synthetic fabrics, and down (for insulation). Cotton is not a good backpacking fabric because it absorbs water and is slow to dry.

WORN CLOTHING

SOCKS: Quality socks specifically designed for hiking are worth the investment when you are spending all day on your feet walking! They usually have some cushioning and are made of wool and/or synthetic materials, which wick away moisture from your feet to help prevent blisters.

GAITERS: Gaiters are garments worn over shoes and over the bottom of your pant leg if you are wearing pants that help keep debris out of your shoes. We recommend pairing trail running shoes with lightweight gaiters so you don't have to stop to dump rocks out of your shoes every few miles.

UNDERWEAR: Antimicrobial underwear inhibits bacterial growth and is a great option for backpacking. Wool underwear is naturally antimicrobial, whereas synthetic underwear requires an antimicrobial treatment. Underwear can double as a swimsuit if you are backpacking near lakes.

BRA: An antimicrobial sports bra is great for backpacking. A thinner bra without padding dries faster, which is convenient for swimming and sweating.

PANTS AND SHORTS: Synthetic pants or shorts are ideal for camping and backpacking. They are lightweight and dry quickly if they get wet. Shorts are nice if it will be hot, but in some regions, pants are preferred; they provide a layer protection against plants like poison oak and ivy, and even in the hot desert, they shield your legs from the multitude of pointy thorns and brush.

SHIRT: There are lots of options when it comes to shirts for backpacking. Synthetic or wool? T-shirt, long-sleeve shirt, or sun hoodie? Some shirts even have UV protection built in. The season, climate, and your personal preferences are all factors to consider when choosing a shirt to wear on a trip. For example, a lightweight sun hoodie is a great option for hiding from the desert sun. A T-shirt combined with a long-sleeve shirt may be a better option for summer hiking in the mountains, when it's hot during the day but cold in the morning and at night. Synthetic shirts are more durable than wool shirts, but wool shirts are more odor-resistant than some synthetic shirts. We recommend experimenting to find what works best for you.

HAT: A baseball cap helps protect your face and eyes from the sun. A sun hat provides additional protection for your ears and neck.

SUNGLASSES: Look for sunglasses with UV protection. Polarized lenses can help reduce glare when hiking in the snow or near water.

CARRIED EXTRA CLOTHING

EXTRA SOCKS: Although we don't recommend carrying an extra outfit, this doesn't apply to socks. It is a good idea to have at least one change of socks in your backpack to minimize the amount of time you are stuck with wet feet. In cold and/or wet environments, we will carry two extra pairs of socks to keep our feet as happy as possible.

EXTRA UNDERWEAR: An extra pair of underwear is also a good idea for health and hygiene. Renee typically carries two extra pairs of underwear to rotate between, and Tim carries one extra pair.

LAYERS

LONG-SLEEVE SHIRT: Depending on the season and climate, it is a good idea to bring along a long-sleeve shirt for an added layer of warmth. Temperatures can drop significantly overnight, especially in the mountains. Wool, synthetic, or even fleece is recommended, with thickness depending on the weather forecast.

BASE LAYER: The primary function of a base layer is to wear overnight as pajamas. Even if you don't wear pajamas at home, they are a good idea for when you are out on the trail. Body moisture soaks into the clothing you wear all day, which cools down the body significantly if you leave your clothes on overnight. Using a dry base layer as pajamas goes a long way to maintain warmth, even on cold nights. The second function of a base layer is to use it as yet another layer to wear during the day if temperatures get unexpectedly cold. Again, choose wool or synthetic, not cotton.

RAINCOAT AND PANTS: Letting yourself get cold and wet is a guaranteed way to ruin a trip. A lightweight raincoat and rain pants are well worth the weight if the weather decides to turn. If we are backpacking in a very dry and warm climate and there is no rain in the forecast, we might omit the rain pants, but we never head out without raincoats. A rain poncho is another option instead of—or in very wet climates, in addition to—a raincoat and pants. Ponchos can cover you and your backpack at the same time. Yet another option is a rain skirt instead of rain pants.

RAIN MITTS: Lightweight waterproof mittens keep your hands dry in the rain. We have found that wet hands can suck a lot of warmth out of our bodies, so we both keep a set of rain mitts with us for extra protection when rain is in the forecast.

PUFFY JACKET: The beauty of a down puffy jacket is that it is extremely lightweight and compressible when not needed, but it provides lots of insulation when the temperature drops. Down jackets lose their ability to insulate if they get wet, so in very wet climates, fleece jackets are a reliable alternative. Synthetic puffy jackets also are very lightweight and compressible and can serve as an alternative to down.

BUFF OR BEANIE: A buff is a multifunctional tube of wool or synthetic fabric. It can be worn on your head as a hat for warmth or on your neck for protection against bugs. A buff or a beanie is very effective to wear in your sleeping bag on cold nights to trap extra heat while you sleep.

GLOVES: Mornings on the trail can be surprisingly cold on our hands. Even in the summertime, we both carry a lightweight set of glove liners (i.e., thin gloves) that fit under our rain mitts.

FIRST-AID & GEAR-REPAIR KIT

There are two extreme schools of thought when it comes to packing a first-aid kit for the trail. The first is that you should be prepared for anything and everything because dangerous things can happen outside and help may be hard to find on the trail. The second is that you can't carry a hospital on your back, no matter how hard you try, so why bother? Just carry an emergency beacon if needed. Every adventurer falls somewhere between these two extremes, depending on their own personal risk tolerance. We are comfortable carrying a first-aid kit with essentials to get us to the nearest hospital if necessary. This attitude does come with accepting a certain amount of risk if getting out of the wilderness proves to be harder than expected.

Inside our first-aid kit, we also carry a few items for in-field gear repairs, which we end up using much more often than our first-aid items.

Following are a few essentials to consider putting in a first-aid kit. These are our first-aid essentials, but you can adjust your own kit to fit your needs. We carry only small quantities of each item. For example, we don't carry a full bottle of 100 painkillers; instead, we put 5 to 10 in a small ziplock bag that we label with the name of the medicine and the expiration date.

PRESCRIPTION MEDICINES: If you take any prescription medicines, be sure to bring them along.

PAINKILLERS: Avoiding painkillers as much as possible can be a good way to stay in tune with your body and avoid injury, but sometimes they are nice to have.

ANTIHISTAMINES: Bee stings, poison oak/ivy/sumac, or seasonal allergies can affect you while out on the trail. We keep antihistamines on hand just in case one of us has an allergic reaction.

ALCOHOL WIPES: It is good practice to disinfect open wounds and popped blisters with alcohol.

FIRST-AID OINTMENT: After applying alcohol, use ointment to help prevent infection in open wounds and popped blisters.

BANDAGES AND GAUZE: Bandages and gauze are good for minor cuts and scrapes. For anything major, a trip to the hospital is probably required.

LEUKOTAPE P: This is an extremely sticky type of sports tape that stays bound to skin for days. We always have Leukotape P on hand to protect hot spots from blister formation.

TWEEZERS: These can be used for removing the occasional splinter or cactus thorn.

NAIL CLIPPERS: On long hikes, it is a good idea to cut your toenails from time to time to avoid blisters and ingrown nails.

RAZOR BLADE OR KNIFE: We keep a lightweight foldable razor blade in our first-aid kit. We have found that full-blown pocketknives are unnecessary 99 percent of the time, but every now and then we find a use for a sharp edge.

NEEDLE AND THREAD: Sometimes, bad blisters call for treatment with a needle. Needles also come in handy for in-the-field gear repairs. In a pinch, dental floss can serve as a very strong thread for sewing ripped equipment and shoes back together.

MINI LIGHTER: We keep a backup lighter in our first-aid kit, just in case our primary lighter breaks or we lose it. We also use the lighter to disinfect our needle before puncturing blisters. Matches are also an option.

REPAIR TAPE: We keep technical tape (e.g., Tenacious Tape) on hand for gear repairs; this is especially important when the shell of a down item such as a sleeping bag or puffy jacket tears. We also make sure to have a little bit of duct tape as a backup, just in case. You do not need to carry full rolls of tape; we like to cut off a section of tape and reroll it on itself.

CONSUMABLES

Outdoor adventures involve several consumable products that have to be replenished before a trip, after a trip, or along the way. These include the following.

FUEL: Whatever type of stove you choose, be sure to bring along enough fuel for your entire trip, or know where you can replenish along the way.

SUNSCREEN: Protect your skin by wearing sunscreen, especially on your face and ears.

BUG SPRAY: Depending on the time of year and location of your trip, bug spray may or may not be necessary.

BEAR SPRAY: If you'll be traveling through areas with bears, especially grizzly bears, carrying bear spray is something to consider. Bear spray is a high-powered can of pepper spray that can repel a bear in case of an attack. Ideally, this won't be a consumable item at all—hopefully, you'll never have to use it! (We have not yet had to use our bear spray despite thousands of miles of backpacking in bear country.)

FOOD: Make a food plan before heading out, and be sure to carry enough food for your entire trip or enough to get to your next resupply stop if you'll be resupplying. If you are unsure how long the trip will take, carry extra food for safety.

PACKING A BACKPACK TO MAXIMIZE COMFORT

Packing a backpack correctly is essential to maximizing comfort, especially for frameless packs that have no built-in support structure. It makes a huge difference for all packs, though, framed or not. You should start with a good base at the bottom of your pack, followed by the heaviest items in the middle of the pack, and then your lighter gear on top.

For framed backpacks, start by stuffing your sleeping bag directly into the bottom of your pack (without a stuff sack) to create a solid base with no gaps. You can push awkwardly shaped items, such as your pot and a plastic bag of toiletries, directly into your sleeping bag—they'll disappear amid the soft insulation. Next, put in the heavier stuff, like food and electronics, directly on top of your sleeping bag, still trying to avoid gaps. On top, put your extra clothing layers and tent.

For frameless packs, try to pack any semirigid items in a way that lets them serve as a pseudo frame. For example, if you have a closed-cell foam sleeping pad, you can put it vertically inside a frameless pack to add structure and support.

Items that you expect to use throughout the day should go in the external pockets. This includes snacks, your phone and maps, a poop trowel, and a jacket and/or raincoat,

depending on the weather. It also works well to dry out things on the outside of your pack, like the socks you wore the day before or anything else that may be wet or damp. The sun does an amazing job of drying damp items during the course of a day on the trail!

TIP

Stuff sacks might sound like a good idea to stay organized, but they don't mold to your pack. They leave gaps and do not build up a good structure within the pack. Using excessive stuff stacks and bags is like trying to tightly fill a water bottle with ice cubes; there's no avoiding gaps. Because the backpack isn't hard-shelled, it ends up being misshapen and sometimes lopsided—not comfortable to wear.

That said, a minimal number of bags do make sense for organization. We recommend using a food bag, or bear-proof food container if required, to keep your food separated from the rest of your gear. We like to carry a water-resistant bag for our clothing (which also doubles as a pillow); we usually leave it open so it molds well to the shape of our packs. When it's raining, we stuff our sleeping bag and clothing into it, squeeze all of the air out of it, seal it, and stuff it into the bottom of our packs as the base.

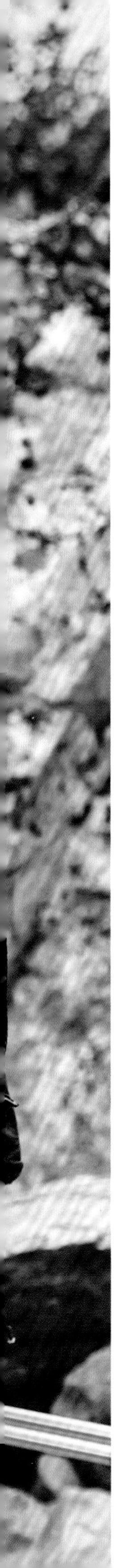

THRUHIKERS' TIPS

GEAR

- Choose a tent that's designed for backpacking (car camping tents are too heavy), and be sure you have all of the pieces with you (tent, rain fly, ground sheet, tent poles or hiking poles, and stakes, as applicable).
- Mummy sleeping bags or quilts are both good options. Consider the temperature rating, length, and weight when choosing a bag or quilt.
- Always bring a sleeping pad for insulation between you and the ground (as well as comfort).
- Less is more when it comes to a camp kitchen. Most backpackers just boil water for dehydrated meals, so a single pot that you eat out of may be all you need. Pots that are taller than they are wide can double as a coffee cup.
- Hollow fiber water filters are quickly becoming the most popular method for filtering water because they are convenient, lightweight, and easy to maintain.
- It is easier to monitor your water intake with water bottles as compared to water bladders.
- For trips longer than a night or two, a power bank is a great way to charge cell phones and rechargeable headlamps.
- The only toiletries we typically carry are a travel-sized tube of toothpaste, a toothbrush, a menstrual cup (when applicable), hand sanitizer, and a poop shovel for digging catholes.
- Lightweight aluminum or carbon fiber hiking poles are helpful for balance and power—and sometimes double as tent poles for non-freestanding tents.
- Hiking boots are heavy and hot, and they dry slowly when wet. Consider wearing hiking shoes or trail runners instead.
- Wear the same outfit every day when backpacking, and bring layers and rain gear adjusted for the weather you may encounter. (We do like to bring an extra pair of socks or two and at least one change of underwear.)
- Choose wool or quick-drying synthetic clothing. Cotton is not recommended.
- Carry a first-aid kit, including prescription medications, and also some gear-repair tape. We recommend assembling your own kit and storing it in a ziplock bag.
- When packing our backpacks, we push our sleeping bags into the bottom to create a nice base, put our heavier stuff (like food and electronics) in the middle, and arrange the lightest stuff on top.

5

TAKING CARE OF & STORING GEAR

After a trip, it's important to ensure all of your gear is clean, dry, and organized. This will prolong its life, so it will last for many years and many adventures, and it will make it easier to pack up and get back out on the trail next time.

EVALUATE YOUR GEAR

Unpacking from any trip is a perfect opportunity to take a close look at everything you brought and ask yourself if you needed it. Items that stayed in a pocket of your backpack from when you left your house until you returned might not justify their own weight. For instance, if you brought an extra power bank, just in case, but didn't need the juice at all, it probably doesn't make sense to carry it along on your next similar-distance trip. Similarly, if you brought along games or a book but were too exhausted to use them, you'll probably be too exhausted to use them next time as well. Just after a trip, when it's fresh in your mind, is the best time to go through your packing list with a fine-tooth comb and trim the fat.

This advice doesn't perfectly apply to safety or backup equipment like your first-aid kit or rain gear. If you didn't use your first-aid kit, that doesn't necessarily mean you shouldn't bring it on your next trip, and if it didn't rain this time, that doesn't mean it never will. Nevertheless, if you did experience the conditions that your backup gear is intended for but you still didn't use it, that is an indication that the gear might be excessive. For example, if you were poured on but never used rain pants, then carrying them on similar trips isn't justified. If you sustained an injury but didn't need many of the items in your first-aid kit, it might be oversized. Being careful but critical about every item that lives in your pack is the best way to simplify your hike and minimize the weight on your back.

PREPARE GEAR FOR STORAGE

Unpacking after a trip is never fun, especially after a backpacking trip. But it's very important to ensure all of your gear is completely dry before storing it. Wet or damp gear can get moldy and break. A moldy tent, for example, can develop little holes and lose its waterproofness.

TENTS: The easiest way to dry a tent is to set it up in your backyard in the sun. The ground sheet and rain fly can be laid out on the ground separately and flipped over halfway through drying to ensure both sides dry completely. If you don't have yard space or if the weather is bad, you can hang the tent, but be sure there is plenty of airflow around it, and move it or reposition it every few hours while it dries so water doesn't get trapped in any folds.

SLEEPING BAGS: Sleeping bags do not need to be washed every time they are used. In fact, they probably shouldn't be washed more than once a year. Like a tent, they also can be laid out in the sun to dry. The sun's UV rays help kill microscopic bacteria that could be growing on or in the sleeping bag. Unzip sleeping bags before laying them out, and flip them over halfway through drying to ensure all sides, inside and out, get completely dry. If it's not sunny, you can hang or lay your sleeping bag indoors on a flat surface instead.

COOKING EQUIPMENT: On trail, we recommend washing your pot, spork, and any other cooking equipment with water only (no soap), so it is a good idea to wash all cooking equipment with soap when you get home to avoid mold growth in storage. Only use the dishwasher for cooking equipment that is dishwasher safe. Be sure everything is completely dry before storing it.

CLOTHING: Puffy jackets and rain gear do not need to be washed after every trip. It is important to be sure they are dry, though. They can be laid out on the ground or hung with plenty of airflow around them until they are completely dry. If you do wash them, they should be washed with special detergent per the manufacturer's recommendations. Other clothing should be washed and dried per the recommendations on the tags.

HOLLOW FIBER WATER FILTERS: Hollow fiber water filters require backflushing to keep them flowing well. It is much easier to backflush at home, where you have plenty of access to clean water, than out on the trail. Some filters can even be connected directly to the faucet, and the additional water pressure allows for a more effective backwash. If your filter is really clogged, it can be soaked in white vinegar for about 30 minutes before backflushing. There is no way to completely dry the fibers of a filter, but before storing one, you should let it air-dry for a while so it is as dry as possible to reduce the likelihood of bacterial growth.

WATER BOTTLES AND BLADDERS: Water bottles and bladders should be washed and dried completely before storage to avoid the growth of mold, mildew, and bacteria.

STORING GEAR

After you've evaluated, dried, and washed all of your gear, the next step is to store it. Backpacking equipment lasts much longer if properly stored, and an organized storage system makes it easier to pack and prepare for your next trip. Gear should be removed from stuff sacks and stored in an uncompressed way that provides airflow. Large plastic bins are an efficient way to store hard products like cookware, while fabrics can require more care.

SLEEPING BAGS: Sleeping bags should be decompressed before storing. If a sleeping bag is compressed for an extended period of time, it loses its loft. When you buy a sleeping bag, it often comes with a large fabric bag to use for long-term storage. These bags provide airflow and are large enough for the sleeping bag to be fully lofted. If you have space under your bed, that's a perfect spot to leave your sleeping bag in its large bag between trips. Sleeping bags can be stored in large plastic bins, but the bins should not be airtight, and you should open them at least every few months to increase airflow.

PUFFY JACKETS: Like sleeping bags, puffy jackets should be decompressed before storing. Some also come with a roomy fabric bag for storage, or they can be hung.

Either way, just be sure they aren't compressed.

RAIN GEAR: Hang rain gear between trips. This helps remove creases and extends the life of the waterproofing.

OTHER CLOTHING: Store your hiking clothes on hangers or in a dresser with the rest of your clothing to maximize both airflow and the garments' life. If you have space, it can be nice to have an "adventure" drawer with all of your backpacking clothing, which makes it easier to find and pack for your next trip and reduces your chances of forgetting something.

COOKING EQUIPMENT: For the sake of organization, we recommend storing all of your camp cooking gear in the same place, such as in a large plastic bin. Your stove should not be connected to your fuel source during storage; they should only be connected when you're cooking. We recommend storing your fuel separate from your gear, like in a garage.

ELECTRONICS: For the sake of organization, we recommend storing adventure-specific electronics (headlamp, power bank, cables, etc.) together.

CARING FOR DOWN

You should always follow the manufacturer's recommendations to take care of your down items, but here are some general tips that apply to common down products like sleeping bags and puffy jackets:

- Washing and drying:
    - Use a dedicated down detergent or, if you can't find one, a mild detergent.
    - Wash in a front-loading washing machine or hand wash. Avoid top-loading washing machines with agitators as these can be rough on the fragile down.
    - Dry in a dryer on the lowest heat setting. It can be helpful to dry with a tennis ball to aid in the fluffing process. Check every 20 to 30 minutes until dry.
    - Be sure the washer and dryer are large enough to fit your sleeping bag with plenty of room to spare. If not, consider going to a Laundromat instead.
- If a feather is popping out through the fabric, avoid pulling it out if possible. Instead, try to pull it back in from the other side.
- If you have a hole in your sleeping bag or puffy jacket, patch it to avoid losing feathers. Sometimes down items are sold along with a small piece of tape for patching. If not, specialized gear-repair tapes, like Tenacious Tape, are best.
- Store down uncompressed to help it keep its loft.

THRUHIKERS' TIPS

TAKING CARE OF & STORING GEAR

- Right after a trip is the best time to evaluate what you brought along and determine what you can leave at home next time.
- Completely dry all of your gear before storing it. For sleeping bags and clothing, dry them out even if you don't think they got wet—moisture from your body builds up in these items.
- Store sleeping bags uncompressed to prevent them from losing loft over time.
- Store sleeping bags and clothing somewhere that allows a bit of airflow around them to prolong their life.
- Do not wash down items every time you use them. No more than once a year, wash them carefully according to the manufacturer's instructions.

PART 2

ON THE TRAIL

snow peak
GIGA POWER

HOKA

6

LIFE ON THE TRAIL

After you've packed your bags with all of the gear you'll need for your trip, you're ready to head out on the trail! In this chapter, we give you a preview of what life is like when you're out there. Whether you're going on an overnight with friends or planning for a long solo adventure, the experience will be very different from your normal life. By setting realistic expectations, you can maximize your chances of having a great time!

A TYPICAL DAY ON THE TRAIL: WHAT TO EXPECT

A typical day on the trail includes walking, eating, drinking, filtering water, and resting, although not necessarily in that order. After waking up, some hikers make coffee and/or breakfast right away, and others immediately break down their tent and hit the trail. In either case, the earlier you get up and get going, the easier it will be to complete the miles that lie ahead. Our usual compromise is to wake up before sunrise for a few coffees and breakfast in our tent (or, when in bear country, away from the tent) and then hit the trail as the sun starts to brighten up the day. We benefit from the sense of calmness this slow breakfast brings us before we really start moving.

After breaking down camp and hitting the trail, we recommend taking breaks as often as your body asks for them and also eating a snack approximately every 5 miles. On short trips or at the beginning of long thruhikes, your body will require breaks more frequently than it will when you are fully trained. That's okay. Don't neglect your body's requests; rather, use this as an opportunity to enjoy some downtime on the trail, relaxing and being a part of nature. There's no harm in taking extra breaks to enjoy beauty or fun along the trail. For instance, on hot days, we have the habit of dropping everything if we come across a nice swimming hole—the miles can wait. Keep in mind that you probably headed out on the trail to enjoy it, not to "crush miles." Don't lose sight of this when you come across a landmark that would be fun to take a moment to appreciate.

Whenever possible, it can be fun to plan your lunch to coincide with such a landmark. Before heading out for the day, we check the map to see if there are swimming holes, mountain summits, or overlooks that we might hit around lunchtime, which for us is between 11 AM and 2 PM. If so, we'll adjust our morning mileage. Lunchtime is when we typically take our longest break of the day, for at least 1 or 2 hours. These breaks usually include taking off our shoes and socks to air out our feet a bit, eat, filter water, and—more often than not—take a nap. Quite often, we treat ourselves to an extra coffee at lunchtime—there's no such thing as too much coffee for us! When you're lucky, multiple hikers will congregate at the same lunch spot, and you'll be able to socialize while eating. The solitude of nature is lovely, but it's also nice to share your experience of the trail and hear about others' experiences. It is amazing how different a trail can be when viewed through different sets of eyes.

After lunch, there's a risk that the miles can feel like a rough slog toward camp. Much of the reason for this is because the next major milestone you'll hit is probably your campsite, when you get to take off your pack and stop walking. At this point in the day, you are probably starting to get tired and hungry from the day's miles and may be thinking about dinner and your sleeping bag. Hiking isn't as fun if you spend it counting down the miles until you get to stop. One strategy to avoid this trap is to look again at your map for excitement along the route: rock formations, old growth forests, meadows, bogs, canyons, hot springs, and more. If you are focused on getting to an exciting place instead of stopping for the day, you'll enjoy each step rather than dreading it.

Eventually, it will be time to call it a day and set up camp. If you are hiking in an area with established campsites and permits, knowing when to call it a day is as simple as making it to your permitted site. If you are hiking in a place that allows dispersed camping along the trail, you get to pick when and where you'll stop. If you've packed light enough to enjoy yourself while walking and succeeded in enjoying plenty of breaks along the way, you don't need to be in a rush to set up camp. We often bump into hikers who rush through morning and early afternoon to get to camp as early as possible, but once they get there, they get antsy and bored because they're in a fixed place with little to do. If you take your time and enjoy your entire day on the trail, there's no need to set up camp before the sun is getting ready to set. (Chapter 8 has lots of pointers for how to select a comfortable campsite.)

On short trips, dinner followed by sitting around a campfire (if they are allowed) and socializing at camp can be a great end to the day. On longer thruhikes, we are usually too exhausted to build a campfire. One of us cooks dinner on the stove while the other sets up the tent, and after we are done eating, we go straight to bed, just to repeat it all the next day.

BACKPACKING WITH OTHERS

Backpacking can be an individual or group activity. The basics are the same either way—walk, drink water, eat, and sleep—yet group trips introduce several nuances that should be treated with care to ensure everybody has as much fun as possible.

SHARING GEAR: A benefit of hiking with a group is that you can share gear, which means you don't need to carry every item yourself. Shareable items can include your tent, cooking equipment, and certain electronics, such as power banks and GPS devices. Backpacking gear is usually sized for up to two, so even if the total group is larger, it is a good idea to approach gear sharing as an activity for pairs: Each pair of people should have a full set of equipment between them. Tents for three or more people are unwieldy to carry, as are cooking pots for more than two. Keep in mind that pairs of hikers who are sharing equipment should get along well and plan to stick together for an entire trip. It is better to carry a few pieces of redundant gear than to be stuck sharing with a partner you no longer want to be around.

THE SPEED OF A GROUP: You might think that a group moves at the speed of the slowest hiker; however, a group moves at a speed that is much slower than the slowest hiker and covers fewer miles per day than the slowest hiker would do alone. This is because each of the individuals in a group will experience their own delays that cause the entire group to slow down or stop. If the fastest hiker in a group has to pause to tie their shoe, this pause slows down everybody. Planning for this phenomenon and setting expectations accordingly ensures that a group trip is enjoyable for everybody.

MANAGING DIFFERENT SKILL LEVELS: When hiking in a group, different hikers have different comfort and skill levels. These vary with the terrain, weather, mileage, and just about any other hiking-related variable. Varying expectations for speed or comfort can cause conflict and tension among hikers. For instance, some hikers are slow to ascend mountains, others are slow to descend, and still others are fast or slow in both directions. During challenging segments of a trail, which can be stressful enough on their own, group dynamics can add an additional stressor.

Empathizing with your hiking partner(s) is one way to manage different skill levels and expectations. Know that in the moment, there is little a hiker can do to change their speed or endurance. It is tempting to assume that fast hikers can slow down more easily than slow hikers can speed up, but changing your base cadence is difficult for anybody. A trick that can help is to put the slower person in front, which sets the pace of the group and keeps people from unintentionally spreading out. However, no rule states that hikers need to hike together 100 percent of the time. Often, it's more effective to split up and hike individually or in smaller groups and then rendezvous during breaks or easier segments of the trail. If you go this route, use common sense about hiking alone. When the trail gets dangerous, such as during stream crossings, it is usually best to stick with a buddy. Regrouping at forks in the trail ensures that nobody accidentally takes a wrong turn and gets separated.

Our strategy is to hike together 95 percent of the time, but on challenging ascents and descents, we often spread out so we can each go at our own pace. We meet back up when we get to the summit and/or base of a mountain, as well as during dangerous conditions like snow traverses and crossing fast-moving water.

NAMING TREES ON THE PACIFIC CREST TRAIL

When we hiked the Pacific Crest Trail (PCT), we were recent transplants from Wisconsin, where we were very familiar with the animals and vegetation of the area. Red pines and white pines are the most common pine trees in Wisconsin, and we knew how to identify these with certainty. But on the trail in southern California, we were out of our element. As the days ticked by, we discovered a tree that reminded us of Wisconsin's red pines, but it was too big to actually be that tree. We also realized it only grew in size as we ascended into mountains. We became fond of the tree because we usually found it in areas that were great for camping. Because we didn't know the tree's true name, we came up with our own: mountain red pine. It was surprising how powerful it was to have a name for the tree. We could talk about it when we saw it, and we learned more about the tree as we saw it in different locations. It typically grew only in drier areas; we never saw it up high or on moist north-facing slopes. Eventually, we looked up the tree while we were resupplying in a town. Our "mountain red pine" was actually a ponderosa pine, a common tree in the West. All of our observations about its growth habits were correct, and learning them through observation instead of via a list of factual statements in a book made them all the more meaningful and enjoyable to discover.

—Tim

PASSING THE TIME

Boredom is a threat that can suck the fun out of any hike. Nature has no television, no bars or restaurants, and often no cell service to keep you socially connected. But it is full of plants, animals, geology, and geography that can be fascinating if you pay attention to it. Being observant and aware of the nature that surrounds you is a wonderful way to pass the time on a hike.

A surefire way to lose interest in a hike and be faced with boredom is to focus too much on the end goal: Whether your objective is to get to the evening's campsite or a trail's terminus, counting down to that goal strips the joy out of the journey. The miles become monotonous, and you'll spend half the hike looking at your map or GPS device, watching the miles slowly tick by. You're spending most of your day hiking, probably because you enjoy it, so remember that! Think of the time spent on the trail and under your pack as the purpose of your trip. If you make sure you are enjoying the hiking itself, you are much less likely to get bored. Following are some activities we employ to stay engaged while hiking.

TRACKING ANIMALS: Like people, animals take advantage of established trails to travel efficiently through the forest. Keep your eyes peeled for the different animal tracks and scat you spot on the trail, and you can learn a lot about animal behavior in the area. It can be fun to download a tracking guide to your phone before you head out or bring along a lightweight tracking guidebook to help match new tracks with the animals that left them. Likewise, you may have luck spotting and hearing different birds that are less common in populated areas.

IDENTIFYING VEGETATION: Every trail goes through a unique landscape and has its own set of vegetation. If you look closely, you'll almost always notice a few plants that are abundant and that you spot over and over. You can learn their growth habits, such as the amount of light they prefer, the soil they grow in, and the other plants that grow around them.

GEOGRAPHY: Together, the animals, plants, rocks, and water in an area make up its geographical history. These pieces usually fit together in a fascinating way that can be deciphered if you pay close attention. For instance, if you are hiking in a valley and notice one side is tree-covered while the other is rocky, this could be due to the direction that each side of the valley faces: South-facing slopes get more sun than north-facing slopes,

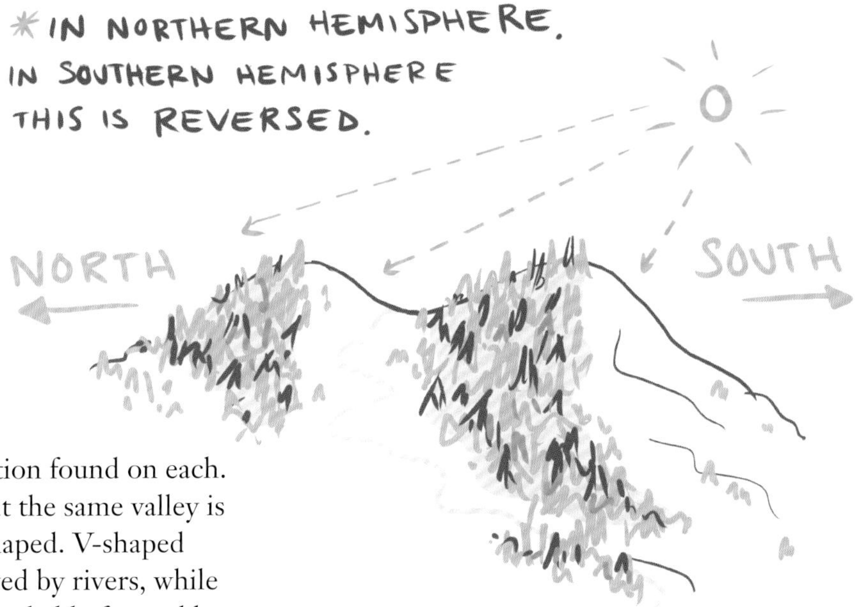

which affects the vegetation found on each. Or you might notice that the same valley is either V-shaped or U-shaped. V-shaped valleys were usually carved by rivers, while U-shaped valleys were probably formed by glaciers. It's rewarding to notice these characteristics of a place while you walk through it.

DECODING GEOLOGY: Rocks and soil along a trail tell the multimillion-year history of the area and how it formed. If you arm yourself with basic knowledge of a region's geologic history, it is remarkable how much you can piece together while hiking to develop a more complete understanding of the area. For instance, by learning how to recognize volcanic rocks and sedimentary rocks, you can imagine your surroundings millions of years ago as either red-hot lava or the cool bottom of an ocean.

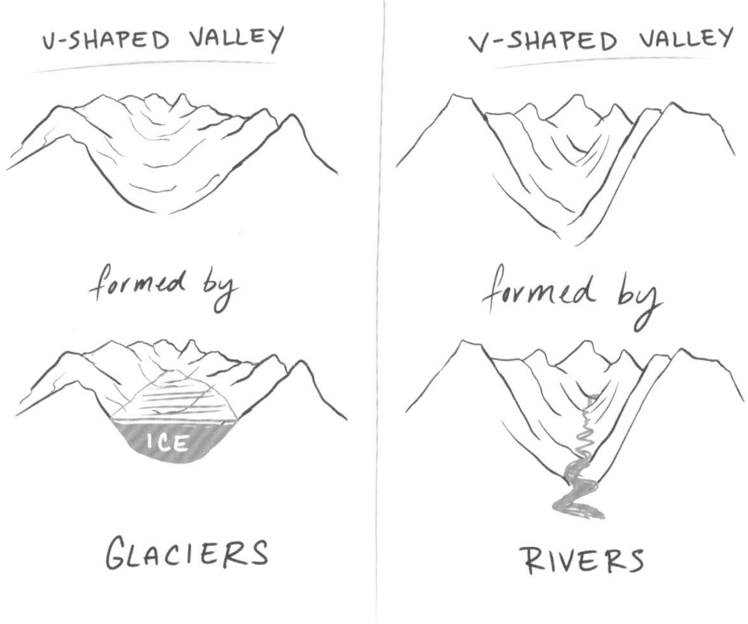

TALKING: While hiking with a partner all day, openly chatting about whatever comes to mind can go on for hours. The rhythm of taking thousands and thousands of steps, one after the other, can lead to remarkable creativity that is fun to work through with a buddy.

GAMES: When you want to chat but conversation isn't coming naturally, games like 20 questions can be an enjoyable way to pass the time and explore your buddy's psyche.

MUSIC AND PODCASTS: Some hikers like to listen to music or podcasts to pass the time, especially when walking solo. Leave no trace by wearing headphones so other hikers and wildlife aren't bothered by your noise. Don't forget to stay alert to your surroundings, though—you may only want to wear the headphones in one ear so you can listen for animals or other hikers.

THRUHIKERS'
TIPS

LIFE ON THE TRAIL

- The earlier you start your day on the trail, the easier it is to accomplish your mileage goal.
- Don't push too hard; take breaks and eat snacks on a schedule that matches your body's needs.
- Take a long "lunch" break when you reach a beautiful place, not necessarily when the clock strikes a particular time.
- Expect a group to move at a pace that is considerably slower than the slowest hiker among you.
- Try not to focus on the end goal for the day or the trip; doing so makes the miles tick by slowly. Instead, connect with nature or chat with your hiking partners to pass the time.

7

SKILLS & SAFETY ON THE TRAIL

For the most part, adventures in the backcountry don't require any skills or experience that are especially difficult to obtain; many are pretty easy to learn. That said, a basic knowledge of outdoor navigation, animal safety, and trail nutrition and hydration will go a long way to minimize the likelihood of finding yourself in a dangerous situation while on trail. In this chapter, we explain some of the strategies to stay safe and healthy on an adventure.

Before leaving home, let someone know how long you plan to be out and the route you are planning to hike. In case something happens on trail and you do not return home when expected, that person can contact rescue authorities and let them know where to look for you.

NAVIGATION

Being able to navigate is extremely important. There was a time when this meant being skilled with a map and compass, which can be intimidating for first timers. Fortunately, technology has made navigating much easier. (See chapter 2 for more information on navigational tools.) But don't just venture into the woods with a cell phone and expect it to get you back safely with no additional preparation. It's critical to have topographical (topo) maps showing your route, including the trails surrounding it and water sources, downloaded to your phone or GPS device ahead of time for offline use. No matter what tool you choose to use for navigating, always have a backup! Paper maps can get wet, and electronic devices require batteries, which can die.

HOW TO FIND YOUR LOCATION ON A MAP: Most smartphone apps and GPS devices have a dot showing you where you are on a map. If not, or if you are using a paper map, you need to know how to locate yourself. Look for landmarks on the map, like peaks, saddles, valleys, slopes, streams, lakes, and forks in the trail. A compass (a physical compass or the compass on your phone or GPS device) can help you figure out where you are relative to landmarks and keep you moving in the right direction.

HOW TO READ TOPO MAPS:

- Pay attention to the scale of your map and the resolution of your contour lines. The contour lines indicate elevation change in regular increments (e.g., 10 feet or 100 feet).
- Contour lines that are nonexistent or far apart indicate a flat area. Contour lines that are close together indicate a slope.
- If your trail crosses contour lines, that indicates that you will be going uphill or downhill. The closer together the lines are, the steeper the slope is.
- If your trail runs with contour lines, the trail is not ascending or descending. If there are contour lines in the vicinity, though, you will be traversing the side of a slope.

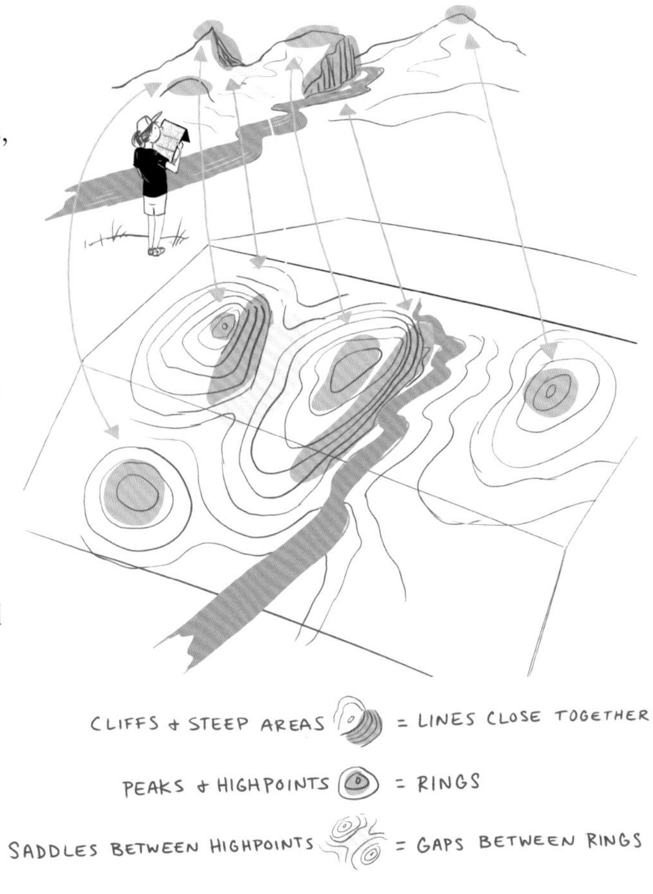

INFORMATION YOU CAN FIND BY STUDYING TOPO MAPS:

- To find a place to camp, look for flat areas on the topo map. Flat spots can be hidden from view of the trail.
- A stream may look like it's right next to the trail when consulting a two-dimensional map. But when you check a topo map and see lots of contour lines between the trail and the stream, that is an indication it may not be accessible due to a steep slope between the trail and the stream.
- The contour lines on a topo map can help you visualize a three-dimensional image of the landscape, which can be useful to orient your position relative to major features like mountains.

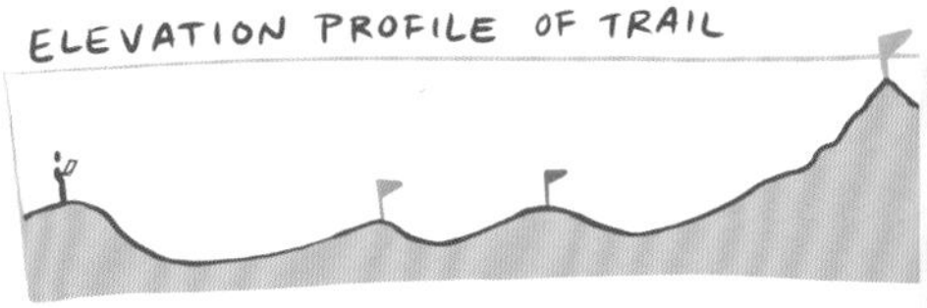

- Some apps or maps show the elevation profile for your route, which can be extremely helpful to know how hard or easy the day's hiking will be. If you don't have an elevation profile, the contour lines on your topo map can tell you the same thing.

NAVIGATION TIPS

It is fun to understand the landscape and your place within it. Here are several points to take note of to be more connected to your location when you're outside. These could be useful if your navigational tools and backups fail, but most often they are simply nice things to notice as you explore and experience the outdoors.

- The sun rises in the east and sets in the west.
- In the northern hemisphere, moss usually grows on the north sides of trees because it gets less sunlight than the south sides.
- South-facing mountain slopes get more sunlight than north-facing slopes. This often leads to major vegetation differences between opposing slopes and means snow will melt earlier on south slopes.
- Small streams flow downhill into bigger streams, but big streams virtually never split into smaller streams.
- The time the moon rises varies during the lunar cycle, but full moons always rise at approximately sunset.
- From high points such as mountain peaks, highways can be heard from many miles away.

ELECTRONICS

Electronic devices are an almost unavoidable part of everyday life, including on the trail. Some of the devices that come in handy in nature include a head lamp, GPS device or watch, cell phone, power bank, and camera. On trips in the backcountry, power conservation is a much more important concern than it is in everyday life, but with a few proactive measures, powering your devices in the backcountry can be easily achieved.

CONSERVE PHONE POWER IN AIRPLANE MODE: You can save your phone battery during your hike by keeping it in airplane mode. Although cellular data and Wi-Fi are off in airplane mode, most hiking apps still work if you have location turned on. Be sure to keep location on so you can see your location on the map, which is based on your phone's separate GPS sensor. (Remember: Download offline maps at home before you go so you'll have them during your hike when you don't have service or are in airplane mode.)

ADDITIONAL POWER CONSERVATION METHODS:

PHONES:

- Put your phone in battery-saver or low-power mode.
- Dim the screen.
- Minimize screen time and cell phone use in general.
- Minimize data use. (Keep your phone in airplane mode.)
- If it is very cold out, keep your phone in a warm place near your body—inside your puffy jacket or in your sleeping bag while sleeping.
- Turn off your phone overnight.

OTHER DEVICES:

- Use your headlamp on its lowest setting.
- If you are tracking your hike using GPS, pause your GPS device during extended breaks.

THINK THROUGH BATTERIES AND CABLE MANAGEMENT: Devices like smartphones run on rechargeable batteries, so the best way to recharge these on a hike is with a power bank. Other electronics, like GPS devices and headlamps, sometimes have built-in batteries that can be charged with a power bank; at other times, they have replaceable batteries. It is extremely convenient for all of your devices to use the same recharging system and same cable; otherwise, you end up hauling a bag full of cables and batteries. As much as possible, select devices that all use the same cable for charging and can charge off the same power bank.

USING YOUR POWER BANK: Page 72 has general advice for selecting a power bank, but once you actually start using it on trips, you may want to make some adjustments. First, determine if your power bank is the right size for your needs. By conserving power, we have found that one 10,000-milliamp-hour (mAh) bank per person is enough for up to a week in the backcountry at our power consumption rates.

If you are a heavy electronics user, you may want to go with a larger size. For weekend trips, a 5,000-mAh battery may suffice. Also, be sure your power bank charges fast enough that it won't slow you down during resupply stops. If you find yourself repeatedly waiting next to an outlet for your bank to finish charging, it may be time for an upgrade.

The most convenient time to use a power bank is usually while in your tent right before bed or overnight. Charge devices only when they need more power. Our GPS watches have to be charged daily, so we plug those in each night. We charge our phones and headlamps only when their batteries get low. Keep an eye on your power bank's battery status so you don't accidentally find yourself in need of juice with nothing left.

BACKCOUNTRY COMMUNICATIONS

The buddy system is a good way to stay safe in the backcountry. When venturing into unknown or dangerous terrain, it is a great idea to go with a group. But adventuring in a group doesn't have to mean spending 100 percent of your time together. It can be nice to spend time alone, or if your group is large, it can be okay to split into smaller groups between campsites or breaks. Because cell phones don't reliably have service in the backcountry, don't rely on them for communicating on a trip. There is no shortage of alternative means to communicate on the trail.

TRAIL REGISTERS: Sign every trail register you encounter! This lets the people behind you know you have made it through, and it's fun to see who's passed the register before you. Even if you don't need to let others know you've come this way, sign anyway. In the unlikely scenario that something happens to you on the trail, signing the trail register ensures that a search and rescue team knows where you have been and makes it easier for them to narrow down the search location.

THINGS OUT OF PLACE: You can temporarily leave items out of place to communicate with hikers who are behind you. For instance, if you are the front person or in the front pack of a spread-out group and have to venture off trail for some reason (e.g., to go to the bathroom), leave something obvious on the trail to indicate that you are there. Stick your hiking pole into the ground on the trail, for example, so nobody passes you without realizing it. If you don't leave a marker, getting passed by your group while you're off trail could be dangerous. You might think you are still the lead person and stop to wait for the others to catch up when they actually passed you while you were off trail. They'll keep hiking on, expecting to eventually catch you, while you're stopped, waiting for them.

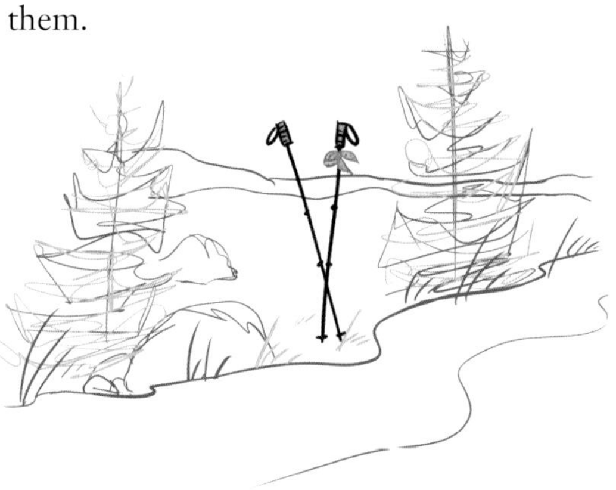

FOOTPRINTS: On hikes, you spend a surprising amount of time looking at the ground. If you know the pattern of the shoes that your hiking buddies are wearing, you can discern whether they are ahead of you. Footprints can do a lot to tell the story of who's ahead and what they were up to. For instance, you can tell where hikers took breaks, and if there is a confusing junction, footprints can indicate the route your partners took.

OTHER HIKERS: The game of telephone works well on the trail. If there is a message you want to send back to the group behind you, it can get there surprisingly quickly if you share it with hikers walking the opposite direction and ask them to relay the information to your partners. This is not 100 percent reliable—the other hikers might take a different route, or they might forget to tell your friends when they pass—but for simple messages, it might work.

SATELLITE COMMUNICATOR DEVICES: When two-way communication is extremely important, you can use satellite communicator devices such as the Garmin inReach or ZOELO messengers. These devices use satellites for service, so they are not restricted like cell phones; they work anywhere on the globe with a clear line of sight to the sky. You can buy a messaging plan that allows text messages to be sent and received via satellite, making communication possible from anywhere. We have never needed these devices to communicate with other hikers on the trail, but we have used them successfully to coordinate a rendezvous with family who were meeting us by car at a road crossing.

Being connected can detract from the wilderness experience, but it was extremely convenient to be able to let those meeting us know our expected time of arrival as we approached. Another way hikers use satellite devices is to keep family and friends at home informed about their whereabouts on the trail. In addition to messaging, these devices offer a feature that sends a regular location update to family and friends that can be viewed online in real time.

CHASING "DIRTY MONEY" BETWEEN CUBA AND GRANTS

When we hiked the Pacific Crest Trail, we met a hiker named Barbara, whose trail name is "Dirty Money." We became great friends with Dirty Money during the course of the 4½-month hike and ended up going to her house in northern Sweden for a reunion every New Year's for several years after. When we set out on the Continental Divide Trail (CDT), it just so happened that Dirty Money decided to hike it the same year. We started a few days apart, but we knew we'd bump into her on the trail, and we couldn't wait. Finally, in the desert of New Mexico, it happened! We ran into each other on the trail and had an amazing few days hiking together. The three of us resupplied in the town of Cuba, New Mexico, but Renee and I were delayed getting out of town in the morning, so Dirty Money hit the trail a few hours before us. We figured we'd catch her within the first few days on our way to the next town, Grants. But it didn't happen. We knew her shoe prints, so we knew for certain that she was ahead, but we just couldn't reel her in. Every day for 7 days, we paid attention to the trail and saw fresh prints, which told us we hadn't accidentally passed her. We eventually started asking hikers headed in the opposite direction, and they confirmed that a short-haired European lady had passed them no more than a few hours before us. It was frustrating to be so close yet unable to catch her. Finally, we made it to Grants just a few hours after Dirty Money did. As it turned out, we were no more than a few hours behind her for the entire 7-day stretch. Although in this case, the knowledge of her signs and information from other hikers didn't lead to the three of us hiking together, it was comforting to know we were on the right track.

—Tim

NUTRITION & FUELING

Nutrition and fueling are very important parts of a successful backpacking trip. But after all the time spent planning your route and choosing your gear, you can easily forget about them. Backpacking is not a stroll through the park. You are carrying a heavy backpack and walking longer distances on rougher terrain. Think of it more like lifting weights or running a marathon.

On the trail, just like at home, everyone has different eating styles and preferences. If you eat three meals a day at home, you should eat three meals a day on trail, plus snacks. If you drink coffee at home, you should drink coffee on trail to help avoid caffeine withdrawal headaches. Our general rule of thumb on the trail is to eat three meals a day plus a 200-or-more-calorie snack every 5 miles.

In part 3, we share lots more information on food and nutrition, including recipes you can make at home and take on the trail.

WATER

There are few places where the importance of water for living is as painfully obvious as it is on the trail. Water is usually one of the heaviest items a hiker carries, so on most backpacking trips, hikers collect water from sources along the route instead of carrying enough to last them from start to finish. In a literal sense, this means that hikers depend on the environment to survive. Especially in dry or desert regions, this can be frightening. But for most hikes, a little bit of planning ahead is all it takes to avoid water shortages. In fact, carrying too much water can be almost as detrimental to a trip as carrying too little. Water isn't lightweight, so you need to know the right amount to carry.

WATER SOURCES

For short trips in populated areas, it is not uncommon for potable water to be provided at campsites or bathrooms along the route. For longer trips in more remote regions, hikers collect water from natural sources, such as natural springs, streams, rivers, or lakes. Such water should always be treated before it is consumed. It is crucial to plan your route to take you past enough of these water sources to refill as much water as you drink. Importantly, water sources can vary drastically during the course of a season. Usually, spring is the wettest time of year, and a raging river in the springtime might be completely dry in late summer or fall. On popular routes, hiking apps such as AllTrails or FarOut often include regular updates from hikers indicating whether water is available from a particular source. On less-traveled routes, historical information about flow rates can sometimes be found in maps or online.

TREATING WATER

Countless water treatment products and devices are available to make naturally collected water safe for drinking, including chemical and physical methods (see pages 70 to 72). All treatment methods have benefits and drawbacks, and virtually no method effectively removes chemical pollutants from human agriculture or industry. That said, in most of North America, pollution is not a common concern in the majority of backpacking areas, but biological pathogens like giardia are. All water collected from natural sources should be treated, no matter how pristine a source appears to be. Most of the hikers we know who have become ill from water drank from beautiful water sources high up in the mountains that seemed cleaner than tap. As it turns out, marmots and other mammals, even at 13,000 feet in elevation, are common carriers of giardia.

CARRYING THE RIGHT AMOUNT OF WATER

Our rule of thumb is to carry 1 liter of water for every 5 miles of trail, plus about a liter for every meal. So if we have a 5-mile stretch between water sources, we each will carry 1 liter, and if we have a 10-mile stretch between water sources that includes dry camping, we each will carry about 2 liters for walking and 2 more liters for eating (4 liters total). There are important exceptions to this guideline: On hot days we carry more, and on cold days we often carry less. Likewise, extra water is a must in difficult terrain—the more we are sweating and breathing heavily, the more water we will consume.

Another factor to consider when deciding how much water to carry is the reliability of upcoming sources. Carrying unnecessary water is a bad idea—it can provide a sense of security, but every liter of water weighs 2.2 pounds, which adds up quickly. It's important to be sure you are carrying enough water to get to the next reliable source, with little or no extra.

If you are absolutely unable to determine how far ahead the next reliable source is, you always know how far back it is to the last reliable source. When venturing into unknown water conditions, keep enough extra water in your backpack to be able to go back to your last source if necessary. This ensures that you will not find yourself in a dangerous situation without enough water to survive.

WATER CARRYING CAPACITY

Before heading out on a trip, consult your maps to determine how much water you will need to carry. Look at the longest water carry you expect to encounter, and bring enough water bottles or bladders to carry the water you will need for that stretch. In the mountains in the springtime, you may need only a couple of liters of carrying capacity. In the desert in the fall, you may need more than 5 liters of carrying capacity.

RUNNING OUT OF WATER ON THE CONTINENTAL DIVIDE TRAIL

The official CDT follows as close as possible to the continental divide, and we decided to stick to it during our thruhike in 2021. This took us into New Mexico's Black Range while most other hikers chose to take the Gila River alternate, which is shorter and has more water sources. We studied our maps before leaving town, using an app that shows waypoints like water sources and allows people to comment on those waypoints to let other hikers know, for example, that a water source has gone dry. Because almost no one else had hiked the Black Range recently, it was hard to know if the less-reliable sources were still flowing or if they had dried up for the season. We focused on the reliable water sources and had enough water bottles to carry water for 20 miles between sources.

We left the town of Winston, New Mexico, knowing we had a 12-mile hike to a spring, our next water source. But when we got to the spring, we couldn't find it. We searched all around, eventually realizing it had gone dry. We knew the next water source was 20 miles down the trail, but we didn't have enough water to make it that far. The only option was to turn around and go back to the road crossing. But there was no water on the trail back to the road or at the road. We looked at our maps and found a dirt forest service road parallel to the trail that would take us back to the road crossing and decided to take it, hoping to run into water. Worst case, we'd make it all the way back to the road crossing and then have to hitchhike back to Winston. As we walked the dirt road, we found a dry cow trough and then a dry cow pond. It was getting late, so we decided to call it a night.

In the morning, we got to a second cow pond and found WATER! It was super muddy and gross, but we were so happy to find it. We spent more than an hour drinking and filling up all of our bottles. The only problem was that the next water source was now 30 miles away, not 20. We didn't have enough capacity for 30 miles, so we "cameled up" (drank lots of water) and filled our cooking pot, too. We headed out and rationed our water as we hiked. As we were hiking, we found a half-full plastic bottle someone had dropped quite a while before, and we grabbed it for our emergency reserves. We continued walking and eventually crossed a road that had a box containing a trail register. When we opened the box, we found two small bottles of Gatorade ... TRAIL MAGIC! Gatorade never tasted so good! Thank you to the trail angel who put it there. The next day, we made it to the next water source: a windmill pumping water into an open-topped, swimming pool–sized cow tank. In total, our trip to get water ended up being a 22-mile and 22-hour detour.

A few hundred miles later, we ran into a guy who was out camping and got to talking. As it turned out, he was our trail angel, the one who had put the Gatorade bottles in the trail register box—the year before. THANK YOU "MOSEY"!

—Renee

DOING THE DISHES

Nobody looks forward to doing the dishes. This is so true on backpacking trips that most store-bought backpacking meals are designed to be cooked directly in the bag they come in, the idea being that carrying a sticky foil bag with you until your next chance to toss it is easier than washing out a dirty pot. But with the right cooking method and recipes (like the ones we share in part 3!), doing the dishes can be simple and painless. Here are some tips to make dish-doing a breeze:

- Cook one-pot meals so you never have more than one pot to clean.
- Don't cook meals that involve frying where food might stick to the pot. The recipes in this book are water based, which makes cleanup easy.
- Don't use a nonstick pan. By using water-based recipes and a metal pan, you can get 90 percent of the cleanup done by adding a bit of water and scraping the pan with your eating utensil. On the trail, 90 percent is good enough.
- Avoid having to deal with waste by knowing your recipes. We never have leftovers to dispose of on the trail. We try out our recipes ahead of time so we know we like them, and we are familiar with our portion sizes so we can finish every bite. (If you do end up with waste, pack it out rather than leaving it behind, so animals can't find it. Leave No Trace: Do not bury or burn it!)
- Don't use soap. After scraping out your pan to clean it, you can just drink the "dirty" water to get rid of it. As long as you don't use soap, the water isn't actually dirty … it is just cold "dinner soup." (If you dump your water instead of drinking it, dump it away from your campsite so animals can't find it, and be sure it isn't full of food residue.)
- Use your pot for every meal. All of our cooked recipes involve boiling water, so every time we bring a pot of water to a boil, we are cleaning out the previous meal's stuck-on residue.
- Cancel out your low cleanliness standards between towns by maintaining high standards when you get to town. Whenever we get back from a trip, or on long trips whenever we get to a resupply town, we wash out our pot and spork thoroughly with hot, soapy water.

ANIMALS ON THE TRAIL

The fear of dangerous encounters with wild animals is a barrier that keeps many people from adventuring into the wilderness. You can use that fear to help ensure you practice good behavior while outdoors, but know that as long as you are careful, the chance of a dangerous encounter is extremely low. During the course of hundreds and hundreds of nights spent outside, we have never had a dangerous run-in with a wild animal.

ANIMALS ON THE TRAIL: The best way to avoid animals on the trail is to be noisy so they hear you coming. Even large predators, such as bears, wolves, and mountain lions, are usually afraid of an approaching group of hikers, and they'll clear out of the way if they hear you coming. It's highly probable that they hear you well before you hear them.

WHAT TO DO WHEN YOU ENCOUNTER AN ANIMAL ON THE TRAIL: The more time you spend outside, the more likely it becomes that you will eventually encounter predators. It could be that you round a rock corner that was blocking your noise, or in rare cases, there are animals who just don't feel like moving. In these situations, the most important thing to do is to be sure the animal does not feel threatened. If a bear thinks it is being attacked, or if a mother bear thinks you are attacking her cubs, it will fight back. Don't let the animal know that you feel threatened. Turning and running can cause a predator to view you as prey and attack, even if it had no interest in doing so in the first place. Face the predator, talk softly to it so it knows you are present but not a threat, and it will probably get out of the way.

BLACK BEARS: Black bears almost always take off running when they hear people on the trail. We have seen many more black bears from behind, running away from us, than we have face-on. Making noise is enough to fend off 99 percent of black bear encounters. Avoid getting between a mother bear and her cubs—no matter how much noise you make, a black bear could attack in this situation. If a black bear attacks you, fight back.

GRIZZLY BEARS: Grizzlies can be dangerous if they're startled. Be sure they hear you coming by periodically making noise. If you encounter a grizzly bear, give it lots of space and do not approach. Carry bear spray when hiking in grizzly territory so you have some measure of protection just in case. As with black bears, be extra careful if you encounter a mother with her cubs. If a grizzly bear attacks you, spray the bear with bear spray if you have it (and be sure you know how to use it). If you don't have bear spray, play dead. If playing dead doesn't work and the grizzly bear starts eating you, fight back.

MOUNTAIN LIONS AND WOLVES: Mountain lion and wolf encounters are extremely rare, and attacks are even rarer. If a mountain lion or wolf approaches you, act large but not aggressive. Fight back if attacked.

MOOSE: Moose are not predators, but they actually injure more people than bears in the United States every year. However, a moose is extremely unlikely to attack a person who does not approach it. If you are lucky enough to see a moose in the wilderness, take pictures from a distance. Unlike with predators, if a moose attacks you, run away. If it knocks you down, curl up into a fetal position and then run away after it backs off.

RATTLESNAKES: Rattlesnakes sometimes get out of the way when they hear somebody coming. If not, take a wide route well around the snake so you don't threaten it, and it will happily continue basking in the sun. If you accidentally startle it, a rattlesnake will almost always rattle well in advance of striking. Rattlesnakes rattle to let you know to back away, and as long as you do so, you'll be fine. In the unlikely event that you get bitten by a rattlesnake, seek medical attention immediately. Bites are rarely deadly if you get to a hospital in time. If you're hiking in a remote area with many rattlesnakes and no cell service, consider carrying a satellite communicator device you can use to call for help if you need to.

ANIMALS AT CAMP: Guidelines for how to camp safely in the presence of wild animals are provided in the camping section of this book from pages 130 to 133, including how to store your food safely in bear country.

MOMMA GRIZZLY AND TWO CUBS

One evening in Wyoming, while we were hiking the CDT, we encountered a mother grizzly bear with her two cubs. We crested a hill, and they were enjoying a wide open space about ¼ mile ahead of and below us. We made plenty of nonthreatening noise as we slowly continued down the hill, talking and singing songs. Eventually we realized they weren't just ahead of us; they were sitting right on the trail. They initially had no desire to move, despite looking up and acknowledging that they knew we were there. We weren't sure how to go around them or how long we'd have to wait until they moved. After a short while, all three bears took a look at us and moseyed out of the way. We walked through, and right afterward, they went back to the exact spot on the trail where they had been and resumed munching on vegetation. At the time we encountered the bear family, we had been looking for a place to camp for the night, but we decided it wouldn't do any harm to continue on for an extra mile before setting up camp. We cooked extra far away from our tent, hung our food even farther in a different direction, and had no problems overnight. Overall, it was an exciting and trouble-free encounter. Upon reflecting, these bears demonstrated for us how different grizzly bears are from black bears. All of our comparable encounters with black bears have ended with the black bears taking off and running far out of sight. These grizzlies only got out of our way when they felt like it. They were much less afraid of us than any black bears we've seen.

—Tim

BUGS ON THE TRAIL

Annoying or painful bugs like mosquitoes and horse flies add to the challenge of a trip. The following techniques will help minimize their impact on your enjoyment.

AVOID THE BUGGY SEASON (IF POSSIBLE): Different parts of the country have their worst insect seasons at different times. Usually, you can expect bugs to peak during or shortly after wet seasons. In the mountains, this means bugs are often the worst a few weeks after the snow melts, and they are much better earlier and later in the season. With little water, deserts typically have few annoying bugs for most or all of the year. In areas with hot, wet summers, bugs can persist for much of the hiking season.

AVOID BUGGY AREAS: Even during the peak of insect season, you will find that some areas have better or much worse bug conditions than others. Mosquitoes breed in water, so swampy areas are often swarming with them. Wind is surprisingly effective at dispersing bugs, so look for dry, windy areas (e.g., the top of an exposed hill), and you are much less likely to be attacked. Ticks love tall grass and vegetation, so try not to tramp through areas that have vegetation brushing against your body.

DRESS RIGHT: When bugs are bad, try to have as little exposed skin as possible for them to find. Long pants and sleeves go a long way toward forming a layer of protection between yourself and annoying insects. Hats and gloves help, too. Mosquitoes can puncture through many types of clothing, but we have found that wearing puffy down jackets at camp is nearly 100 percent effective at keeping them away. You also can treat your clothing with permethrin, an insecticide that repels mosquitoes, ticks, and other bugs. When bugs are absolutely terrible, wearing a mosquito head net can help, but beware that these diminish visibility, are unpleasant on hot days, and are not 100 percent effective because mosquitoes can still get to you wherever the net comes into contact with your skin or thin clothing.

USE BUG SPRAY: We have found that by avoiding buggy areas and the worst of the season, and by dressing right, we rarely need to use bug spray. But when the bugs get really bad, spray can make the difference between having a fun trip and calling it quits early. Several types of bug sprays and repellents are available, from natural oils like lemon eucalyptus to chemical repellents such as picaridin and DEET. Our experience is that natural products have limited effectiveness, and harsh chemicals are much more effective to keep the bugs at bay. We recommend experimenting with different products to establish which one works best for you. If you do choose to use a DEET-based repellent (which is what we often go with), be careful and avoid getting it on plastic materials or fabrics. DEET reacts with plastic and can strip away or smear colors.

TURNING BACK IN THE OLYMPIC MOUNTAINS

When we hiked and canoed the Pacific Northwest Circuit (PNC), we had to set an ambitious schedule. The trip started with the 1,200-mile Pacific Northwest Trail (PNT), which hikers usually start in July. Our plan was to hike the PNT from the Pacific Ocean to Glacier National Park, head 300 more miles north into Canada to the headwaters of the Columbia River, and finally canoe the entire 1,200-mile Columbia River back to the ocean. To be sure we'd have time to complete the trip before fall rain set in in the Pacific Northwest, we decided to start the hike early, in mid-June. It was a high-snow year, so we knew that crossing the Olympic Mountains would be a challenge. We talked to a park ranger, but because we were among the first hikers of the year crossing the mountains, he wasn't able to give us a preview of the conditions. As we got up to high elevations, we encountered lots of snow. We'd hiked in snow many times before, so we were optimistic that we could handle it. But conditions got worse and worse as we ventured higher on the High Divide Trail. Everything was completely snow-covered, and the trail was steep. We were traversing thousand-foot drop-offs, which meant moving extremely slowly as we kicked footsteps into the snow. We were moving less than 1 mile per hour when I slipped and slid several yards down the mountain and was caught by a tree. I was okay, but this was the wake-up call we needed. We were prepared for a long-distance hike, not for mountaineering. Continuing would have meant more risks and more chances for severe injury.

We swallowed our pride and turned around. We had wanted to do all of the "official" PNT, but safety is always more important than an arbitrary goal. So we found a lower, alternate route around the mountains that was snow-free. We weren't on the official PNT, but we were still able to walk the route, following a continuous foot/boat path with no skips necessary. It was not as scenic as the high route, but it had its own perks—we got to spend more time on the ocean. While hiking this alternate, we met a biker who told us that a few weeks prior he had traversed the exact route we turned around on. This was a momentary blow to our pride, but in talking, we realized he had approached it as a mountaineering trip, completely different from our approach. He had snowshoes, an ice axe, a helmet, and mountain gear. We had hiking shoes with simple microspikes for traction.

In hindsight, the only thing I'd change is that I would have turned around sooner. We can always go back and hike in better weather or try a mountain expedition with proper gear, but if we had pushed our limits and gotten seriously injured, our hiking days could have been over forever.

—Tim

KNOWING YOUR LIMITS

A trip can change from a fun adventure to an unpleasant or even dangerous experience when you exceed your limits. This could mean setting unrealistic distance goals, venturing into weather you aren't prepared for, or taking on terrain that is beyond your abilities. Keep a log of your hiking trips so you have a good handle on the conditions you can manage with ease and those that might be beyond your current abilities. It is much better to be safe than sorry.

THRUHIKERS'
TIPS
SKILLS & SAFETY ON THE TRAIL

- Before your trip, let somebody know where you're going and when you expect to return.
- If you opt for electronic maps for navigation, be sure you have the entire region downloaded ahead of time because you may have no cell service on your trip.
- If you use paper maps, ensure they are topo maps that cover the area of your entire trip at a high-enough resolution to be useful on the trail.
- Look at the elevation profile of your trail or at a topo map to get a sense of how difficult it will be—going up and over mountains is much more challenging than hiking something flat.
- Conserve power by keeping your phone in airplane mode with the screen brightness low. Don't use any of your electronic devices more than necessary to avoid running out of battery. Carry a power bank for longer trips.
- Our rule of thumb for eating on trail is three meals a day plus one snack of 200 or more calories every 5 miles.
- Carry enough water to comfortably get to the next reliable water source, but minimize pack weight by not carrying more than necessary.
- Expect to drink about 1 liter of water every 5 miles, but more if it is hot out or if you are traversing difficult terrain. Adjust this guideline to match your body's own needs.
- Doing the dishes is easy if you have only one pot and your recipes are all water based.
- Learn which animals are present in the area where you are hiking, and follow the area's regulations to avoid attracting them.
- Know your limits—don't take on a trip that is more challenging or dangerous than you can comfortably complete. Don't be embarrassed to turn back if you become uncomfortable.

8

CAMPING

Camping in the backcountry is peaceful and fun, but it is rarely as simple as jumping in bed and turning off the lights like you might do at home. Depending on where you are going, you may be allowed to camp anywhere you please (i.e., dispersed camping), or you may have to get permits and follow strict regulations to be allowed to camp. Either way, knowing how to select an ideal site and making it warm and comfortable is a skill that will maximize your enjoyment overnight. In this chapter, we discuss campsite selection, fires, minimizing your impact on the area, and doing what you can to ensure you don't disturb animals and they don't disturb you.

CAMPSITE SELECTION IN AREAS THAT DON'T ALLOW DISPERSED CAMPING

On certain routes and trails, camping is only permitted in designated sites. This makes campsite selection straightforward: Plan your route ahead of time, and choose sites based on a map of the area. Check to see if permits are required before you go. If not, it's possible to have multiple sites in mind, depending on how far you make it on a given day. If yes, be sure you don't overestimate your mileage so you can get to your permitted site. It is no fun to push past when your body says stop because you were too optimistic when getting permits. Be aware that when hiking with a group, you'll cover less ground than the slowest member of the group would do alone.

CAMPSITE SELECTION IN AREAS THAT ALLOW DISPERSED CAMPING

On lots of public land, especially out west, you can camp anywhere. Check the regulations before you head out. Dispersed camping provides lots of freedom to stop when and where you wish, but don't expect to find a great campsite the exact moment you decide you've hiked a complete day. Several factors dictate a good versus bad campsite.

CLEAR OF VEGETATION: It's impossible to set up a tent on top of trees, bushes, or cacti, and although it's possible to set up on grass, doing so can damage the landscape. Ideal campsite surfaces are dirt, sand, leaves, or needles. Being aware of the area you are hiking will help you find a good surface; deserts, old-growth forests, and arid areas are full of great sites, while lush vegetation (found in new-growth forests and plains) makes campsite selection more difficult.

FLAT: For a good sleep, aim for a campsite that is as flat as possible. Camping on a hillside leads to a remarkably poor sleep. In steep areas such as mountain slopes, finding a flat campsite can be difficult. A topographic map can indicate saddles, mountaintops and hilltops, and valleys that are more likely to harbor flat areas.

SOFT GROUND: Dirt is usually a soft and comfortable place to set up camp. Camping on large rocks is uncomfortable. Camping on small rocks and gravel are better, but these can be difficult to get tent stakes into. Abandoned dirt roads that are no longer used for cars can serve as great campsites, but be wary of abandoned gravel roads; these can be some of the most difficult surfaces for inserting tent stakes because of how packed down they've become after vehicle use.

FREE OF DEAD TREES AND BRANCHES: Never camp near unstable dead trees or under dead branches. People are killed by trees and branches falling on their tents every year.

SHELTERED FROM THE WIND: Windy nights shake tents, causing unpleasant noise or worse, blowing tents over. Mountain summits are particularly prone to high winds. If it is windy when it's time to set up camp, avoid exposed areas by looking for shelter provided by forests or valleys.

TEMPERATURE: During the hiking season, it's usually true that the higher your elevation, the colder the temperature is. When crossing mountainous areas, it can be wise to camp at lower elevations to avoid the cold. However, in certain areas during certain times of the year, this pattern can be reversed. Valleys can be some of the coldest places to camp because cold air and condensation settle down into the valleys overnight, and the sun rises later when shaded by steep valley walls. Pay attention while hiking, especially in the morning, to determine if valleys are colder than the surrounding area, and if so, avoid them for a warmer night.

WATER: Hikers often want to camp near water sources because it's easy to fill up and filter water for dinner and breakfast if water is nearby. This drastically limits the potential areas to camp in, though. Also, condensation is much worse near bodies of water than away from them. Being willing to fill up your water bottles before choosing a campsite lets you find the best campsites on trail.

FIRES

When many people think of camping, they think of campfires. Having a relaxing campfire can be a great end to a day on the trail, but it isn't a requirement. Sometimes the stress of getting to camp in time to set up and enjoy a fire isn't the ideal way to spend an evening, and no rule says you have to. We have found that we often enjoy a campfire on short hikes, but on long-distance hikes, we almost always forgo evening fires because we'd rather go to bed.

If you do choose to have a campfire, only collect dead and naturally fallen wood to burn. Live wood burns terribly, and chopping down trees leaves unsightly evidence for future hikers. Pay attention to the region you are hiking in, too. During dry seasons, especially in the western United States, campfires often are forbidden due to the risk that they'll cause forest fires. If campfires are permitted, use a fire ring if one is provided at your campsite. If not, use rocks to build a ring and clear the area of flammable materials like dead leaves and needles. Keep your fire small and away from your tent so that sparks don't burn it. Before going to bed, be sure your fire is completely out. In the morning, practice Leave No Trace by dispersing ashes and any rocks you used for a campfire ring so that there is no evidence you ever had a campfire there.

LEAVE NO TRACE AT CAMP

Camping and hiking become more popular every year. This is a great thing; more people enjoying the outdoors means more people will preserve and protect it. It also means there are more people sharing outdoor spaces, and Leave No Trace camping is the best way to ensure the experience remains wild for future users. The simplest guideline for Leave No Trace camping is to take only pictures and leave only footprints. At your campsite, this means the following.

CAMPFIRES: Keep your campfire small if you have one at all. Use only dead and down wood to build a campfire. Don't burn garbage or leftover food, which leaves residue that can attract animals. After your fire is completely out, distribute coals and any rocks you used to build a fire ring so there is no lingering evidence that it was ever there.

CAMPSITE SELECTION: Don't trample vegetation to clear a space for your tent. If you move rocks, return them to where you found them after you're done with the site.

FOOD: Don't leave food, food residue, or crumbs at your campsite. This changes animal behavior, teaching them to associate humans with a free meal.

Several additional guidelines for practicing Leave No Trace are provided in chapter 11.

ANIMAL-PROOFING YOUR CAMPSITE

Encountering a wild animal at your campsite can be a frightening experience. Fortunately, it is not difficult to minimize the chances of attracting animals to your campsite.

CAMP CLEANLINESS: Most animals have a much better sense of smell than humans do. But just like humans, animals are almost never looking for a fight. If they do head toward your camp due to yummy smells, they'll stay far away as long as you are awake and making noise. When you go to sleep, or if your campsite is empty, curious animals like bears or mice might decide they want to take a look around. Avoid this by making sure there are no scents coming from your campsite. This includes the obvious like leftover food and drinks, but also less-obvious items they could confuse with food, such as scented deodorants, toothpaste, and lotions. Put all scented items in an odor-proof or odor-resistant bag. If you're not in bear country, ensure you store your food out of reach of rodents. If you're camping in bear country, follow the guidelines for bear-proofing your camp below. Always keep your campsite clean and scent-free, and you may never have to deal with an animal in your camp.

BEAR-PROOFING YOUR CAMP: There are three ways to store food safely from bears while camping in the wilderness. Different regions have different requirements, so be sure to check the regulations for the area where you go camping.

Hanging: The first way to store your food is to hang it. Carry a food bag and 40 to 50 feet of rope. Before you go to bed, hang all of your scented items, including food, dishes, and toiletries, in a tree about 100 feet from your campsite. The bag should be 10 to 12 feet high and 6 to 10 feet out from the nearest tree trunk. Some areas allow you to tie the rope off to the trunk of the tree, but in others (like the Sierra Nevada mountains in California), the bears have learned how to get the rope down when this method is used. In these areas, a counterbalance method with two bags that offset each other's weight keeps the bags, and ropes, out of reach of the bears. Check the regulations ahead of time.

Bear-proof canister: The second method is to use a bear-proof container. These are plastic, metal, or carbon-fiber jars that bears can't open. You simply put your scented items in the jar and place it away from camp overnight. The National Park and Forest Services recommend 100 yards from camp. The downside of these canisters is that they weigh 2 or 3 pounds and are bulky. In areas where bears are common, these are often required, so check regulations ahead of time to know if you need one.

Bear-resistant bag: The third method is a bear-resistant bag. These are canvas bags that bears can't bite through. Just like a bear canister, you put all of your scented items in the bag overnight, and to ensure bears can't run off with the bag, you tie it to the trunk of a tree. Bags are much lighter weight than a bear-proof canister, and they conform to the shape of your pack. However, they're not permitted everywhere, so double-check regulations before heading out.

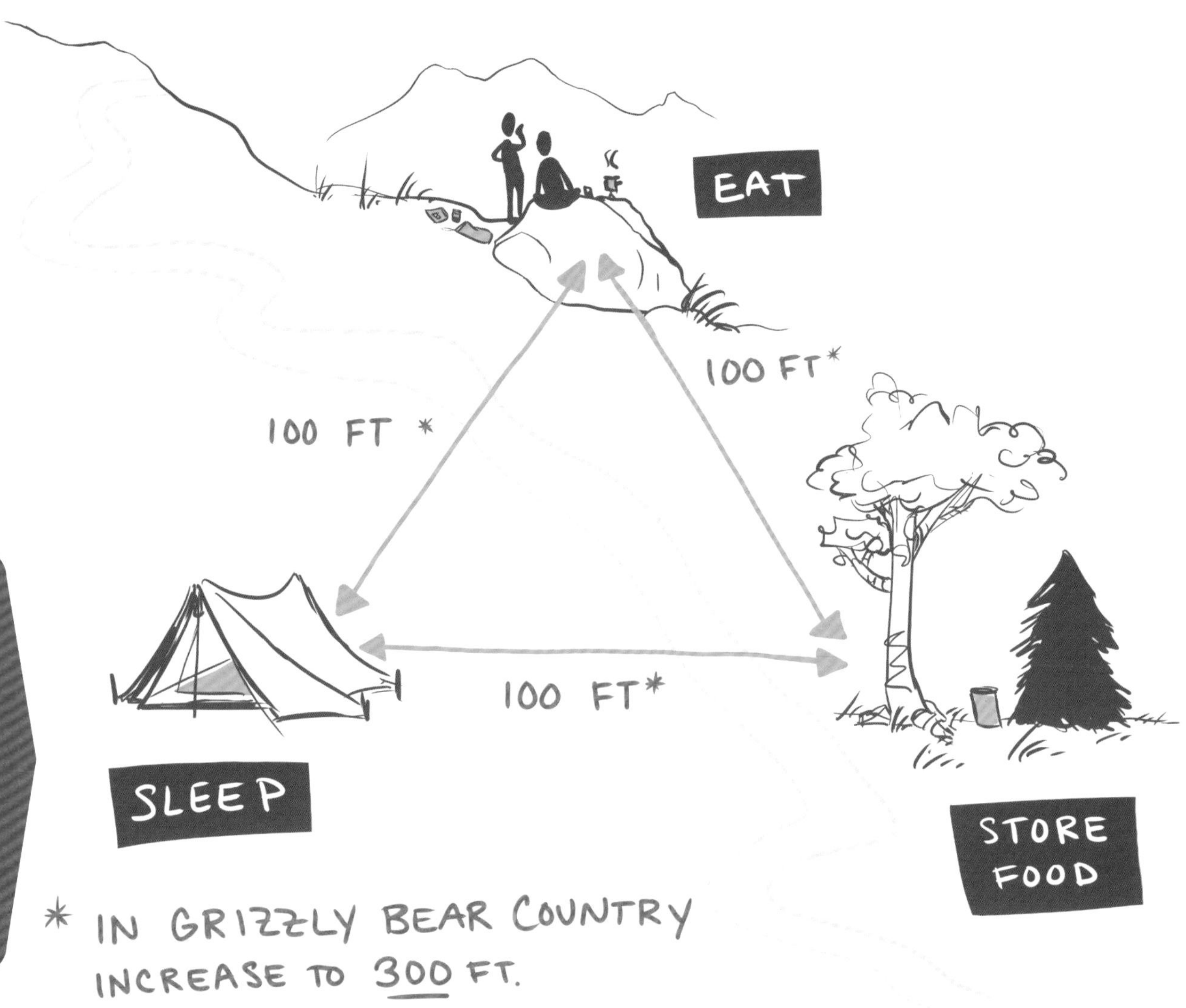

BEAR-MUDA TRIANGLE: Regardless of which approach you use to store food, practice the "bear-muda triangle" when in bear country: Your sleeping, cooking, and food hanging/storage areas should be arranged in a triangle, with each point approximately 100 feet away from the other. In grizzly bear country, increase that to 300 feet.

OTHER PREDATORS: Aside from bears, few predators are attracted to campsites. Wolves, coyotes, and mountain lions rarely venture into campsites looking for food. The same guidelines that apply for bears will serve as an extra measure to keep these animals away, too, but in areas that do not have bears, they are not necessary.

NON-PREDATOR ANIMALS: Most negative encounters with wild animals at camp come from non-predator species, especially rodents. Mice will happily chew through your tent or backpack to get that open bag of trail mix you accidentally left in there. In more popular areas, we have even seen a raccoon decimate a campsite where food was left out and a crow fly away with a wrapped granola bar. Deer love salt, and they'll lick or steal any salty items you leave lying around, like hiking poles that have come into contact with your sweaty hands. The good news is that the guidelines for bears work for nuisance animals, too. Keeping a clean camp helps keep rodents, birds, and deer away. When talking to a ranger at Olympic National Park, where bear canisters are required, we learned that the requirement has much more to do with keeping rodents out of campsites than it does with preventing bear encounters; bears are not too common in the park, but rodents ransacking camps are. Always check the regulations, but typically if you are not hiking in bear country, hanging an odor-proof or odor-resistant bag will suffice.

DEER LIKE SALT

While we were on the Northern California section of the PCT, it became clear that the deer had learned to associate humans with salt. It was not uncommon to hear noises outside our tent at night and then peek out and see a deer enjoying the salt in our urine by licking the ground where we had peed. One evening, we camped near a few other hikers, and when we woke up, one could not find one of his hiking poles. After a long search, it was recovered at least 50 yards away from where we had all camped. All we can figure is that a deer had wandered into the campsite overnight and enjoyed the salt from sweat on his hiking pole handles so much that it tried to run away with the pole. Ever since, we've slept with our hiking poles safely out of reach of deer.

—Tim

THRUHIKERS' TIPS

CAMPING

- Know if the area where you are headed allows dispersed camping or camping only in designated sites, or if it requires permits for specific sites. Plan accordingly.
- Plan your route so that you aren't doing too many miles to comfortably make it to camp each day.
- If dispersed camping, look for a site that is flat, clear of vegetation, and shielded from the wind.
- Camping doesn't have to include a nightly campfire. Never have a campfire where it's prohibited, and consider forgoing campfires altogether in dry, fire-prone regions. Keep your campsite clean, and minimize smells by not leaving any food lying around. Rodents searching for food can cause considerable damage to your gear and rations.
- Follow the area's regulations to make unpleasant wildlife encounters unlikely. If camping in bear country, hang your food or use a bear canister or bear-resistant bag. Always check regulations for which method(s) are allowed before heading out.

9

BODY & HEALTH ON THE TRAIL

Even though it's not a race, walking miles outside with a heavy pack is undeniably an athletic endeavor. Being in tune with your body is key to avoiding injury, preventing overuse, and having a good time. Being outside also means you are away from amenities like toilets, showers, and running water. This chapter describes ways to make sure you treat your body well on the trail and includes some tips for hygiene, including pooping and peeing on trail.

LISTEN TO YOUR BODY

Regardless of the length of your trip, the best thing you can do for your body is listen to it. If you're thirsty, drink. If you're hungry, eat. If you need a break, take it. Most ailments on the trail can be avoided by paying attention to how you feel physically and mentally and adjusting accordingly.

AVOIDING PHYSICAL INJURY

Common physical injuries on the trail include blisters, sunburn, chafing, scrapes, bruises, sore or strained muscles, twisted or sprained ankles, knee pain, and back pain. Some of the most common overuse injuries experienced by backpackers include stress fractures, plantar fasciitis, and Achilles tendinitis. A primary cause of injury on the trail is pushing your body too hard for too long, especially if you do so too early in a trip. It is demanding and fatiguing to walk miles under the weight of a backpack day after day. Overuse injuries develop when muscles, tendons, ligaments, and bones are tired and are pushed beyond their limits without any chance to rest.

To reduce the risk of physical injury on long-distance hikes, we limit our daily mileage for the first week of every trip. No matter how good we are feeling, we won't hike extra miles in a day until we've given our bodies enough time to get used to the rigors of walking all day, every day. Specifically for us, that means we keep our daily distance limited to 15 miles or less during this period. All hikers are different; depending on your experience level and base level of fitness, starting out with no more than 5 or 10 miles per day could be a better idea for you. Regardless, be aware that it takes significant discipline to limit your mileage during the early days of a hike. On popular trails, this might mean letting other hikers fly past as they cover more miles per day, and reminding yourself over and over that being conservative for the first week helps guarantee that you will make it to the last week of the trip without getting injured on the way.

Worn-out gear, especially shoes, is another common cause of injury. After about 500 miles of use, the soles of most hiking shoes become compressed and stop providing support. Depending on factors like weight and the terrain you're on, shoes can last longer or shorter than that, so pay attention to your body to be sure you don't push your shoes too far. If you start getting sore knees, your plantar fascia acts up, or the bottoms of your feet start to hurt, this may be a sign that your shoes need replacing. If your shirt or pants form holes under your backpack, this means your pack is now cutting straight into your skin. Foam sleeping pads compress over time, and using a pad that is beyond its useful life can lead to hip pain and soreness.

PEEING

Peeing in the wilderness is extremely easy for people with penises. For people with vaginas, options include air-drying, carrying toilet paper, or carrying a reusable cloth wipe that can be attached to the outside of a backpack. Companies have recently started to make reusable cloth wipes specifically designed for peeing that are absorbent and made with antimicrobial fabrics, which help reduce the risk of infection. Before these antimicrobial options existed, it wasn't uncommon for people to use something like a handkerchief. Remember, pee clothes should only be used for peeing, not pooping! On trail, they can be rinsed in streams. When you get home from a trip or while resupplying on longer trips, be sure to wash the pee cloth with your laundry. If you do choose to carry toilet paper, follow the area's guidelines to determine if it can be buried (6 to 8 inches deep) or if it needs to be packed out. If the latter, bring a ziplock bag to hold your used toilet paper so it doesn't contaminate the other items in your backpack. When peeing, be careful not to splash onto your shoes or clothing, and be aware that pee flows with gravity, so don't squat or stand with your shoes immediately downhill from the spot where you pee.

In most areas, it is okay to pee in any secluded spot off the trail. Don't go too close to obvious campsites or potentially popular places to take a break; when the same spot is used over and over, a smell can accumulate. In some fragile environments, such as high alpine regions, pee can do damage to vegetation. It also can attract animals like deer because of its high salt content. When possible, pee onto a rocky surface or, on sparsely populated trails, directly onto the trail itself.

POOPING

There is nothing glamorous about pooping in the woods. Use the bathroom before you head out, and if there are bathrooms or outhouses provided along your route, use them—this is the best way to minimize the amount of human poop left in the wilderness. On overnight or multiday trips, pooping in the wilderness becomes necessary. Here are guidelines to make it as pleasant and low-impact as possible.

LOCATION: Most importantly, do your business away from water sources. Even buried poop can contaminate nearby water, and you or other hikers are likely collecting your drinking water from those same sources. Your chosen spot should also be in a secluded area that's unlikely to be utilized by others for camping or breaks.

BURY IT: Don't just poop on top of the ground because that's what animals do. Human poop can carry diseases like norovirus that may get other hikers sick, and it's just plain gross to encounter somebody else's poop near the trail. Most wilderness areas permit burying poop 6 to 8 inches underground. In some dry, fragile, and/or heavily used environments, you may be required to poop into a bag and pack it

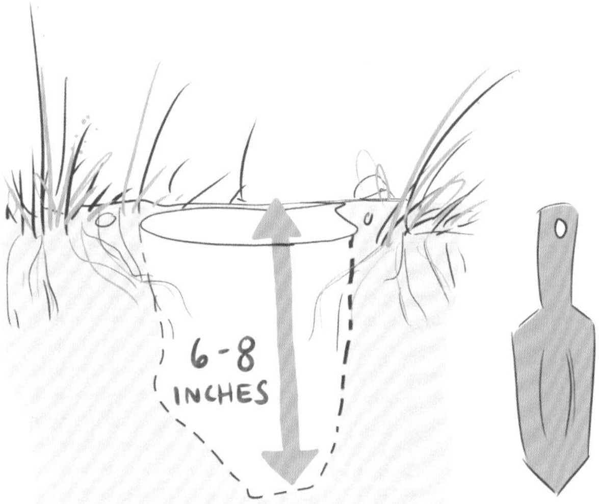

out of the wilderness with the rest of your trash. Outfitters sell special bags that seal very securely and do not leak, so if you need these, be sure to stock up before you head out!

TOILET PAPER AND OTHER OPTIONS: Guidelines for toilet paper disposal vary by location. Many areas allow the burial of human waste but require or recommend packing out toilet paper. Others allow toilet paper to be buried right in the same hole as your poop. Nowhere is it okay to leave your toilet paper on the ground or to burn it.

Another option is to forgo the use of toilet paper completely and instead opt for natural materials. This sounds gross, but in fact, many cultures around the world do not use toilet paper, instead opting for water as a cleaning substrate. Leaves make a poor wiping material (and may be poisonous or cause irritation), but smooth sticks and rocks work surprisingly well. Many long-distance hikers opt for a combination of sticks, rocks, and water to clean themselves after pooping. Additional benefits of this approach are that it produces less waste to bury or pack out, and it saves the weight and space of toilet paper in your pack.

A final option is to carry a portable bidet, which is a small and light plastic device that attaches directly to the threading of a standard water bottle and can be used to squirt yourself clean.

HAND SANITIZER: Regardless of how you choose to clean up after pooping, don't forget to wash your hands with hand sanitizer. A small bottle is well worth the weight and space it takes up in your pack to keep your hands clean. Squatting in the woods and potentially using awkward wiping materials increases the risk of getting poop on your hands, and the wilderness does not provide soap and sinks. Sadly, breakouts of fecally transmitted diseases do occur among hikers from waste matter on their hands getting onto their food and/or the food of people they are hiking with.

PERIODS

Just like at home, there are many options to deal with periods on trail.

MENSTRUAL CUP: A menstrual cup is a lightweight, low-waste option. Menstrual cups should be emptied every 8 to 12 hours, and you can dig a hole to bury the blood. It's important to keep clean to avoid infections, so clean your hands with hand sanitizer before and after emptying the cup, and use clean, filtered water to rinse the cup. When you're back in town, wash your cup with a mild soap. You can also boil it to sanitize it.

TAMPONS AND PADS: If you're using tampons and/or pads on trail, be sure to pack out all waste, including the wrappers and the used tampons or pads. Do not bury them. It is convenient to carry an extra ziplock bag to collect the used tampons or pads. Use hand sanitizer for your hands before and after changing your tampons or pads.

It is important to eat and hydrate well on trail, especially when you're on your period. Exercise can help with cramps, but be sure to take extra breaks as needed. Periods can make elevation sickness worse, so give yourself time to acclimate and rest as needed. On longer hikes, like multiple-month thruhikes, increased exercise can cause lighter, irregular, or missed periods.

When hiking in bear country, all scented items should be stored in a bear-safe container—this includes clean and used tampons, pads, and menstrual cups.

HYGIENE

It's almost impossible to maintain the same standards of hygiene while on the trail as you do in daily life. The number-one thing to focus on is your health. It's important not to sacrifice the things that keep you healthy, but it isn't necessary to keep your appearance as beautiful and nice-smelling as you would if you were headed to work. Depending on the length of your trip, you can either wait until the end of the trip to return to your normal state of hygiene or take a break every few days in a town to shower and feel almost as clean as you normally would.

WHAT *NOT* TO SACRIFICE:

TOOTH HEALTH: You should brush your teeth just as frequently on trail as you would off trail. Extended periods of time without brushing your teeth can cause permanent damage and tooth decay. Remember to leave no trace when brushing your teeth on trail because curious animals could eat a glob of toothpaste spat onto the ground. Instead, toothpaste should be buried in a cathole, swallowed, or sprayed over a large area away from where you are camping. Our preferred approach is to swallow toothpaste.

AVOIDING GERMS: Prevent the spread of germs on the trail by using hand sanitizer when soap isn't readily available and avoiding contact with dead animals or fecal matter.

FOOT HEALTH: Your feet take a beating when you're walking miles under the load of a heavy pack. Clip your toenails, keep your feet as clean and dry as possible, and treat any punctured blisters with alcohol and antibiotic ointment and cover to prevent infection. Maintaining foot hygiene is a key factor to ensure you don't have to stop your hike early.

FEMININE HYGIENE: Washing yourself with clean, filtered water or feminine wipes can help prevent infections.

WHAT CAN BE SACRIFICED:

APPEARANCE: Makeup and other beauty products are not practical on the trail, and the other hikers you'll interact with won't expect you to have a perfect appearance.

SHOWERS: Society has come to expect frequent showering, but for thousands of years, humans survived without them. Showers are rarely available in the backcountry, so a little bit of dirt on your skin can be worn as a badge of honor that does no long-term damage.

SHAMPOO AND CONDITIONER: Nobody likes to have greasy hair, but attempting to use shampoo and conditioner in lakes and streams is unpleasant and can leave residue in water sources that is harmful for the ecosystem. After several days, hair tends to adjust to not being washed frequently and begins producing less of its natural oil.

SOAP: Rinsing off your body in lakes and streams is a good way to get dirt off your body. Soap is not necessary and is harmful for the ecosystem.

DEODORANT: Few long-distance hikers wear deodorant daily because it isn't practical, and scented deodorants can attract animals. On short trips, it usually does little harm to carry a stick of deodorant if you choose to, but if you decide to forgo it, it will only take a few days before you and your hiking partners adjust and become immune to the smell. In fact, if you spend a long time in the backcountry, you will probably notice the strong smells emanating from deodorants and perfumes worn by the day hikers you pass much more than the natural body odors of other long-distance hikers.

SUNBURN

Wearing sunscreen, a hat, and/or long sleeves and pants is the best way to avoid getting a sunburn. Bad sunburns on the trail can blister, peel, and make hiking uncomfortable. Sunburns aren't just a risk in hot weather; on trail, you will spend 100 percent of your time outside under the sun, regardless of the temperature, so sunburns are just as likely and can be just as bad when the weather is cold. When you're hiking in the snow, sunburns can occur more easily than they do during summer because the snow reflects the sun up at you while the sun is also casting its rays down.

HEAT EXHAUSTION & HEAT STROKE

Heat exhaustion is one of the most common physical ailments affecting hikers and sometimes requiring rescue. When you're hiking in hot weather, drink plenty of water and take extra breaks—in the shade if possible. Our rule of thumb is usually to drink 1 liter of water for every 5 miles hiked, but we increase that number when temperatures are high and the sun is out. Because we also sweat more when it's hot, we make sure to drink extra electrolytes, like Gatorade powder. When temperatures are extremely high, the worst temperatures can be avoided by hiking in the morning and evening with a long "siesta," or midday break, during the worst of the heat. If shade is hard to find, you can always pitch your tent for shelter from the sun.

According to the Centers for Disease Control and Prevention, symptoms of heat exhaustion include heavy sweating, weakness, tiredness, cool or clammy skin, a fast and weak pulse, cramps, dizziness, nausea, vomiting, headache, and potentially fainting.[1] If you experience these symptoms, get out of the sun and to a cooler location as soon as possible. Heat exhaustion can progress to heat stroke, which is an emergency situation. Signs of heat stroke include a hot body temperature, red skin, an elevated pulse, confusion, and potentially passing out.

HYPOTHERMIA

Cold temperatures and wet conditions can also lead to dangerous conditions on the trail. When subjected to cold for a prolonged period of time, your body can lose heat faster than it produces it, causing hypothermia. The risk is greater when you are wet because moisture conducts heat away from the body. Even when it's well above freezing, the combination of cold temperatures and wet conditions make hypothermia a risk. To avoid hypothermia, bring appropriate layers for the conditions you're hiking in. Even if it's hot during the day, it can get very cold at night, especially at high elevations.

According to the Centers for Disease Control and Prevention, symptoms of hypothermia include shivering, exhaustion, confusion, slurred speech, and drowsiness.[2] If you experience these symptoms, remove any moist clothing and use whatever means possible to warm yourself immediately, including skin-to-skin contact with another person if no better heat sources are available.

POISON IVY & POISON OAK

Poison ivy and poison oak are prevalent in much of the United States. These plants like to grow in disturbed areas where sunlight gets through dense vegetation; in other words, they like to grow right along trails. Poison ivy and poison oak are closely related; both contain an oil called urushiol that many people have an allergic reaction to if it gets on their skin. The oil causes red itchy skin and, in bad cases, swelling and weeping blisters. If the oil gets on your

1 "Warning Signs and Symptoms of Heat-Related Illness." Centers for Disease Control and Prevention. September 1, 2017. https://www.cdc.gov/disasters/extremeheat/warning.html.
2 "Hypothermia and Frostbite." Centers for Disease Control and Prevention. November 2, 2023. https://www.cdc.gov/disasters/winter/staysafe/hypothermia.html.

shoes, clothing, or hands, it can be transmitted to the rest of your body. Poison ivy and poison oak both have three leaves and can grow as plants, bushes, shrubs, or vines. The leaves turn a reddish color as the season progresses. High in the mountains, the plants are less common.

If you come into contact with poison ivy or poison oak, wash the affected area immediately with soap and water. If you don't have soap, water and friction to remove the oil is better than nothing. Over-the-counter medications like Benadryl and hydrocortisone cream can alleviate the itching and pain. For bad cases, doctors can prescribe steroids to reduce the reaction quickly and dramatically.

Additional irritating plants to be on the lookout for include stinging nettles, poison sumac, poodle-dog bush, and others that may affect fewer people or are prevalent in more isolated regions.

DISEASES TO LOOK OUT FOR

LYME DISEASE: A tick-borne disease that can be transmitted to humans through the bite of an infected blacklegged (aka deer) tick, Lyme disease symptoms include a bull's-eye rash, fever, headache, and fatigue. Lyme disease needs to be treated with antibiotics; untreated Lyme disease can lead to infection of your joints, heart, and nervous system. To avoid Lyme disease, use bug spray, wear long pants and shirts, and remove ticks promptly. We recommend checking your body for ticks every night before heading to bed.

GIARDIA: This disease is caused by parasites in drinking water and causes diarrhea and vomiting that can last for 2 to 6 weeks. Giardia can be avoided by always using a filter before drinking from springs, streams, lakes, or other natural water sources. Don't trust mountain streams based only on the fact that they look safe to drink and are at high elevation—several wild animals, including marmots (found only at high elevation), are common carriers of giardia.

NOROVIRUS: This very contagious virus causes diarrhea and vomiting that typically lasts for 1 to 3 days. It can be transmitted on trails from fecal matter getting into food.

AVOIDING & TREATING BLISTERS

Bad blisters can be debilitating on hiking trips. They are caused by friction on your feet, so hours of walking coupled with extra weight on your back elevates the risk of blisters forming. Moisture increases the amount of friction between your feet and socks or shoes, as do swollen feet. Hot weather is particularly bad for blisters because it means your feet are more likely to swell and sweat. Hiking socks with a little bit of extra padding (but not too much) can reduce friction. If your socks get wet, dry them out whenever possible. A good trick is to rotate your socks daily; dry out the pair you aren't wearing by hanging it off the back of your backpack. Consider wearing hiking shoes that are bigger than you'd wear for everyday use—this allows extra space for padded socks and for your feet to swell during the course of long days on the trail. We have found that there are very few drawbacks to using shoes that are bigger than our around-town shoes, and this makes the most difference for blisters. One more avoidable factor that increases the likelihood of blisters is having rocks and debris in your shoes. Using gaiters that cover the gap between your shoes and ankles dramatically reduces the amount of debris that gets in. When you do feel something in your shoe, take the time to stop and remove it before a blister has the chance to form.

Despite taking all of these precautions to reduce blisters, for most hikers, blisters still form from time to time. Small blisters can be a simple annoyance that goes away over time. Severe or persistent blisters make a hike miserable, and in the worst-case scenario, they can lead to infection that takes you off the trail. When a hot spot or blister forms, cover it with a sticky medical tape like Leukotape P to reduce friction—the friction will be between the tape and your socks or shoes instead of your feet. Alternatively, apply Vaseline to the hot spot to reduce friction before a blister forms.

Occasionally, it is appropriate to drain a swollen blister to reduce pain. To drain a blister, sterilize a needle with alcohol and your lighter, and sterilize the blister and your skin around it with alcohol. Then, gently and carefully puncture the edge of the blister with the tip of the needle and push out the fluid. Apply first-aid ointment liberally to cover the blister and then cover the area with enough Leukotape P that it doesn't fall off. For example, if the blister is on the pad of your foot, don't just put a small piece of tape over the blister because it will fall off when you start walking. Instead, put a strip of tape over the blister and around to the top of your foot.

BLISTERS ON THE CONTINENTAL DIVIDE TRAIL

At around mile 450 in the desert section of our Continental Divide Trail (CDT) thruhike, I started to get blisters on my feet. At first, they were manageable and in places I had gotten them before: on my little toes and on the outsides of my heels. They were a bit uncomfortable but pretty easy to ignore. A few days later, I had blisters on the balls of my feet (very painful), on every single toe, and on both sides of both heels. Every step was painful. I would take off my shoes and socks at breaks and elevate my feet to try to reduce the swelling. Toward the end of every day, I was almost in tears, and Tim played podcasts for me to try to help me forget about the pain. At our next resupply stop, I ordered new shoes that were a half size bigger than the shoes I had been wearing and solicited advice from other thruhikers. They gave me some Leukotape P, which is the only tape we have found that doesn't fall off while hiking. (Band-Aids and moleskin become loose almost immediately.) I drained some of the larger blisters and then applied first-aid ointment and the Leukotape P to all of them. We continued hiking, and the Leukotape P helped a lot. Seven days later, I got my new shoes, and they made all the difference! My feet were so swollen from the hiking and the desert heat, and I needed that extra space. My blisters healed, and I didn't get any more after that.

—Renee

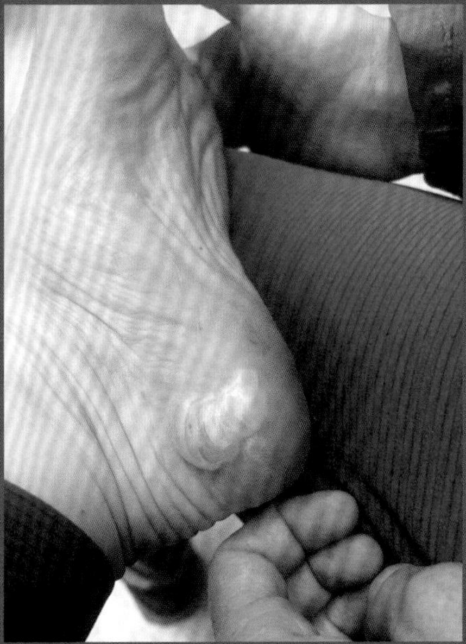

AVOIDING LONELINESS

A mental ailment that has the potential to grip hikers, particularly on long-distance trails, is loneliness. In regular life, we interact with friends, colleagues, and many other people, such as store cashiers, in person as well as via social media every day. On trail, most of these social stimulants are reduced or completely eliminated. For some, the break from social engagement is a perk. For others, being alone with just your thoughts is a real challenge.

On most trails, you are not truly alone. If you're looking for social engagement, don't hesitate to chat with other hikers you bump into. Trail conversations can be surprisingly long and engaging. If those you meet aren't in the mood to talk, the conversation will be short before everybody moves on, but even in this case, saying hi is almost never perceived as offensive or invasive.

Many hikers take up journaling to share their thoughts and experience with a future audience, whether that audience is only their future self, friends and family, or an online blog. This form of expression can help satisfy the desire to communicate even without immediate feedback.

For finding a community in nature, long-distance trails are their own beast. The majority of thruhikers set out alone but start at approximately the same time. For example, the Pacific Crest Trail (PCT) issues 50 permits per day, which are all quickly reserved for start dates ranging from March to May. A sense of community forms rapidly among any group of thruhiking adventurers, all of whom have a difficult-to-comprehend challenge ahead and no or few long-term friends at their side to share it with. Hikers readily introduce themselves, chat about their lives, and quickly start forming trail families, or "tramilies," of friends hiking more or less together. Fifty hikers spread out across approximately 20 miles still gives more than ample solitude for those who want it. But for hikers seeking a community, a long-distance trail provides a remarkable opportunity to meet lifelong friends.

GETTING TO KNOW LIFELONG FRIENDS ON THE PCT

When we set out from the Mexican border to hike north on the PCT to Canada, we didn't quite understand everything we were getting ourselves into. We knew being out for 4 or 5 months while walking 2,650 miles would be physically and mentally demanding. We knew we would travel through some of the most beautiful wilderness areas around. But we thought the trail would be a solitary experience, and it was anything but. The PCT Association gives out up to 50 permits per day for northbound hikers, which is not a small number of people to share an 18-inch-wide trail. You can't avoid seeing and interacting with other hikers at water sources, at campsites, or in trailside towns. On top of that, most people starting out share similar fears, expectations, and insecurities about what lies ahead, all of which they want to discuss with others. This leads to frequent and fulfilling conversations with other hikers about vulnerable topics, which is just the right setting for friendships to form. Among the subset of hikers who started at about the same time as we did and hiked at about the same pace, we remain friends with several, all these years later.

Right after we finished the PCT, we moved to Germany, and one of our good PCT friends, Parmesan, lived only 30 minutes away from us by train. We began hiking with him all around Germany, and although we no longer live there, we still keep in touch with Parmesan and visit regularly. Another friend from the PCT, Dirty Money, remains among our closest friends. For four winters in a row, we traveled to northern Sweden, above the Arctic Circle, to visit her. Our latest move brought us to California, where another good PCT friend, Alix, lives. Almost instantly, our PCT friendship was rekindled in California's Santa Cruz mountains, and the years in between melted away. It's remarkable how sharing an experience as powerful as a thruhike builds bonds that are comparable to those between childhood friends.

—Tim

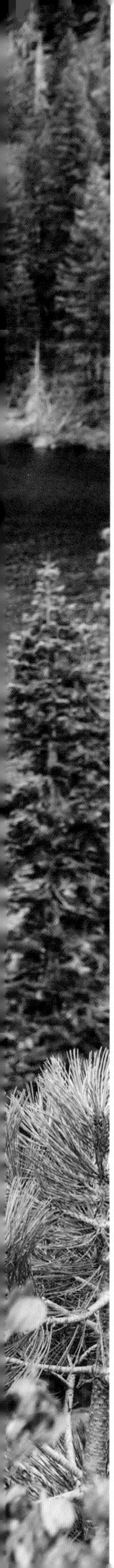

THRUHIKERS' TIPS

BODY & HEALTH ON THE TRAIL

- The best thing you can do for your body is listen to it. Don't push hard when something hurts, eat when you're hungry, drink when you're thirsty, and slow down if you're constantly exhausted.
- On long trips, start slower to let your body acclimate to the rigors of walking all day.
- Replace your gear, especially your shoes, when it is worn out.
- Never leave toilet paper or human waste on the ground. In some areas, it is fine to bury it, and in other areas, it needs to be packed out.
- Use hand sanitizer frequently, especially after going to the bathroom, because soap and running water are hard to come by in the backcountry.
- Backpacking while on your period is very doable. Eat and hydrate well, and be aware that you will be more susceptible to elevation sickness while on your period.
- Don't sacrifice hygiene practices that could affect your long-term health, such as brushing your teeth.
- You can sacrifice your short-term beauty; on the trail, you probably will shower less frequently and sometimes be covered in dirt.
- Pay attention to the weather, especially during extreme heat and cold, and take measures to avoid being struck by heat exhaustion or hypothermia.
- Do everything you can to keep your feet dry, healthy, and blister-free. You demand a lot from them on a backpacking trip.
- Avoid loneliness by journaling or chatting with other hikers out on the trail.

10

ENVIRONMENTAL CHALLENGES

Life on the trail necessitates dealing with whatever environmental conditions Mother Nature throws at you. From heat to cold to treacherous conditions, the trail constantly reminds hikers that they are not in control. Learn about and be prepared for the region that you are hiking in and the extremities that you may encounter before you set out. This chapter highlights several of the environmental challenges that hikers are likely to encounter.

EXTREME TEMPERATURES

We have been reminded more times than we care to admit that the temperature on trail rarely matches the temperature back in town. At different elevations and depending on factors like wind, temperatures are highly variable. Extreme heat can make hiking during the hottest part of the day unpleasant or even unsafe, and extreme cold without the right equipment can quickly transform a hike from fun to frightening and even dangerous. Always check the forecast before heading out, but know that even the best forecasts are only a guess, especially in mountainous regions where weather patterns can suddenly and unexpectedly change.

HEAT: If heat is a risk, wear lightweight, light-colored clothes and carry plenty of water. Drink electrolyte drinks, such as Gatorade powder mixed in water, to replenish electrolytes lost to heavy sweating. Take extra breaks during the day, and if hiking in the heat is uncomfortable, take advantage of cooler mornings and evenings for hiking, with a long midday break during the hottest part of the day. (See page 142 for information on how to pay attention to your body and avoid letting the heat cause heat exhaustion or heat stroke.)

COLD: On the trail, particularly at high elevation, temperatures can quickly and unexpectedly drop to frigid levels, even during the summer. Be prepared by carrying layers that will keep you warm in the coldest conditions you might encounter. Layering lets you adjust your insulation to match the temperature; big, heavy coats do not.

Carry a sleeping bag rated for at least the coldest temperature you might experience overnight, but be aware that ratings often indicate the temperature at which your sleeping bag will keep you alive, not at which you will sleep comfortably. Trial and error is the only way to figure out if you "sleep cold" or "sleep warm"; on chilly nights, pay attention to how cold it can get before your sleeping bag isn't doing enough to keep you happy. Everybody is different, but both of us are comfortable using 20°F bags down to about freezing, and if it gets much colder than that, we use sleeping bags with a warmer rating. (See page 59 for more information about choosing the right sleeping bag.)

A surprisingly high proportion of hikers do not use mummy-style sleeping bags correctly. The purpose of the bag is to trap warm air inside and hold it close to your body. For the greatest warmth, zip up your sleeping bag all the way to the top and cinch down the drawstring to tighten it around your face. Putting loose clothing items or a jacket inside your sleeping bag around your head and neck can also help trap warm air down below. If you feel a draft coming in, that means your sleeping bag isn't tightened enough. To remain comfortable with the bag so snugly around you, roll with the bag instead of separately from it—this way your face always has a little opening to breathe through.

If using a quilt in cold temperatures, ensure there are no gaps around it to let drafts in. Achieve this by wrapping the quilt's straps around the bottom of your sleeping pad to keep the quilt snugly around you. Cinch the top tight around your neck.

Wear a hat overnight, and avoid sleeping in damp clothes. Moisture conducts heat away from your body and cools you down quickly. Even the moisture and/or sweat lingering in your clothes after a normal day of hiking is enough to cool you down overnight. Changing out of your hiking clothes and into a set of dry pajamas or sleeping clothes contributes significantly to a warm night's sleep.

Always use a sleeping pad. These aren't just for added padding; they provide insulation between you and the ground. Beneath your body, your sleeping bag compresses, rendering the insulation almost useless. A sleeping pad provides an additional insulating material that works even with the weight of a body on top. Sleeping pads come with varying amounts of insulation, so if you are camping in the cold, be sure your sleeping pad is up for the challenge. It can be a good idea to use two sleeping pads, one closed-cell foam and one inflatable, if you will be camping on top of snow. (See page 62 for more information about choosing the right sleeping pad.)

In cold weather, certain pieces of gear require special care. Hollow fiber water filters should never be allowed to freeze. Water expands when frozen, so lingering water in your filter, which is impossible to remove, will burst the fibers, making the filter ineffective. On nights with the potential to drop below freezing, put your filter inside your sleeping bag when you go to sleep. If temperatures remain below freezing during the day, keep your filter inside your jacket while you hike. Also, pay attention to the batteries in your electronic devices when temperatures drop. Most batteries do not work as well in the cold, but putting electronics in your sleeping bag overnight or inside your jacket during the day can help keep them working well.

CAUGHT IN A COLORADO BLIZZARD IN LATE JUNE

On June 27, 2021, we were hiking near Mount Poor on the Continental Divide Trail (CDT) in Colorado. It had been raining on and off all day, but we were mostly at a relatively low elevation so the temperatures were not too bad. With evening approaching, we decided to push for a few extra miles. The trail ahead would take us up to about 12,500 feet before we descended to our intended camp at a lower elevation. Because of the rain, the day had been slow and unpleasant, so we hadn't covered nearly as many miles as we had hoped. Instead of accepting that the weather wasn't on our side, we blamed ourselves for the low mileage and wanted to push to make up for it. As we climbed toward 12,000 feet, the intermittent rain changed to increasingly heavy snow. Eventually, it was a heavy, wet blizzard with huge snowflakes that stuck to our wetted-out raincoats (even though they were waterproof, they were becoming so saturated, water was starting to seep through our raincoats) and soaked right through them. We had gloves, but they, too, quickly became wetted-out and almost useless.

The novelty of the late June blizzard was lost on us as we became soaked through and through. The wind picked up, the temperature plummeted, and we were miserable. We realized that if we got injured and needed to be rescued, no helicopter could fly in to save us. That was a scary thought. Our bodies were freezing, but our only option was to walk on, hoping to get to lower elevation—to warmer temperatures and a safer place to set up camp—before nightfall. We did not take any breaks to pee or snack; we just walked and walked. As we descended, the snow changed to rain and then lighter rain, and we joyously grabbed the first flat and clear spot we found to set up camp. Our hands were so cold that unbuckling our backpacks was a challenge—we had to help each other get them off. Our usual process of setting up camp took many times longer than usual as we fumbled with cold and wet fingers. Only when we had changed into dry clothes, we were finally tucked tightly into our sleeping bags, and the feeling was returning to our hands and feet did we finally feel like we had survived. Our takeaway lesson from the experience was to hike as the weather dictates, not based on arbitrary daily goals, and to always remember that no matter what the weather is like, it will be worse at higher elevation.

—Tim

SNOW

Snow on the trail will slow down your hiking speed considerably and make every step take more effort. Most backpackers avoid trips in the snow, but with the right equipment and experience, snow can present an exciting challenge and extra solitude on the trail. That said, even if you are hoping for balmy weather but your trip has the potential for snow, or if your trip includes mountainous snow crossings, be sure you are prepared.

For a snow-only trip, our typical recommendation of trail running shoes instead of hiking boots does not apply. Trail runners do not provide enough insulation to keep your feet warm through snow.

For trips that only include a few hours of snow at a time, trail runners can work fine, but be sure they have enough traction for where you're walking. Microspikes, metal spikes that you can attach to the outside of your shoes, can give you more traction on snow and ice. On steep, snowy traverses, whether or not you are using microspikes, it is effective to kick or carve footsteps into the slope, rather than just placing your foot on top as you normally would walk, to avoid slipping and sliding down the side. Wearing waterproof socks over your hiking socks can help keep your feet warm and dry when crossing snow and streams.

Deep snow requires even more special equipment like snowshoes, and slick ice through mountainous terrain necessitates mountaineering abilities, crampons, an ice ax, and potentially ropes plus a helmet. Only venture into extreme conditions like these if you are experienced or traveling under the guidance of somebody who is.

RAIN

Unexpected rain can make a wilderness trip miserable. Use rain gear to avoid letting your layers, sleeping bag, or the inside of your tent get wet. If you check the forecast and see that heavy rain and low temperatures lie ahead, there is no shame in spending extra time in town to wait for the weather to improve. If you are caught in endless rain on the trail, it can be wise to spend extra time (or a full day) in your tent, which protects you from precipitation better than a raincoat does. If temperatures are cold and your gear does get wet, consider heading off trail and into civilization to dry out and warm up before venturing back out.

We have learned that almost no raincoats or rain pants are actually fully waterproof. In an effort to be comfortable and breathable, raincoats sacrifice waterproofness. Raincoats are water resistant for a long time, but eventually they wetout and water starts getting through. However, almost every rain poncho *is* waterproof, including the extremely lightweight disposable ones made of cheap polymers sold at gas stations. Because ponchos are open at the bottom, they are inherently breathable. In continuous rain, we carry ponchos in addition to our raincoats and rain pants and put them on right over our backpacks.

TWO STRAIGHT WEEKS OF RAIN ON THE PACIFIC CREST TRAIL

When hiking the Pacific Crest Trail (PCT), we were treated to almost perfect weather for 4 months. It barely rained, the desert temperatures were tolerable, and snow levels in the Sierras weren't bad. But the total trip took 4½ months. The rain began as we moved through Washington in September, and we hiked through almost constant rain for the last 2 weeks of the trip. We didn't want to wait it out because we knew the weather would only get worse as fall progressed. But the rain was a real challenge. We foolishly had sent home our rain pants after so much great weather, so we had only raincoats and a tent to protect us. We quickly learned that one day of hiking in the rain is a very different experience from day after day of rain hiking with nowhere to dry our things in between. We picked up ponchos as an extra layer of rain protection. We learned to pack our rain fly and ground sheet in separate bags from the rest of our tent. We strung up a clothesline inside our tent every night in an attempt to dry our socks, underwear, and pants as much as possible, although this did essentially nothing because it always rained through the night so the air was 100 percent humid and we had to put on wet clothes every morning. Most importantly, we learned that if and when we did get a moment of sunshine, we should stop everything right away and dry our gear as much as possible. It was a rough 2 weeks, but when we made it to the northern terminus of the trail, we didn't regret a minute of it.

—Tim

In rain, it's important to keep not only your body dry, but also your gear. Down jackets and sleeping bags lose virtually all of their insulating properties when wet. Wet clothes against your body suck away the heat and increase the risk of hypothermia. Be aware that most "waterproof" backpacks are only water resistant, and lightweight waterproof dry bags are often the same. Many hikers use a heavy-duty garbage bag to add a waterproof liner to the inside of their pack. Common tent materials like nylon and polyester are not waterproof, so use a ground sheet to prevent water from seeping into the bottom of your tent. Never pack a soaking wet tent into your backpack alongside the rest of your things—water will drip out of the tent and into your stuff while you hike. Store the dry body of your tent separate from the wet ground sheet and rain fly to protect it from getting wet, too. After a night of heavy rain, we recommend using at least two bags for your tent: one for the wet parts and another for the dry parts. Store the wet bag on the outside of your pack if possible, or keep it in a truly waterproof container like a garbage bag. Closed-cell foam sleeping pads are usually carried on the outside of packs, but they can soak up water in the rain. Put your sleeping pad inside your backpack or wrap it in a garbage or similar bag when it is raining. We like to use Tyvek (a waterproof, lightweight construction material) as our ground sheet under our tent, and when hiking in the rain, we wrap our sleeping pad in the Tyvek to protect it.

WATER CROSSINGS

When venturing away from populated trails and farther into the wilderness, bridges over small to mid-sized streams become a rare luxury. Rock-hopping or finding a log across a stream can be options when possible, but often the trail will take you right up to the edge of a big stream with no way across other than walking through the water.

Don't cross barefoot—you might injure your feet and/or fall into the water thanks to slippery, unstable footing. Keep your shoes on and head straight across. Your shoes will dry as you continue hiking (or get wet again at the next crossing). Some hikers who despise wet shoes carry dedicated water shoes or sandals for water crossings, but these come with a sizable weight penalty. If the water is high and/or fast moving, unbuckle your backpack so you can slip out in case you do fall over. If you are swept downstream, being attached to a backpack that can get waterlogged or tangled up in fallen trees or hanging limbs greatly increases your chances of drowning. Check your pockets for loose items or electronics that aren't waterproof, and be sure they are securely attached higher on your body or pack before crossing.

Don't ever cross high and/or fast-moving water alone. Wait for a friend or another hiker to cross.

During spring and early summer while the snow is melting, water will be much higher than later in the summer and fall. Cold temperatures overnight reduce snowmelt, so streams tend to be lower and easier to cross in the morning than in the afternoon. Be aware that some water sources may be uncrossable during certain times of the year, even if there is a trail that takes you right through them. Streams don't have to be very deep to be very dangerous. Fast-moving water can sweep you off your feet and downstream even when it is well below waist deep. If you are unlucky and get caught between fast water and trees or rocks, the situation can become deadly. When a crossing seems dangerous, check upstream and down for a safer way across, and if you can't find one, find an alternate route. It is better to backtrack and detour than it is to drown.

FEET FISSURES ON THE CONTINENTAL DIVIDE TRAIL

Colorado is a beautiful state. But in June, Colorado is also a state full of snow and water crossings. Between the two, our feet were constantly wet as we traversed the Rocky Mountains on the CDT. Smartly, Renee likes to take off her shoes and socks during lunch breaks. I often opt to keep on my uncomfortable, wet shoes instead of going through the hassle of taking them off only to put them back on an hour later. Colorado taught me that this is a mistake. Big miles every day took a toll on my wet feet, and multiple large fissures started to form in my right foot. These are deep, painful cracks in the skin—in my case, between my toes and into the ball of my foot. I was convinced that the fissures would heal on their own, but they just kept getting bigger. Eventually, I realized that there was no way I would heal without getting off trail, and neither of us had any intention of stopping before we made it to Canada. I continued walking on my fissured foot for another 2,000 miles after the fissures first formed in Colorado. After we finished the hike, it still took several months for the fissures to completely heal. Even as I write this, more than 2 years after completing the CDT, I still have a scar on my foot as a reminder of the fissures. The pain was unpleasant but rarely unbearable. In hindsight, I can't help but feel foolish for letting the fissures form in the first place. Had I been more careful and taken the time to let my feet completely dry once or twice each day, I probably would have been fissure free for the entire hike.

—Tim

ELEVATION

In addition to being tiring and difficult, hiking at high elevations can cause elevation sickness. Air is thinner at high elevation, so each breath you take contains less oxygen than at lower elevations. Most people can adjust to the decreased oxygen levels on almost all trails, even those over 14,000 feet, but if you suddenly travel from a low elevation to a high one, it's not uncommon to experience a few days of elevation sickness. The most common symptoms of elevation sickness include drowsiness, nausea, and/or headaches. In more severe cases, dizziness, vomiting, and even confusion can occur.

Often, the best solution for elevation sickness is to slow down and take extra breaks as your body adjusts. Our experience is that physical exertion, menstruation, and cold all increase the symptoms, but taking it easy helps. We have even stopped to nap on the way up big mountains to help the acclimation process. However, in extreme cases, the best solution is to return to a lower elevation. If you or a hiking partner is acting strange and/or sick from elevation, head back down. More likely than not, after a little while at lower elevation, they will feel better and can give the mountain another try when they are ready.

On longer trips, after a person's body acclimates to high elevation, they should be fine for a long time. Elevation sickness isn't typically something that happens from one mountain to the next, but rather from one trip to the next. For example, the John Muir Trail repeatedly takes hikers from 8,000 feet to 12,000 feet and back again. After a hiker adjusts to their first time above 12,000 feet, they should be fine for the rest of the trail.

OBSTACLES

The less populated a trail is, the more likely it is to contain obstacles. These can include fallen trees, wash-outs, overgrowth, and burned areas. Sometimes obstacles are simply an annoyance, but occasionally they can be dangerous hazards that require care or detours. If obstacles render a trail closed, don't put yourself or rescue teams at risk by trying to venture through it.

DOWNED TREES: All trees eventually die and fall over. When they fall over and block a trail, hikers have to go over, under, or around them. Be careful getting past fallen trees because you and/or your gear can be poked or scraped by pointy limbs. Extreme wind events can litter miles of trail with fallen trees. When this is the case, the best plan of attack may be a detour; spending hours upon hours moving extremely slowly while climbing over or under trees can be a demoralizing experience.

ELEVATION SICKNESS IN KINGS CANYON NATIONAL PARK

Long before we started thruhiking, when we were first discovering the Sierra Nevada mountains of California, we ventured to Kings Canyon National Park for a 2-night backpacking trip. We drove up from near sea level on a Friday, intending to car camp the first night and then start the hike from a trailhead near our campsite. We arrived late and went straight to bed. It was a cold October night, with overnight lows less than 20°F, and I woke up early, freezing. Renee, on the other hand, insisted that she was burning up and kept removing articles of clothing. That seemed odd, but everybody's different, so at first I didn't think much of it. Then she said she wasn't feeling well and wanted to go to the bathroom. Our campsite was no more than 100 feet from the outhouse, but she asked to be driven. I told her that made no sense. It would take much longer to get into the car and drive than just to walk. Nope—she insisted she had to be driven.

At this point, I knew something was off. We debated for a while, but I ultimately caved and drove her 100 feet to the outhouse. Afterward, she was still burning up and wanted to take off more layers, which I now realized was dangerous in the cold temperature. We hadn't taken seriously the possibility of elevation sickness because we were only at about 8,000 feet. But whether she was experiencing that or another ailment, it seemed like heading downhill to a ranger station was a good idea. As we drove down, Renee started feeling better almost immediately, and she was completely fine when we got to the ranger station a few thousand feet lower. We chatted with the ranger about alternative routes and then sheepishly asked if it is possible to get elevation sickness at 8,000 feet. The ranger said it is possible and, without skipping a beat, asked Renee if she was on her period. She was. Dealing with unacclimated campers day after day had taught the ranger, who taught us, that elevation sickness can affect people well below extreme mountain elevations, and that it has a much greater likelihood of affecting people during their periods.

—Tim

WASHED-OUT TRAILS: Severe rain events sometimes wash away sections of trail. If you can safely continue around the washed-out section, do so while trying to minimize additional erosion or damage to vegetation.

OVERGROWTH: In areas with thick vegetation, trails are cut right through the growth to create a pleasant route for human travel. But if a trail has not been maintained for a while, vegetation will do its best to reclaim the trail. When traveling through overgrowth, be careful with light or fragile clothing because it may snag and tear on branches. Keep your eyes peeled for poison oak and poison ivy, which love growing alongside trails. Finally, if there is morning dew, be prepared to get wet. Hiking through dew-covered overgrowth can leave you wetter than if you'd been in a downpour.

BURNED AREAS: Hazards remain well after forest fires are extinguished or die out. Burned trees can fall over and injure hikers. Erosion and mudslides are more likely after a burn. A lack of leaves reduces shade, and charred black ground absorbs the sun's heat, so recently burned areas can be some of the hottest to walk through. It can be frustrating when officials keep burned forests closed to hiking for several years after a fire, but they do so based on an analysis of the conditions and the decision that travel is not yet safe. When hiking through a burned area that is not closed to travel, stay alert and avoid camping in it.

THRUHIKERS' TIPS

ENVIRONMENTAL CHALLENGES

- During extremely hot weather, drinking electrolytes in addition to water can help prevent dehydration.
- When it is cold out, moisture is the enemy. Do everything you can to keep your gear and yourself dry, especially overnight.
- Bring layers and rain gear to be prepared for any weather you encounter on trail.
- Hiking in the snow is guaranteed to be much slower than hiking on solid ground.
- Keep your shoes on when crossing streams to avoid injuring your feet. For mountain streams fed by snowmelt, water levels are lower in the morning than at night. Don't cross a stream with deep, fast-moving water because you could be knocked off your feet and swept downstream.
- Expect more obstacles, such as downed trees and overgrowth, on less-populated trails.

11

LEAVE NO TRACE PRINCIPLES

Leave No Trace is a philosophy for enjoying the outdoors that maximizes the number of people who can enjoy an outdoor experience while minimizing the impact on the environment and experience of others.[1] Leaving no trace means striving to have zero impact on the places you visit. Traces to be avoided include the obvious, like littering or damage to vegetation and wildlife, as well as subtler things like excessive noise and being unprepared. This chapter describes ways to minimize the evidence that you were ever enjoying the outdoors so that those who travel after you can enjoy a similarly pristine experience.

1 Leave No Trace is a philosophy that focuses on minimizing the impact people leave on the places they visit. The Leave No Trace principles described in this book are our interpretation of those provided by the Leave No Trace organization. For more information, visit lnt.org.

BE PREPARED

Having a plan and being prepared reduces the risk of finding yourself in a dangerous situation or requiring a rescue. Running out of food or water can mean you negatively impact the experience of other hikers by asking them to share some of theirs. Getting lost or injured can require the assistance of a search and rescue team, which impacts the wilderness and puts the rescue workers' safety at risk. Accidents happen, and are sometimes unavoidable, but do what you can to minimize the chances of finding yourself in a dangerous situation. Bring a map or app loaded with offline maps and enough extra battery power to charge your devices, have a plan for your daily route and mileage, know where to find water sources, and bring adequate supplies for your adventure.

STAY ON THE TRAIL AS MUCH AS POSSIBLE

Hiking on marked trails and staying on them restricts the impact of many people onto a single strip of land. Don't cut "switchbacks," which are zigzagging trails going up or down steep hills, because this causes erosion and makes the actual trail hard for the next hikers to follow. If you intend to do any off-trail travel, stick to durable surfaces like rocks, gravel, dirt, and sand as much as possible so you minimize damage to vegetation.

DISPOSE OF WASTE

Carry all of your garbage back to civilization and throw it away in the trash. Waste left behind on the trail or at campsites can be harmful to the environment and can attract animals. Often-overlooked waste includes organic litter like orange or banana peels as well as eggshells. Even though organic litter decomposes eventually, it is just as unsightly as inorganic garbage and can attract animals before it does. Burning garbage leaves residue and attracts animals.

HUMAN WASTE & TOILET PAPER

Proper disposal of human waste and toilet paper is important to avoid polluting water sources and spreading disease. Depending on an area's popularity and soil composition, acceptable disposal methods vary. At minimum, human waste and toilet paper should be buried at least 6 to 8 inches deep and about 70 paces away from water sources. Always pack out wet wipes and feminine products. In drier climates, toilet paper should be carried out, not buried. In very dry or popular areas, even human waste should be packed out instead of buried. National parks and other public lands publish their guidelines and requirements for human waste disposal, so look these up before heading out.

POOP BAGS ON THE SIDE OF MOUNT WHITNEY

At 14,505 feet, Mount Whitney is the tallest mountain in the contiguous United States. It's a short detour from the Pacific Crest Trail (PCT); it is the southern terminus of the John Muir Trail; and it is accessible for long day and overnight trips from the Whitney Portal parking lot. These factors make Mount Whitney a very popular mountain, enjoyed by approximately 20,000 people each year, according to the US Forest Service. Because so many people frequent the mountain, and it is mostly hard rock instead of diggable dirt, burying human waste is prohibited. Hikers are asked to use a waste bag for poop and carry it off the mountain when they leave. For hikes starting at the Whitney Portal parking lot, rangers distribute special bags for this use.

When we summited Mount Whitney, we did it as a 1-day detour from our PCT thruhike. Our PCT permit allowed us to hike to the summit, but it did not include a designated waste bag. We didn't even know they were a thing! As we hiked up the mountain, we kept seeing plastic bags on the side of the trail and had no idea why they were there. Eventually, we were curious enough to peek inside one, and we were shocked to find it full of human poop! We quickly learned the purpose of the bags but were disgusted by finding so many of them abandoned on the side of the trail. The hikers who left them there were definitely not adhering to Leave No Trace principles. They got the message that they should poop in a bag, but they didn't grasp the bigger purpose: to avoid littering the trail with human poop!

—Tim

LEAVE WHAT YOU FIND

Items you find in nature should stay in nature. This includes natural objects such as antlers, feathers, flowers, and rocks as well as cultural artifacts like arrowheads. Take only pictures, and leave what you find for others to enjoy in the future.

HAVE NO OR LOW-IMPACT CAMPFIRES

Know the local regulations for campfires, and have one only if fires are allowed. If you do have a campfire, use an established ring if possible, or build a small ring that you'll disassemble later. Only collect dead and downed wood to burn. Always attend your fire and thoroughly extinguish it when you are done; the next morning, if you built a fire ring, widely scatter the ashes and any rocks you used to build the ring so nobody can tell you ever had a campfire in that spot.

RESPECT WILDLIFE

Observe wildlife from a distance. Quick movements and loud noises are stressful to animals. If you're hiking with a pet, be sure it is fully under your control or on a leash so it does not chase wildlife. Do not feed wild animals; this is bad for their health and can alter their behavior toward humans. Protect your food, including crumbs and scraps, so animals cannot get to it and learn to associate humans with an easy meal.

MAXIMIZE THE ENJOYMENT FOR OTHERS

Excessive noise, uncontrolled pets, and damaged surroundings take away from other people's outdoor experience. On narrow trails, downhill hikers should yield to uphill hikers. Bicyclists should yield to hikers. Both hikers and bicyclists should yield to equestrians.

Additional information about Leave No Trace camping can be found at lnt.org.

THRUHIKERS' TIPS

LEAVE NO TRACE PRINCIPLES

- Practice Leave No Trace to keep an area beautiful for future users.
- If you pack it in, pack it out. Don't leave trash behind, and don't burn trash.
- Dispose of toilet paper and waste in accordance with the area's guidelines.
- Take only photos. Don't take souvenirs from the land so others can find and enjoy them later.
- Don't make excessive noise that could bother animals or other hikers.
- Respect wildlife by keeping a distance and never feed wild animals.

AFTER THE TRAIL: BATTLING THE POST-TRAIL BLUES

After any trip, many hikers find it difficult to return to normal life. There is something about the freedom of the outdoors that feels missing after you return to the daily grind. To recover from a weekend or weeklong trip, it's usually just a matter of going through your regular routine for a couple of days until it feels normal again.

For longer trips or thruhikes, it is not uncommon to feel sad for a much longer time after the trip is over. In thruhiker lingo, this is called "post-trail depression" or the "post-trail blues." After a life-changing event like a thruhike, transitioning from trail life back to normal life is difficult. Days may not feel as fulfilling, potentially because you are less connected to your basic needs of food, water, and sleep. Work and life goals may not feel as precise; on long hikes, it is very straightforward to break down the hike into single-day objectives—just walk every day, and you have been a success. In normal life, goals can be complex and have more pieces, and assessing progress toward them is not as straightforward.

To deal with the post-trail blues, we find it helpful to keep in touch with friends we've met on our thruhikes or other backpackers. It can also be helpful to share your experience with friends and family by telling them stories from the trail and showing them photos and videos. The sadness may cure itself over time as you repeatedly go through the motions of regular life, but the recovery period can take a long time. Do not hesitate to seek professional help if needed.

ANALYZING OUR DATA AFTER THE CONTINENTAL DIVIDE TRAIL (CDT)

One way we cope with normal life after our thruhikes is to make maps and analyze the data we collected on the trail. This allows us to relive our trips together. Tim is a statistician and scientist, and I am an engineer, so we are both data nerds. We have been recording all of our hikes, runs, and bikes with GPS watches for more than 10 years, so it was only natural for us to record all of our thruhikes as well. We did a statistical analysis of the CDT, which gave us some interesting insights into hiking in general. For instance, we found that as the 3,000-mile trail went on, our miles and hours walked per day increased, and the steps we took per mile also increased. We attribute this to shortening our stride length and increasing our step rate, which increased our walking efficiency as we got more and more accustomed to hiking.

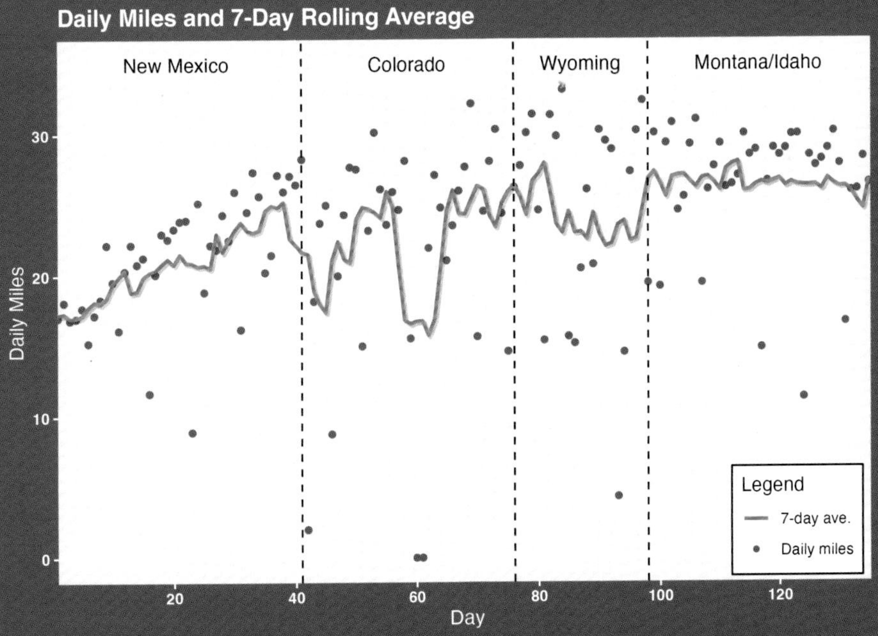

—Renee & Tim

PART

3

RECIPES & FOOD PLANNING

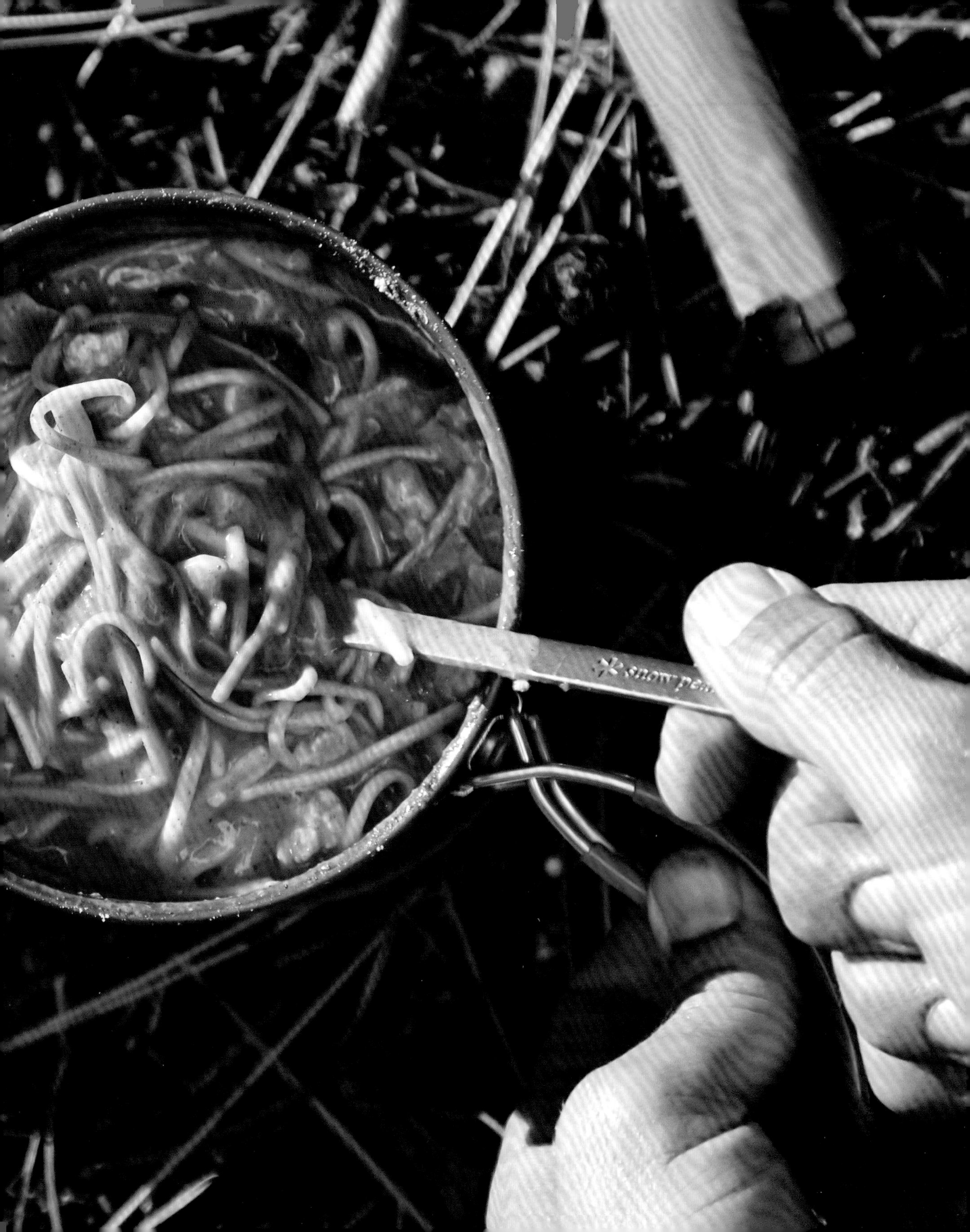

12

FOOD PLANNING FOR A TRIP

One thing all people have in common is the need to eat. We have found that food is far more rewarding on the trail than in normal life because you are much more connected to your basic needs on trail; each day involves little more than eating, drinking, sleeping, and walking from point A to point B. With a little bit of planning, it's not difficult to carry satisfying food in your backpack that is easy to cook, fills you up, tastes great, and doesn't weigh a lot. In this chapter, we share advice on meal planning for long and short trails, from general strategy, to specific meals, to hydration. We provide two sample menus, one for a weekend and another for a weeklong trip, that will make it easy to feel fulfilled at the end of each day you spend hiking.

STRATEGY FOR FUELING HIKES

Short day hikes of a few miles or less don't require special nutrition. For these, it is fine to eat before hiking, after hiking, or maybe munch on a granola bar while on trail. As distances increase above 5 miles, as pack weight becomes substantial, and/or as you hike over grueling terrain, fueling your body with nutritious food becomes increasingly important. For overnight trips and beyond, have a plan to take in as many calories as your body needs, and follow that plan. It can be the difference between an enjoyable trip and a miserable one—or worse, an unsafe one.

But food on a backpacking trip is a double-edged sword. Every pound of food in excess of what you want or need to eat is extra weight in your pack that has to be carried. And carrying excessive weight is a surefire way to be uncomfortable on a trip. Food and water can weigh approximately as much as everything else you're carrying combined, especially on trips longer than a weekend. We use this strategy to find the right balance between a happy stomach and a happy back:

- We plan our meals with as much precision as possible to ensure we have enough calories and nutrients—but not too much.
- We dehydrate our meals to make them lightweight and long-lasting.
- We consume filling snacks on a regular schedule while out on the trail.
- We hydrate well, which includes a mix of water and electrolyte drinks, to keep our bodies operating at their top levels.

DEHYDRATING

The primary benefit of eating dehydrated food on the trail is weight savings. Dehydrating removes the water from food, which makes it much lighter. For instance, tomato sauce is more than 90 percent lighter after being dehydrated. Although people often imagine that hikers carry dehydrated food because it is nonperishable, weight is just as, if not more important. In fact, a diet composed of hiker-friendly non-dehydrated foods like granola bars, blocks of cheese, and canned foods like chili, tuna, and Spam is much heavier than a diet made of dehydrated foods. (See chapter 13 for information on how to dehydrate food and chapter 15 for recipes.)

THE ORIGIN OF OUR APPROACH TO FOOD ON TRAIL

For as long as we've known each other, we have loved exploring the outdoors together. But we were not always long-distance hikers. Early in our relationship, our joint feats of physical exertion were more traditional forms of exercise like swimming, biking, and running. Our first dates often involved biking around the lakes of our college town, Madison, Wisconsin. Years later, we were running the Chicago Marathon side by side when we made the decision to get married. We both took the sport of triathlon very seriously for several years, competing across the country, including in an Ironman race. Because of our athletic backgrounds, we are brutally familiar with the impact that nutrition can have on physical performance. For example, during a 140.6-mile Ironman race, if you run out of calories, you will bonk, or crash, hard and fast.

While we were still focused primarily on endurance sports, we started going on longer and longer backpacking trips. With our knowledge of nutrition for performance, we approached backpacking food the same way we approached food for any sport. We wanted to control exactly what we ate, how much we ate, and when we ate it. The easiest way to achieve this was by planning our backpacking menus in advance, which led to curiosity about dehydrating. As we got into dehydrating our own meals, we loved that it gave us total control over the portion size, taste, weight, and most importantly, nutritional content of our meals on the trail. As we graduated from weekend hikes to weeklong hikes and eventually to multiple-month adventures, we refined our approach and improved our menu. We are able to ensure that all of our meals have enough protein, starch, and nutrients to keep us moving on the trail, and we have learned how to make meals that taste great. It is hard to imagine backpacking without this level of control over the food we are putting into our bodies.

—Tim

MEALS ON TRAIL

Different people have different eating habits in regular life, and that doesn't change out on the trail. When it comes to base eating for the day, it is a good idea to mimic what works for you off trail. We both like to have three meals a day, so on trail we have breakfast in or near our tent, take our longest break at lunch, and have dinner when we get to camp. For people who prefer no breakfast or who like to stretch their lunch throughout the day, the same should be fine to do on a trip.

SIZE

Appetites vary, but one thing that is almost universal is that a person's on-trail calorie requirements are higher than their off-trail requirements. Trail meals, coupled with snacks eaten along the way, should be large enough to keep a hiker satisfied. It is surprising how few calories are in most prepackaged dehydrated backpacking meals sold at stores. It can take two to four "servings" of these meals to feed a single person. We like to have trail dinners that are a minimum of 500 calories per serving … and we never have leftovers.

BALANCE

A complete meal includes carbohydrates, protein, vegetables, and flavor. When putting together recipes for home or the trail, we make sure all categories are fulfilled for each meal (except breakfast; we usually don't have vegetables for breakfast). Carbohydrates we eat on the trail include rice, noodles, and potatoes. Proteins can be dehydrated beans, nuts, seeds, or dehydrated meats. Using a variety of vegetables in different recipes adds nutrients and makes trail food more exciting and unique. Flavor on trail is important—nobody wants to eat bland food at camp. Moreover, because you'll probably sweat out lots of salt while hiking, it is okay to boost flavor for trail food with a bit more salt than would be healthy at home.

CONVENIENCE

There's something romantic about waking up, starting a fire, and cooking a hearty traditional breakfast on the trail, complete with bacon, eggs, potatoes, and percolated coffee. For car camping trips, or maybe even very short social backpacking trips, meals like this make sense. For most backpacking trips, however, cooking complex recipes is a guaranteed way to slow down your trip and increase pack weight. Practical backpacking meals can be quickly cooked in one pot with just a few steps. The less work it takes to do the cooking, the easier it is to enjoy the scenery and make progress down the trail.

BREAKFAST ON TRAIL

Not everybody is a breakfast eater. For those of us who are, a large breakfast is a great way to start off a day on the trail. In regions where wildlife like bears isn't a concern, we love lazy breakfasts in our tent, cooked right through the tent door before we even head out. From the comfort of our sleeping bags, we'll have a cup of coffee, followed by breakfast, followed by a second cup of coffee, and sometimes a third cup of coffee after that!

On-trail breakfast should be as large as is comfortable to provide sustained energy through the morning. Not all calories are created equal, though. The body is extremely efficient at burning through sugary foods like sweet cereals and instant oats. Breakfasts based on whole grains, protein, and healthy fats provide energy for much longer. Our go-to breakfasts skew toward oat-based foods (old-fashioned oats, not instant) with added seeds or nuts for protein and fat.

LUNCH ON TRAIL

While out on the trail, it's a good idea to continuously snack throughout the day. This makes it tempting to view lunch as nothing more than a glorified snack. But this approach can make days long and monotonous. We've found that it works well to think of lunch as a distinct component of the day that includes both food and rest. Our lunch recipes vary, sometimes amounting to a complex meal (e.g., Cold-Soaked Rice & Beans; see page 231) and at other times being very similar to our snack foods (e.g., a pack of instant ramen). In either case, by coupling food with a long break and calling it lunch, we have a reward to look forward to all morning.

In the recipes in chapter 15, we do not distinguish between lunch and dinner recipes. The same dishes can be eaten for either lunch or dinner. We prefer to eat cold-soakable meals for lunch. Cold soaking is a method of "cooking" food without heat; many foods can be rehydrated on trail by simply soaking them in cold water. (See page 214 for more information on how to cold soak.) Lunchtime is typically during the heat of the day, so a warm meal may not be as appealing. Plus, cold soaking saves effort, time, and fuel.

DINNER ON TRAIL

Dinner is the best meal of the day! After miles and miles of travel, it's hard not to build up a sizable appetite. Putting in hard miles is easier when you know that when it's all over, a filling, nutritious, and tasty meal will be your reward. We love getting to camp and having a hot, satisfying meal that is simple and fast to prepare. It can be nice to have a small dessert after dinner, too, for a tasty treat as well as some extra calories.

NORTHERN CALIFORNIA LUNCHES ON THE PACIFIC CREST TRAIL

Our first long-distance thruhike was the Pacific Crest Trail: 2,650 miles over 4½ months. The experience was completely new for us, and we spent the first 1,000 miles just adjusting to life on the trail. The food was different, the amount of exercise was different, and the social interaction was different. By the time we were about 1,000 miles into the hike and had reached northern California, we finally had our routine figured out. The day-to-day tasks that a thruhike involves hadn't become easy, but they were no longer surprising or confusing; we knew we could hike 20 miles a day, accomplish all of our chores like cooking and filtering water, and that we would have some time left over for fun, too.

Northern California in July can be extremely hot, but just about every day we were hiking past beautiful wooded mountain lakes. We figured out that lunchtime should overlap with lake time. Whenever we hiked past a lake between 11 AM and 3 PM, we would declare it time for lunch. We'd take off our packs and eat a lunch that we had started cold soaking at a previous water source and then spend a couple of hours taking a break. Renee would always lay out her sleeping pad on the ground and take a nap, and I would swim. Occasionally, Renee would convince me to take a nap or I would convince her to swim, but our individual priorities were always the same. On subsequent hikes, we have stuck to this pattern of long lunch breaks spent relaxing. These are some of the most pleasant and tranquil memories I have of life on the trail.

—Tim

SNACKS ON TRAIL

Trail life is active and full of exertion, which makes it unrealistic and/or unpleasant to limit food to three meals per day. Snacking is necessary to stay fueled.

FREQUENCY: A good rule of thumb is to eat one snack approximately every 5 miles on the trail, in addition to breakfast, lunch, and dinner. For example, on a backpacking trip where we will be hiking 10 miles per day, we bring two snacks. This guideline will vary depending on a person's size, metabolism, and appetite. We have found that for the first few hundred miles of a thruhike, we don't quite need a snack every 5 miles, but after we're thousands of miles in, our bodies have burned off practically all of their excess fat and one snack every 3 or 4 miles becomes necessary.

CALORIES: Our guideline to ensure our snacks are big enough is that if a snack is fewer than 200 calories, it doesn't count. Nuts and bars are some of our go-to snacks. Bars from the grocery store breakfast aisle often don't meet the 200-calorie threshold, but bars from the sport or health section usually do. (Check out brands like Clif, LÄRABAR, and LUNA.)

LITTLE MUNCHIES: We often carry some extra, small munchies, such as a few pieces of dehydrated fruit or a handful of chips. These don't meet the 200-calorie threshold, so we carry them in addition to our snacks and allow ourselves to munch on them for a sweet or salty kick any time we need one.

NUTRIENTS: High-protein snacks and nuts are satisfying for much longer than sugary snacks like candy or pastries. Your body processes sugary snacks very quickly, and before you know it, you'll be hungry again. Snacking on too many sweets while hiking can cause bonking, which is when your body runs out of calories to burn and you suddenly feel tired and heavy. But when bonking does happen, a sugary snack like candy or dried fruit can be just the thing to provide a quick boost and get you reenergized. Salt is another important nutrient you lose throughout a day of hiking that can be replenished by snacking. On hot days especially, salty snacks help replenish salt lost through sweat.

RECOMMENDED HIKING SNACKS

- Granola bars
- Nuts
- Graham crackers with powdered peanut butter
- Crackers with dehydrated hummus
- Cold-soaked store-bought ramen packets
- Homemade dehydrated fruit (We like to bring dehydrated bananas or pineapples in addition to the other hiking snacks listed here. We don't typically include it in our snack count.)
- Electrolyte powders or tablets

HYDRATION ON TRAIL

Drinking enough liquids to stay hydrated is extremely important. What makes this challenging during hiking trips is that all liquids have to be either carried or collected along the way. (See page 114 for more information on how to find and filter water on trail.) Incorporating either electrolyte drinks or sports drinks into a trail diet is a good idea, too. This is an easy way to consume additional calories and helps prevent dehydration.

FREQUENCY OF DRINKING: Our rule of thumb is to consume about 1 liter of liquid each every 5 miles. On hot, dry days we drink more. On cold, rainy days we drink less.

DON'T CARRY MORE WATER THAN NECESSARY: At 8.34 pounds per gallon, water is one of the heaviest items you'll put in your pack. It is a good idea to carry no more of it than necessary to get from one water source to the next. Although carrying more water than necessary is unpleasant, carrying not enough quickly becomes unsafe if you allow yourself to become dehydrated.

ELECTROLYTE DRINKS: You'll probably sweat more while hiking than you would at home, especially if it is hot and/or you are exerting heavily to cover rugged terrain with weight on your back. Electrolyte drinks replenish the salts your body loses while sweating. We recommend the type that is sold as a powder so it can be added to water you collect from natural sources. Electrolyte drinks aren't absolutely crucial on a hike, but the hotter it is and the more you are sweating, the more beneficial they are. They come in no-sugar varieties (e.g., Nuun tablets) and sugar varieties (e.g., Gatorade powder). Both types provide electrolytes, but the latter can also give you a calorie boost. We use both on our hikes, depending on our need for the extra calories.

VARIETY

We have two cats, and for years, we fed them the exact same dry food every day. They got older and we got softer, and we eventually gave in and started feeding them a variety of more exciting wet foods before bed. They love it! We have happier cats now because they have something to look forward to every evening. Hikers are no different; time spent eating is one of the most satisfying parts of being on trail, especially when the food is varied and exciting.

We make sure not to pack too many of the same meal on a single trip, and we rotate through repeated recipes using a semi-random schedule. This is mostly for fun (after all, variety is the spice of life), but there is a safety component, too: If we do something wrong and a meal goes rancid, we wouldn't want to find ourselves with nothing to eat. Even though we often cook large batches of a single recipe at once, rotating what we pack ensures that a single bad batch won't affect multiple consecutive days in the wilderness. For trips of a few days, we usually have a different dinner recipe every night. For longer trips, we rotate through about 12 different recipes. The same strategy applies to snack foods.

APPETITE

Appetite can vary considerably from person to person, so experiment to find out what works best for you. Appetites can also vary during the course of a multiday trip. Hikers often find that as their body first adjusts to being on trail, they have a smaller appetite than they usually do off trail. As time goes by, the calorie deficit builds up, and before they know it, their appetite is huge. A favorite topic among backpackers is what they are going to eat as soon as they return to civilization.

We have also found that appetite varies with the weather. On very hot days, our appetites are smaller than on mild days. When the outside temperature is very cold, your body will automatically burn extra calories to keep warm. This is hard to notice in normal life, when most days are spent in heated buildings, but on camping trips, the extra calorie burn is substantial. All else being equal, the portion size your body requires on a cold day will be more than on a mild day. It is a good idea to pack larger meals for winter camping than you do for warm-weather trips.

EATING ON A LONG-DISTANCE TRIP

For any trip lasting longer than a week, food planning becomes significantly more complicated. The main difference is that, for long trips, it can be impossible to carry all of the food you'll need from the beginning all the way to the end—it's just too much weight. Instead, you'll need to make a resupply plan to replenish your food along the way.

KNOW YOUR ROUTE: Most long-distance hikes cross roads or pass near towns. When planning a trip, peruse maps of the area surrounding the trail and choose which towns are ideal for resupply stops.

PLAN YOUR RESUPPLY TOWNS: We always make a spreadsheet of our intended resupply towns and the trail mileage to get to each. Our criteria for choosing resupply towns include proximity to the trail, ease of off-trail travel to the town (e.g., is it a short side trail, a simple hitchhike, or a multistage hitchhike?), size of the town, and services available (post office, groceries, gear shops, camping, hotels, showers, etc.).

MAILING FOOD: Mailing food to post offices in your resupply towns makes preparing dehydrated meals in advance of a long hike possible. However, sometimes it is a challenge to get from the trail to the post office and back. (See page 40 for more information on how to mail food to yourself on the trail.)

BUYING FOOD: Mailing food is not absolutely necessary for most long-distance trips. Many successful hikers shop for groceries during their resupply stops and stock up on easy-to-find nonperishables such as instant potatoes, flavored instant rice packets, bags of precooked tuna or chicken, Spam, ramen, cheese, beef jerky, nuts, bars, instant oatmeal packets, and so on. In larger towns this strategy works well, but in smaller towns hikers often leave with frustratingly unhealthy food and little variety.

HYBRID RESUPPLYING: Our approach is a blend of mailing and buying. Because almost every town with a post office also has a grocery or convenience store, we have found that we don't have to ship all of our food to ourselves. We dehydrate and mail our dinners ahead of time, along with extra bags of beans and vegetables, and we buy our breakfasts and snacks when resupplying. For our lunches, we buy the carbohydrate components (like instant potatoes and instant rice) and some flavor (like soup or spice packets) while resupplying, and we assemble our lunch recipes along the trail by supplementing these with the extra veggies and beans we sent in the mail.

SOURCING SNACKS ON LONG HIKES: Appetites and tastes vary over time, so it is difficult to accurately preplan all of the snack food you'll need for a long-distance hike before heading out. We recommend buying snack food during resupply stops. Even gas stations usually sell a reasonable assortment of bars, nuts, and trail mix. That said, there are reasons you may opt to mail a subset of your snacks with the rest of your resupply shipments, especially if you want specific or homemade snacks (like dehydrated fruit) or for when you plan to resupply in a tiny town that might have few or no snack foods available.

TIP

Peanut butter is the ultimate trail snack. A couple spoonsful of peanut butter provide more calories than most bars, along with a huge amount of protein. For longer food carries, we usually like to add a jar of peanut butter to our packs, just in case.

SAMPLE MENU: WEEKEND BACKPACKING TRIP

	Friday (0 miles)	Saturday (10 miles)	Sunday (5 miles)
Breakfast		Instant coffee Overnight Oats (page 222)	Instant coffee Tofu Scramble (page 229)
Morning Snacks		Granola bar	Granola bar
Lunch		Cold-Soaked Rice & Beans (page 231)	
Afternoon Snacks		Sports drink powder Nuts Dehydrated fruit	
Dinner	Curry Rice (page 249)	Creamy Tomato Rotini (page 253)	

TIP

Bring a variety of granola bars, nuts, and dehydrated fruit (we love dehydrated bananas, pineapple rings, and mangoes), so you don't get sick of any one type.

SAMPLE MENU:

ONE-WEEK BACKPACKING TRIP

	Day 1 (5 miles)	Day 2 (15 miles)	Day 3 (15 miles)	Day 4 (15 miles)	Day 5 (15 miles)	Day 6 (15 miles)	Day 7 (5 miles)
BREAKFAST		Instant coffee Overnight Oats (page 222)	Instant coffee Tofu Scramble (page 229)	Instant coffee Homemade Granola (page 226) with dry milk	Instant coffee Strawberries & Cream Oatmeal (page 225)	Instant coffee Overnight Coconut Chia Pudding (page 230)	Instant coffee Homemade Granola (page 226) with dry milk
MORNING SNACKS		Granola bar Nuts	Granola bar Nuts	Granola bar Nuts	Granola bar Nuts	Granola bar Nuts	Granola bar Nuts
LUNCH		Cold-Soaked Rice & Beans (page 231)	Cold-Soaked Shepherd's Pie (page 234)	Hot or cold-soaked Homemade Ramen (page 237)	Cold-Soaked Tomato & Nut Couscous (page 232)	Hot or cold-soaked Spaghetti Ramen (page 238)	
AFTERNOON SNACKS	Granola bar	Easy Bean Dip with Chips (page 259) Dehydrated fruit Sports drink powder	Graham crackers with store-bought dehydrated peanut butter Dehydrated fruit Sports drink powder	Crackers with store-bought or homemade dehydrated hummus Dehydrated fruit Sports drink powder	Graham crackers with store-bought dehydrated peanut butter Dehydrated fruit Sports drink powder	Crackers with dehydrated hummus (store-bought or homemade) Dehydrated fruit Sports drink powder	
DINNER	Curry Rice (page 240)	Creamy Tomato Rotini (page 253)	Mushroom Risotto (page 245)	Peanut Butter Pasta (page 250)	Chili Mac (page 249)	Dal with Rice (page 242)	

THRUHIKERS' TIPS

FOOD PLANNING FOR A TRIP

- Aim to eat three meals a day plus one 200-or-more-calorie snack every 5 miles, but adjust this guideline to match your own needs and preferences.
- For a successful trip, variety is key when planning food. You will get very sick of ramen if you eat it every night for a week straight.
- Bring balanced, nutritious meals that include carbohydrates, protein, veggies, and flavor. Not only is this good for fueling your hike, but it's also good for your taste buds.
- Adapt to your changing appetite and caloric needs as you progress through a trip.
- Look for granola bars and other snacks that contain more than 200 calories. (Check the sports or health section of the grocery store for high-calorie granola bars.)
- Bring electrolyte tablets and/or sports drink powder, especially if it will be hot and you will be sweating a lot. These also can be nice to add some flavor to your water when you're filling up from a water source that doesn't taste great, like some ponds or lakes.

13

DEHYDRATING FOOD

Dehydrating food may seem overwhelming at first, but it's a lot of fun and is a great way to start getting excited for a trip. Dehydrating also lets you manage your diet and your calorie and nutrient intakes more precisely. If you have a dietary restriction, dehydrating your own meals lets you control what is in them. Plus, homemade dehydrated meals usually taste better than store-bought dehydrated meals, and they're almost always significantly less expensive.

DEHYDRATING EQUIPMENT

A full dehydrating setup requires a moderate investment to purchase a dehydrator, additional dehydrator trays and accessories if needed, and storage supplies. Fortunately, getting started requires none of this. All you need is an oven, a baking sheet, and a few sheets of parchment paper. Before you spend lots of money on a full collection of dehydrating gear, it's a good idea to first try dehydrating some food in your oven to be sure dehydrating is an activity you enjoy. Following is a breakdown of the supplies needed for dehydrating in the oven and dehydrating with a dedicated dehydrator.

EQUIPMENT NEEDED FOR OVEN DEHYDRATING

OVEN: To use an oven as a dehydrator, it just needs to be able to heat to a low-enough temperature. If your oven can heat to a temperature below 150º, it should work. Convection ovens, which circulate air as they heat, are the best option. With convection turned on, an oven is very similar to a dehydrator, just with fewer shelves.

WOODEN SPOON: Ovens trap air inside while they cook, which means they trap moisture, too. When using an oven for dehydrating, the door should be left cracked open with something like a wooden spoon to let out the moisture.

THERMOMETER: At low temperatures, oven dials can be inaccurate. Use an oven thermometer to ensure you are maintaining a temperature below 150º.

BAKING SHEET: You'll spread food to be dehydrated in a single layer on a baking sheet.

PARCHMENT PAPER: Line your baking sheet with a sheet of parchment paper to be sure your food doesn't stick.

NOTE

Ovens are a good tool to begin dehydrating, but they are not optimized for it. They are larger and don't have as many shelves as dedicated dehydrators, meaning they use more energy to dehydrate less food.

EQUIPMENT NEEDED FOR DEHYDRATING WITH A DEHYDRATOR

DEHYDRATOR: Several different styles of dehydrators are available, and they range from very affordable to extremely expensive. Here are some factors to consider when shopping for a dehydrator:

- Dehydrators with top- or rear-mounted fans last longer than those with bottom-mounted fans. Sticky droplets can drip into bottom-mounted fans while food is dehydrating and gunk them up. This is especially likely to happen with fruit or other high-moisture foods.

- When dehydrating food for weekend trips, any dehydrator works well. When dehydrating for longer trips and thruhikes, capacity becomes a major consideration. A single round of dehydrating takes anywhere from 8 to 24 hours, so it is nice to be able to do many meals at once. Dehydrators with rectangular trays have a much larger capacity than circular dehydrators. Plus, they're easier for dumping dehydrated food into storage containers.
- Temperature control is a nice feature to have because it helps the machine work ideally for different foods. Leafy greens are usually dehydrated at lower temperatures than fruits, which are dehydrated at lower temperatures than meats.
- A timer is a nice feature on a dehydrator so it can turn off while you are away or sleeping. For dehydrators without a built-in timer, a simple plug-in timer from the hardware store—the kind you would use to set lamps on a schedule—works just as well. (The drawback of running the dehydrator for too long without a timer is wasted energy, not the risk of over-dehydrated food. Most backpacking foods, especially veggies, are difficult or impossible to over-dehydrate; the goal is to remove as much water as possible.)

DEHYDRATOR ACCESSORIES: Additional dehydrator sheets are convenient to have on hand as a permanent alternative for parchment paper. Solid sheets (sometimes called fruit leather sheets) are great for dehydrating sauces. Fine mesh sheets work well for dehydrating smaller veggies that fall through the cracks of standard dehydrator trays.

EQUIPMENT NEEDED FOR FOOD STORAGE

PLASTIC BAGS: We've experimented with all sorts of storage options and have found that simple, resealable plastic bags (i.e., ziplock plastic bags) work perfectly for storing assembled dehydrated meals.

PLASTIC FOOD STORAGE CONTAINERS AND GLASS JARS: For longer-term storage of bulk dehydrated ingredients, it is effective to place food in airtight plastic containers or glass jars to ensure that moisture can't get in. For long-term storage of prepared meals, it doesn't hurt to place your meal-filled ziplock bags inside a plastic container for a second layer of protection from the air.

VACUUM SEALER: Some people like to vacuum seal dehydrated food to ensure that no moisture gets in. This costs extra and is not necessary in our experience, but it's another storage option for those who want to be super careful. Dried veggies can be surprisingly pointy, so if you do choose to vacuum seal, be sure to stop before the bag gets so tight that the veggies puncture the plastic. Vacuum-sealed meals will take the shape of your resupply boxes, backpack, and bear box better if they have a bit of air inside and remain somewhat flexible.

DEHYDRATING VEGETABLES

Dehydrated vegetables last a remarkable amount of time on a shelf or in a backpack. Because most vegetables are primarily water, dehydrated vegetables are very lightweight—dehydrating reduces the weight of most vegetables by 90 percent or more. The process to dehydrate vegetables is simple: rinse and cut vegetables into smaller, uniformly sized pieces for even drying, lay them flat on a dehydrator tray in a single layer, and dehydrate at 135°F for at least 8 hours, or until they are completely dry and crispy. Dehydrated vegetables will be brittle and hard. If they are flexible and soft, they're not done yet. The table on pages 197 and 198 outlines how to prepare the vegetables needed for the recipes in this book along with their raw amounts and the corresponding dehydrated volumes and weights.

STEPS FOR DEHYDRATING VEGETABLES:

1. Rinse and cut the vegetables according to the table on pages 197 and 198.
2. Distribute the vegetables in a single layer on dehydrator trays.
3. Dehydrate at 135°F until crispy (no moisture remains), 8 or more hours.

PREPARATION INSTRUCTIONS, QUANTITIES, AND WEIGHTS FOR DEHYDRATING VEGETABLES

Vegetable	Raw Amount	Preparation Instructions	Dehydrated Volume	Dehydrated Weight
Bell peppers	1 large (9 ounces)	Remove ribs and seeds, and cut into ½-inch square pieces	¼ cup	0.4 ounce
Broccoli	2 medium stalks (1 pound, 7.3 ounces)	Cut into ¾-inch pieces	1¼ cups	1 ounce
Cabbage	1 small head (1 pound, 12.8 ounces)	Cut into ½ × 2-inch strips, broken apart	4 cups	1.9 ounces
Carrots	3 medium (9.1 ounces)	Peel and julienne (cut into matchsticks)	1 cup	1.3 ounces
Cauliflower	1 medium head (1 pound, 7.5 ounces)	Cut into ¾-inch pieces	1 cup	1.2 ounces
Corn (frozen)	16-ounce bag, frozen	Boil 1 to 2 minutes, drain, and let cool	1⅛ cups	3.6 ounces
Garlic	1 medium bulb (2.9 ounces)	Peel, separate into cloves, and cut ⅛-inch slices	⅓ cup	0.9 ounce
Grape tomatoes	1 pint (11.3 ounces)	Cut into quarters	⅔ cup	1 ounce
Green onions	1 small bunch (3.7 ounces)	Cut into ⅓-inch slices	½ cup	0.3 ounce

continues

PREPARATION INSTRUCTIONS, QUANTITIES, AND WEIGHTS FOR DEHYDRATING VEGETABLES (CONT.)

Vegetable	Raw Amount	Preparation Instructions	Dehydrated Volume	Dehydrated Weight
Jalapeños	2 medium (1.5 ounces)	Cut into ¼-inch rings	⅛ cup	0.1 ounce
Mushrooms	8 ounces	Cut into ⅓-inch slices	1¾ cups	0.8 ounce
Onions	2 large (1 pound, 0.7 ounce)	Cut into ¾-inch squares, broken apart	1⅔ cups	1.4 ounces
Zucchini	2 medium (15.6 ounces)	Cut into ⅓-inch semicircles	½ cup	0.9 ounce

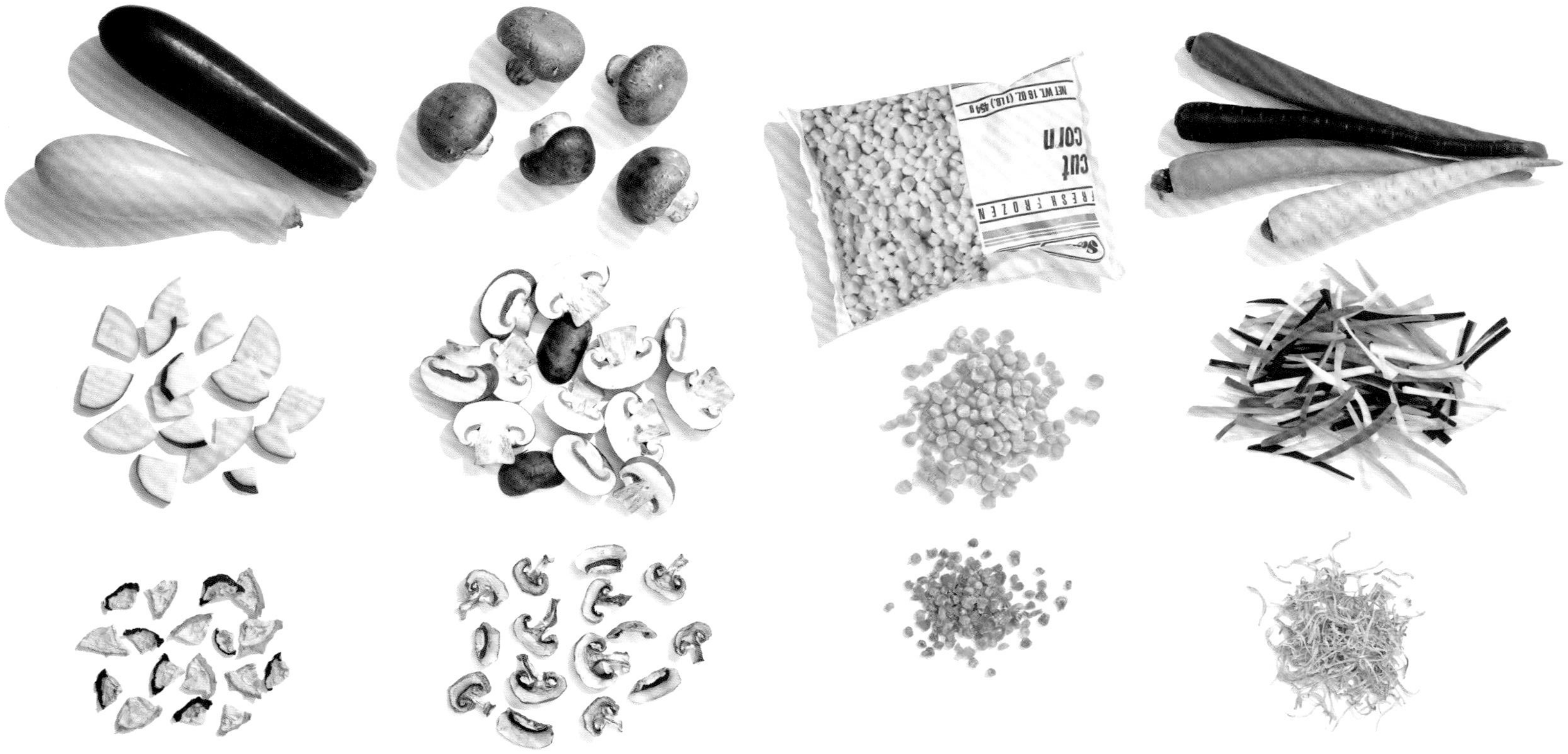
FRESH FROZEN
cut
corn
NET WT. 16 OZ. (1 LB.) 454 g

DEHYDRATING BEANS

Beans are our preferred and primary source of protein on the trail. They are easy to dehydrate in bulk, and they rehydrate to the right texture almost every time. Dehydrated beans are very different from the dry beans sold at the grocery store. Dry beans have never been cooked. Depending on the bean variety, cooking dry beans requires anywhere from 2 to 12 hours of soaking and boiling. Dehydrated beans are cooked before being dehydrated, so rehydrating them is a quick and easy process.

We like to skip the cooking step entirely by dehydrating canned beans. When cooking dry beans, it isn't easy to know when they are fully cooked but not overcooked. Undercooked beans will rehydrate too hard, but overcooked beans rehydrate into mush. Canned beans are perfectly cooked by the canner and ready to eat when you bring them home from the store. All they require before being dehydrated is draining and a quick rinse.

Our favorite beans to dehydrate are kidney, black, pinto, white, and refried. Most beans are very easy to dehydrate; they just need to be spread out evenly on dehydrator trays. This applies to refried beans, too; just spread into a thin layer on a solid dehydrator tray (or parchment paper) with a spatula. Chickpeas (garbanzo beans) are more challenging; they take longer than other beans to rehydrate, which often results in a harder-than-desired texture on trail. The table below outlines how to prepare beans for the recipes in this book.

STEPS FOR DEHYDRATING BEANS:

1. Drain canned beans and rinse well.
2. Distribute the beans in a single layer on dehydrator trays.
3. Dehydrate at 135°F until crispy (no moisture remains), 8 or more hours.

QUANTITIES AND WEIGHTS FOR DEHYDRATING BEANS

Beans	Can Weight	Dehydrated Volume	Dehydrated Weight
Black	15.5 ounces	¾ cup	2.1 ounces
Kidney	15.5 ounces	1 cup	2.3 ounces
Pinto	15.5 ounces	¾ cup	2.2 ounces
White	15.5 ounces	⅔ cup	2.5 ounces

FINDING DRY RICE AND BEANS IN "HIKER BOXES"

We learned about hiker boxes on our first thruhike, the Pacific Crest Trail (PCT). They're usually just cardboard boxes labeled "hiker box" located in popular resupply spots in trail towns, like an RV park where thruhikers go to take showers. Hikers leave behind food and/or gear that they no longer need for other hikers to take if they want or need. We love getting into town and checking the hiker box before heading to the grocery store to do our resupply. Sometimes we find yummy snacks, like fancy granola bars, and sometimes we leave behind things we aren't using and reduce the weight on our backs.

During the first 500 miles of the PCT, we found lots of bags of dry rice and dry beans in the hiker boxes—not useful! Rice and dry beans are lightweight, but they take way too long to cook on trail because they are dry, not dehydrated. Minute or instant rice needs to be boiled for only a minute, but regular dry rice needs to be boiled for about 20 minutes. Dry beans need to be boiled for at least 2 hours! Seeing so many of these items in hiker boxes made us realize that many hikers had set out thinking they would be cooking dry rice and beans each night at camp. As we made it farther along the trail, dry rice and beans became less and less common in hiker boxes because everybody had learned that if not precooked, both are terrible foods for backpacking. Luckily, we knew about cooked and dehydrated rice and beans ahead of time and had prepared and mailed ourselves plenty of both before setting out.

—Renee

DEHYDRATING TOFU

We use tofu in lots of our dehydrated recipes because it adds a unique texture along with tons of protein. But if you dehydrate tofu by simply taking it straight out of the refrigerator, cutting it, and dehydrating it until no moisture remains, it will be very difficult to rehydrate. This method leads to tofu that has to be boiled for a very long time before it finally starts soaking up water and rehydrating; when the rest of the meal's food is ready to eat, the tofu will still be extremely rubbery and chewy, kind of like trying to eat a leather belt or a car tire.

This simple trick makes tofu dehydrate and rehydrate well: Freeze it and then thaw it before dehydrating it. After buying a package (or several) of firm tofu, put it into the freezer until the tofu and all of the water surrounding it is completely frozen, about 8 hours. Remove it from the freezer, and let it completely thaw on the counter for about 4 hours or in the refrigerator for about 24 hours. Cube or crumble the tofu, spread in a single layer on a dehydrator tray, and dehydrate at 135°F until no moisture remains, 8 to 12 hours or more. This freeze-thaw cycle breaks the tofu's internal structure, allowing it to absorb water while rehydrating just fine. There still may be an occasional chewy piece, but for all except the pickiest of eaters, this method will lead to tofu that is enjoyable to eat.

STEPS FOR DEHYDRATING TOFU:

1. Completely freeze the tofu in the package.
2. Completely thaw the tofu at room temperature or in the refrigerator.
3. Cut into ½-inch cubes or crumble, depending on the recipe, and distribute in a single layer on dehydrator trays.
4. Dehydrate at 135°F until crispy (no moisture remains), 8 to 12 or more hours.

PREPARATION INSTRUCTIONS, QUANTITIES, AND WEIGHTS FOR DEHYDRATING TOFU

Tofu	Raw Amount	Preparation Instructions	Dehydrated Volume	Dehydrated Weight
Firm tofu, crumbled	16-ounce package	Freeze, thaw, and crumble by hand	1½ cups	2.5 ounces
Firm tofu, cubed	16-ounce package	Freeze, thaw, and cut into ½-inch cubes	1¼ cups	2.75 ounces

DEHYDRATING RICE

Rice is dry when you buy it, you might be thinking, *so why bother dehydrating it?* Dry rice from the store is lightweight because all the water is gone, but it is not cooked. Twenty minutes of cooking time isn't a big deal in the comfort of your kitchen at home, but on the trail, the time, fuel, and dedicated pot it takes to cook rice is hard to come by. By precooking and then dehydrating rice ahead of time, you can rehydrate it back to cooked rice almost instantly in boiling water on the trail. It can even be "cooked" in cold water; it just has to soak for about an hour. (See chapter 14 for more information on how to cold soak.)

Basmati rice is our favorite, so we eat it most often on the trail. The dehydrating method given here works for any type of rice, though, including sticky, long-grain, and brown.

Instant rice is cooked and dehydrated by the manufacturer. It can be used instead of self-dehydrated rice in any of our recipes. But it tends to have a less-exciting texture and flavor than homemade dehydrated rice.

STEPS FOR DEHYDRATING RICE:

1. Cook rice according to package directions. (We recommend using a rice cooker.)
2. Gently spread the cooked rice in a single, ½- to 1-inch-thick layer on dehydrator trays. Try not to break or smush the rice while spreading it out.
3. Dehydrate at 135°F until completely dry and crispy, at least 8 hours.

QUANTITIES AND WEIGHTS FOR DEHYDRATING RICE

Rice	Raw Amount	Dehydrated Volume	Dehydrated Weight
Dry, uncooked basmati	1½ cups	3⅓ cups	9.2 ounces

DEHYDRATING SAUCES

Dehydrating sauces feels a bit like magic. You start with a messy liquid and end up with a smooth and dry sheet of "sauce" that resembles a piece of paper and is about 90 percent lighter than the original sauce. Most sauces rehydrate very well when added to hot water. Tomato sauce is what we dehydrate most often for our recipes, but almost any low-fat sauce can be dehydrated. We've also enjoyed dehydrating pasta sauce and applesauce for our trips. If a sauce has too much sugar, it will take a long time to dehydrate. If a sauce is oily or cheesy, like many store-bought pasta sauces, it will go rancid much sooner than a fat-free sauce.

STEPS FOR DEHYDRATING SAUCES:

1. Pour the sauce onto a flexible plastic dehydrator tray. For thin sauces like tomato sauce, let gravity distribute the sauce into a circle. For thick sauces like applesauce, spread out the sauce using a spatula.
2. Dehydrate at 135°F until no longer sticky, 8 to 24 hours. (It's okay if they're leathery.)
3. About two-thirds of the way through the dehydrating time, the sauce should form a solid sheet. Peel it off the tray, flip it over, and continue dehydrating.

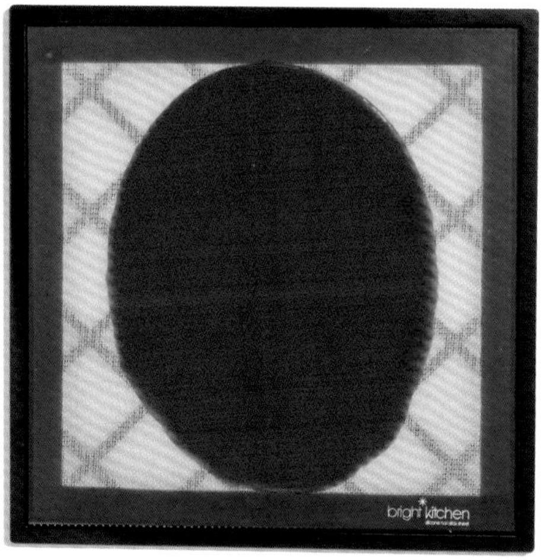

Step 1

Dehydrated sauce

QUANTITIES AND WEIGHTS FOR DEHYDRATING SAUCES

Sauce	Raw Amount	Dehydrated Weight
Tomato sauce, fat free	Two 8-ounce cans	1.5 ounces

DEHYDRATING STEWS

For thick stews and chilis, ingredients do not have to be dehydrated separately. The stew can be cooked similarly to how you'd cook it for immediate consumption and then dehydrated en masse. The volumes and weights for the stews are given within the recipes in chapter 15. Following is the basic process that applies to each.

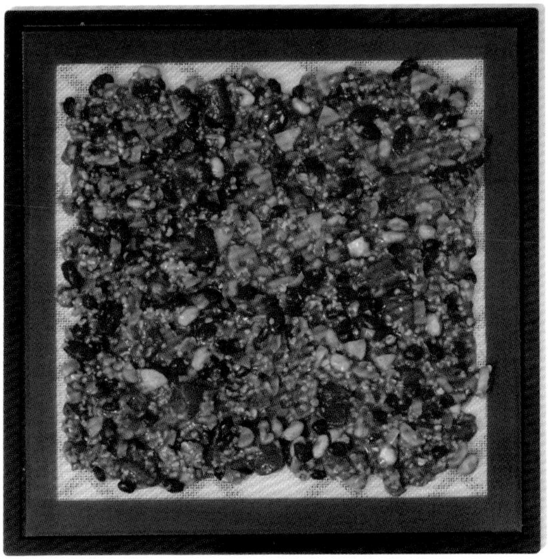

Step 2

STEPS FOR DEHYDRATING STEWS:

1. Cook the stew as you normally would, but omit the oil and fat. If your stew calls for sautéed vegetables, sauté them in water instead of oil. (Oil and fat shorten the shelf life of dehydrated food, so we avoid using them.)
2. Pour the stew onto flexible plastic dehydrator trays, and spread thinly (less than 1 inch thick).
3. Dehydrate at 135°F until the moisture is gone, at least 8 hours. Flip over the stew about halfway through the dehydrating time, or as soon as the stew has formed into a solid sheet or flippable pieces.

Dehydrated stew

DEHYDRATING FRUIT

In the wilderness, dehydrated fruit tastes like candy. It is extra sweet in part because sweets are harder to come by on trail and also because removing the water concentrates the sugar in the fruit. In principle, fruit could be rehydrated in water, but it will never regain the texture of fresh fruit, so we just munch on it in its dehydrated form as a snack or treat while we are hiking. On long hikes, we try to eat at least a little bit of dehydrated fruit every day. Be careful, though; dehydrated fruit is very small and concentrated compared to fresh fruit, so it is easy to overeat! For example, eating 10 dehydrated bananas will give you the same stomachache that eating 10 fresh bananas would ... but they'll weigh less than ½ pound, so you might not notice that you ate so many bananas until it is too late.

STEPS FOR DEHYDRATING FRUIT:

1. Cut the fruit into bite-sized pieces. Cubes or strips both work well, depending on the fruit and your preference; ½-inch cubes are a good starting point for experimentation. Fruits that are bite-sized to begin with, such as blueberries, don't require any additional cutting.
2. Most fruits don't require any pretreatment before dehydrating. However, some dehydrate better when blanched or frozen before dehydrating. (See the table below for suggestions.)
3. Distribute the fruit in a single layer on dehydrator trays.
4. Dehydrate at 135°F until crispy, at least 12 hours. The more sugary a fruit is, the longer it will generally take to dehydrate. The fruit is done when it is no longer sticky, but ideally it still will be flexible and leathery.

PREPARATION INSTRUCTIONS, QUANTITIES, AND WEIGHTS FOR DEHYDRATING FRUIT

Fruit	Raw Amount	Preparation Instructions	Dehydrated Volume	Dehydrated Weight
Bananas	4 medium (1 pound, 2.9 ounces)	Peel and cut into ⅓-inch rounds	1⅓ cups	3 ounces
Blueberries	32 ounces	Blanch or freeze to break skin	1½ cups	3.25 ounces
Mangoes	1 large	Peel, pit, and cut into ¾-inch slices	1⅓ cups	3 ounces
Pineapple rings, canned	20 ounces	Drain	1 cup	1.9 ounces
Strawberries	16 ounces	Cut into ⅓-inch slices	1 cup	1.9 ounces

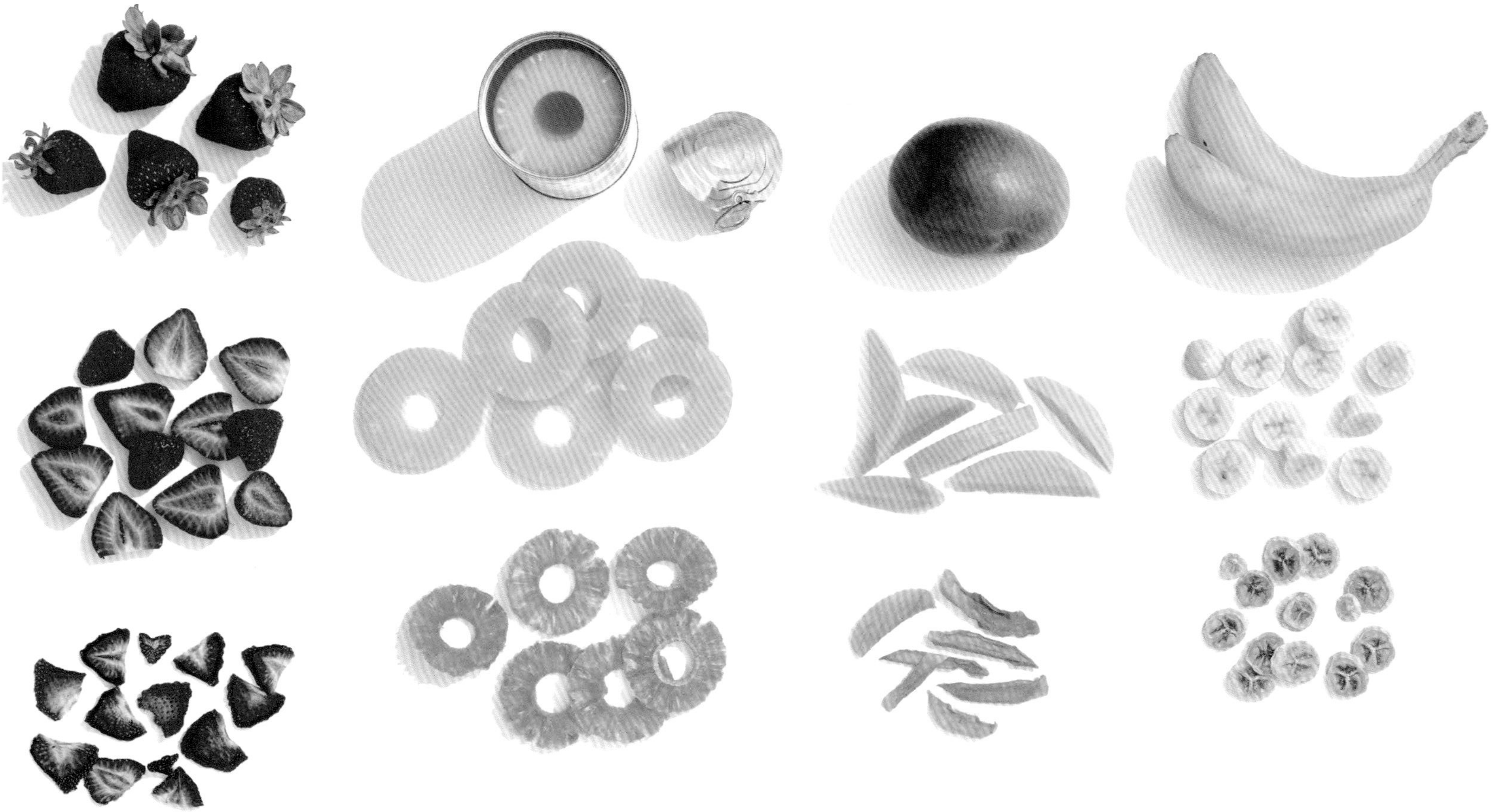

HOW TO STORE BULK DEHYDRATED FOOD

Dehydrated food storage is simple and straightforward. The most important thing is to keep the food dry because dehydrated food will happily absorb moisture from the air. There are two stages of preparing meals for the trail: dehydrating ingredients and assembling meals. As such, there are two stages of storage: The first is bulk storage of dehydrated ingredients. After individual meals are assembled, the second stage is to store those meals, which we cover in chapter 15.

PROCESS: Dehydrate bulk ingredients individually and then place into separate containers (e.g., peppers go in one container, onions in another, and strawberries in another). Leave at least 10 percent of the container empty to allow air to circulate inside and evenly distribute any remaining moisture. For the first week after dehydrating, shake the container every day or two to help redistribute moisture. If you see condensation on the inside of the container, that means the food isn't fully dehydrated and it should go back into the dehydrator. For extended storage, after you've verified that there is no condensation inside the container, keep containers of dehydrated food in a cool, dry, and dark place to prolong shelf life. When properly dehydrated, packaged, and stored, dehydrated food should last at least a year.

BULK STORAGE CONTAINERS

AIRTIGHT PLASTIC FOOD STORAGE CONTAINERS: Large airtight plastic containers serve as excellent storage for dehydrated ingredients. They come in sizes ranging from tiny to huge.

MASON JARS: Mason jars have many of the advantages of plastic containers, but they are easy to see through and sometimes have measurement indicators on the side, which makes it easy to assess how much of each ingredient you have.

ZIPLOCK PLASTIC BAGS: If you don't have enough plastic containers or mason jars, bulk ingredients can be stored in ziplock bags. These should provide enough protection to keep moisture out for up to a year.

THRUHIKERS'

TIPS

DEHYDRATING FOOD

- If you want to try dehydrating but aren't yet ready to invest in a dehydrator, you can use your oven.
- For best results, look for dehydrators with temperature control and a fan on the top or in the back.
- Dehydrate food in a single layer, or spread sauces thinly, on dehydrator trays to maximize efficiency.
- Cut fruits and veggies into uniform pieces for even dehydrating.
- The main objective of dehydrating is to get out as much of the water as possible; if noticeable moisture remains, regardless of how long the dehydrator has been running, the food is not done yet.
- Store dehydrated food so it's protected from the air. If air gets into the food, it will reabsorb moisture and may spoil.
- It is not necessary to vacuum seal food for the trail, but if you do, don't pull out so much air that the bag becomes hard, which can cause pointy dehydrated foods to puncture the bag.

14

REHYDRATING FOOD ON THE TRAIL

In chapter 13, you learned the steps involved in planning and dehydrating meals. All of that preparation has you now ready for the fun part: rehydrating. It's time to eat! The recipes in chapter 15 rehydrate easily and quickly, with a minimal amount of equipment, so they can be cooked even on long, tiring days of hiking. In this chapter, we describe the equipment needed to rehydrate food and the methods for rehydrating: boiling and cold soaking.

REHYDRATING EQUIPMENT

POT OR JAR: All of our recipes are designed to be rehydrated in a single pot or, for cold-soaked recipes, in a single jar. The capacity of a cook pot should be at least 2½ to 3 cups per person, to fit the food and water without boiling over. If you're using a cold-soak jar, 2 cups is enough capacity for one person. A pot that is taller than it is wide is nice because it can double as a coffee cup. A pot with a heat sink will boil water faster and consume less fuel on the trail. Titanium pots are the most expensive and lightest option; steel is usually the cheapest and heaviest; aluminum is a happy medium between the two. Our cook pot for two-person meals is also our coffee cup and cold-soak jar. It is aluminum, has a 5-cup capacity and a heat sink, and weighs just under ½ pound. Plus, by carrying only one pot, there is only one dish to do. (See page 118 for more information on doing the dishes on trail.)

UTENSIL: Choose an eating utensil or utensils that you like to use. A single titanium spork is not very expensive and is much lighter than a steel fork, spoon, and knife set. Some hikers prefer long-handled titanium spoons. The options are endless, and every hiker has a unique preference.

STOVE: A stove is required for hot meals in the backcountry. (See page 66 for more detail about stove options.)

FUEL: Different stoves require different types of fuel, so be sure your fuel and stove match. The following rehydrating method preserves fuel, which will lighten your load on a trip. After all, one fuel canister is half as heavy as two.

REHYDRATING HOT FOOD

After a day spent logging miles on the trail, cooking dinner should not be another ordeal. Fuel is weight, so cooking should require as little fuel as possible. The rehydration system we use for our recipes is as simple as possible to minimize effort and fuel use.

1. **MIX WATER AND FOOD IN A POT.** All of our recipes are one-pot meals. Food should be added to cold water before turning on the stove unless otherwise noted. Powders should be added after boiling so they don't burn.
2. **BRING TO A BOIL.** Set your stove to high heat to bring the water to a boil quickly.
3. **BOIL FOR UP TO 2 MINUTES.** Reduce the heat to the lowest level that maintains a simmer. Generally, pasta dishes should be boiled for 2 minutes, rice dishes for 1 minute, and oat dishes for 0 minutes.

LOSING OUR SPORK ON THE PACIFIC NORTHWEST CIRCUIT

We purposefully carry as little gear as possible on our backpacking adventures. When we switched to our current pot, which is narrower than it is tall, our eating habits changed—we began passing the pot back and forth to eat rather than taking alternating sporkfuls because the pot is just too small for two heads to fit above it. After a few weeks of using the new pot, we realized we were passing a spork back and forth with the pot, so we no longer had a use for our second spork. Even though sporks are light, useless weight is useless weight, so we shipped the spork home during our next resupply stop. For months, we barely noticed it was gone. Then, while hiking the Pacific Northwest Circuit (PNC), we managed to lose the one spork we still had. We had camped right on the peak of a mountain with an amazing view, so during breakfast, we probably focused too much on the beautiful sunrise and not enough on keeping track of our spork. We didn't realize it was gone until our lunch break 10 to 15 miles later, which was too great of a distance to go back. We had no backup, and it turns out it is very difficult to eat with no utensil.

Before lunch was over, Renee had solved the puzzle: We actually did have *eight utensils* with us—our tent stakes! They made excellent chopsticks, which became their second purpose for several days until we hit the next town. Oatmeal isn't easy to eat with tent-stake chopsticks, but it can be done. We hoped to be able to grab a new spork in town, but the small outfitter there didn't have any for sale, so we repurposed a plastic spoon from a gas station as our utensil for the next segment of the trip. After a few weeks with the plastic spoon, we eventually found the exact model of spork we had lost at an outfitter along the trail. We have since considered carrying an extra spork to avoid this happening again, but because the experience wasn't bad enough to justify more weight and equipment, we haven't bought spork number two yet. We still live on the wild side by sharing a spork!

—Tim

4. **TURN OFF THE HEAT, COVER, AND WAIT 10 MINUTES.** Boiling starts the rehydration process, but most of the rehydration happens after the heat is turned off. Turn off the stove completely, mix in powders or other ingredients as needed, and cover the pot. Don't worry if it still looks soupy. Be patient—all of our recipes call for 10 minutes of wait time while the food soaks up the water. We use this time to set up camp, or if we're totally exhausted, we take 10 minutes to relax!

A NOTE ON CONSERVING FUEL

The recipes in this book are designed to use as little fuel as possible. Boil water for only the time listed, which is how long it takes to soften the ingredients and get the rehydration process started. We never drain water (e.g., for pasta); instead, the proportions should be just right so the cooking water will be incorporated into the sauce fully. In addition to saving water, this saves fuel because it means no heat is dumped out. When we are focused on conservation, this cooking method gives us 11 days of use from an 8-ounce fuel canister while cooking two coffees per day and a two-person dinner per day. (We cold soak breakfast and lunch. See page 215 for cold-soaking tips.)

WHAT IS COLD SOAKING?

It is possible to "cold soak" many backpacking recipes, which is essentially cooking them without heat. Cold soaking is exactly what it sounds like: Instead of rehydrating quickly by adding boiling water to food, you rehydrate slowly by adding cold (or lukewarm) water to food. Certain ingredients, like dehydrated rice, cold soak very well, but others do not. Dry, store-bought pasta noodles will not rehydrate via cold soaking, but ramen noodles will.

To cold soak a meal, we combine the food and water in a sealable container for about an hour before we intend to eat that meal. We throw the sealed container into one of our packs (upright), continue walking, and by mealtime, it's ready to eat. For breakfast, oats can be soaked overnight. Many of the recipes in this book can be cold soaked or cooked depending on your preference.

The cold-soakable recipes in chapter 15 are labeled accordingly.

On long-distance trails, a surprising number of hikers opt not to carry a stove at all and instead do all of their cooking by cold soaking. This approach saves weight and complexity, but it is a no-go for hikers who, like us, are unwilling to give up hot meals and hot coffee. Rather than forgoing all hot food, we have found that a hybrid approach to cold soaking works well for us. We cold soak almost all of our lunches and cook almost all of our dinners.

TIPS FOR COLD SOAKING:

1. Cold soak in a sealable container that can be placed in your backpack without spilling. This makes it easy to cold soak while you hike.
2. Know which foods cold soak well and which don't. Most dehydrated vegetables cold soak well, as do ingredients that were cooked before being dehydrated, like rice and beans. Uncooked foods like pasta noodles usually require heat to cook properly.
3. An hour is usually long enough to cold soak the recipes in this book, but the time required depends on the water temperature. It takes longer to cold soak with ice-cold water (e.g., from a mountain stream) than it does with warm water (e.g., from a pond on a hot day).

LEAVE NO TRACE

We covered the general Leave No Trace principles in chapter 11. For cooking and eating, the following reminders will help you practice Leave No Trace on a trip:

- Pack out everything you packed in. Even biodegradable items are unsightly for future hikers and/or can be found and eaten by animals. Less-obvious items that should be packed out include the following:
    - Coffee grounds
    - Tea bags
    - Fruit pits
    - Fruit peels
    - Leftover food
    - Everything!
- Do not try to burn or bury leftover food because animals may find it. Pack it out.

DINNER ON THE GROUND

During our long adventures, dinner is always a highlight of the day. We usually walk at least 20 miles per day, and sometimes more than 30, so our calorie needs are through the roof. Often it isn't long after lunch that we start discussing which meal we'll pull out of our bags and have for dinner when we finally make camp. On one section of the Continental Divide Trail in New Mexico, spaghetti was on our minds! We were only a few days into a long and remote stretch, so our packs were full and heavy with just enough food to get us to the next town.

We made it through a long day by discussing how wonderful our newly developed Creamy Tomato Rotini recipe (page 253) would taste after we arrived at camp. It took longer to get in our miles than we expected, so it was getting dark when we finally called it a day. Renee usually sets up the tent while I cook dinner. Between the increasing darkness and my exhaustion from the hard day, I wasn't paying enough attention to balancing the pot on the stove, and when I wasn't looking, it flipped over onto the ground. Our yummy rotini was just a pile of noodles in the dirt!

We pondered what to do. We could cook another dinner, but we'd run out of food before making it to the next town. We could skip dinner, but we were hungry and wanted to eat. Either way, we'd still have to clean up and pack out the mess because we were in bear territory, and that would make our backpacks even heavier. We didn't like any of the options, so I tried a noodle—they were just about fully cooked! Renee took some convincing, but she decided a little bit of dirt wouldn't kill her. We ate the pasta piece by piece right off the ground. The dirt added a little bit of extra texture, but it really wasn't too bad. In the end, we did get to eat our Creamy Tomato Rotini after that hard day of hiking, and as the saying goes, we have a story to tell about it.

—Tim

PS: This has now happened to us twice. I also spilled Creamy Tomato Rotini after dark in Washington while hiking the PNC, and we ate it off the ground then, too. There are some lessons I may never learn.

THRUHIKERS' TIPS

REHYDRATING FOOD ON THE TRAIL

- You can save fuel by boiling meals for 0 to 2 minutes and then covering and letting them sit for 10 more minutes with the heat off. Generally, we boil pasta dishes for 2 minutes, rice dishes for 1 minute, and oat dishes for 0 minutes.
- One-pot meals are easy to make on trail and only require one pot to cook in and clean after.
- Cold soaking meals can be a great way to save weight, time, and fuel. (Cheese and sausage for lunch is much heavier than cold-soaked rice and beans.) Cold-soakable foods include cooked and dehydrated rice (or store-bought instant rice), dehydrated beans, dehydrated vegetables, and ramen.
- Always practice Leave No Trace when cooking on trail.

15

RECIPES

The recipes in this chapter were designed to be lightweight and easy to cook on the trail. There's nothing like arriving at camp and having very little to prepare before enjoying a delicious and filling meal. These recipes are all one-pot meals—just boil, wait, and eat. Extra pots and pans add weight to your pack and complications at dinnertime. No draining is required for any of these recipes; all of the water used will be absorbed during the rehydrating process. Each of the recipes can be dehydrated and assembled well in advance of a trip. As long as the ingredients are fully dehydrated, they'll last at least a year.

PACKAGING MEALS FOR THE TRAIL

Assemble meals for the trail by packaging ingredients in individual sandwich- or quart-size sealable ziplock bags. You can put one serving in each bag or, if you plan to cook for a pair or small group, you can package up to four servings in a single bag (assuming your pot is large enough to cook them all at once). For recipes that include powders or semimoist ingredients like raisins, seal the powder or semimoist food in a small bag, such as a fold-over sandwich bag, twisted or tied shut, that is placed directly into the larger ziplock bag with the rest of the ingredients. Write the name of the meal, the amount of water needed, and the boil time on the bag with a Sharpie to be sure you don't forget what is required for cooking while you're out there.

THE EVOLUTION OF OUR RECIPE-MAKING FOR BACKPACKING

Our first foray into preparing our own backpacking food was for a trip with Tim's family to Isle Royale National Park. We volunteered to be in charge of food preparation, and we wanted to impress. We scoured the internet, searching for instructions for easy backpacking meals, and spent hours and hours putting together a spreadsheet to capture the itinerary. It was hard, but we succeeded—nobody starved on the trip. Our meals consisted of some ingredients that we dehydrated ourselves and some that were store-bought. For instance, we were meat-eaters at the time, and we relied on plenty of tuna and chicken packets for protein.

As we started doing longer distances, we realized that by taking on more of the dehydration process ourselves, we could make amazing food and save weight in our packs. We found a book called *Recipes for Adventure: Healthy, Hearty and Homemade Backpacking Recipes* by Backpacking Chef Glenn McAllister (highly recommended!), and we got to work. We learned lots of techniques from Chef Glenn as we took our dehydrating to the next level.

When we were getting ready for our first long-distance hike on the Pacific Crest Trail, we had enough experience dehydrating that we thought it would be fun to start developing recipes of our own. We dehydrated about 150 meals for the trip, and during the process, we had lots of time to experiment with flavors and methods to create unique recipes that hit the spot for us.

On each of our long thruhikes, we have brought along an assortment of new recipes, but we have stuck with some old favorites since the beginning. We made our Curry Rice (page 240) on that first trip to Isle Royale National Park, and we have brought an evolving version on virtually all of our trips since.

—Renee

OVERNIGHT OATS

Overnight oats are one of our go-to breakfasts on trail. They are easy to prepare both at home and on the trail. Plus, it's so nice to wake up with breakfast already made! This recipe is just a starting point. To mix it up, swap in any other nuts or seeds for the sunflower seeds. Try adding cocoa powder, peanut butter powder, or dehydrated fruit, or top with coconut flakes. If you have any filling left over from our Apple-Pear Crisp (page 256), that can be a great addition, too.

Serves 1 | **290 calories** | **Cold Soakable**

BEFORE THE TRAIL

½ cup old-fashioned oats (not instant)

2 tablespoons raw sunflower seeds

2 teaspoons brown sugar, or to taste

¼ teaspoon ground cinnamon, optional

ON THE TRAIL

⅔ cup water

BEFORE THE TRAIL

1. Combine the oats, sunflower seeds, brown sugar, and cinnamon, if using, in a sandwich-size ziplock bag, and seal the bag.

ON THE TRAIL

1. The night before eating, place the oat mixture in a sealable container and add the water. Seal the container, and shake or mix well. Store in an animal-safe way, and soak overnight.
2. In the morning, stir and enjoy.

HOT OATMEAL

This can also be cooked and served hot as oatmeal: Bring the water to a boil over high heat. Reduce the heat to low, and stir in the oat mixture. Remove from the heat, cover, and let sit for 5 minutes. Stir and enjoy.

ULTRALIGHT COFFEE & OATS

Before we realized how much more pleasant hiking is with lightweight backpacks, we carried several pots and cups with us. But over time, we learned that our backs would be happier if we minimized all of the unnecessary gear we were used to hiking with, including coffee cups. We will never give up hot coffee in the morning, so we stopped carrying dedicated coffee cups and began using our cook pot as our coffee cup as well. We still carried two recycled Talenti ice cream jars as dedicated vessels for cold soaking. They make overnight oats the ideal breakfast food—we could enjoy hot coffee from our pot at the same time as we ate cold oatmeal from the jars.

Later, we realized we could switch to a cook pot with a lid and get rid of the cold-soak jars altogether, but now we faced a problem: How could we cold soak the oats overnight but still use the pot first thing in the morning for coffee? I was ready to throw in the towel and carry a coffee cup, but Renee figured it out. We can't rely on the ziplock bags that we package our food to be waterproof, but we can count on them to have no more than a slow leak. With this realization, our system is now to add the water right in the ziplock bag with the oats. We place the bag in our cooking pot, which we then place upright on the ground or in our bear bag overnight (depending on location). When morning comes, we take out the bag of oats and use the pot for coffee. There are never more than a few drops of oat leakage. After finishing our first coffee of the day, we dump the bag of oats into the pot and enjoy.

—Tim

snow peak

STRAWBERRIES & CREAM OATMEAL

Flavored instant-oat packets always leave us feeling hungry, and after eating them for days on trail, we get really tired of them. Old-fashioned oats are less processed than the instant variety, and we've found they keep us full longer. Plus, we can add different fruits, nuts, and flavors to keep them exciting, like strawberries and coconut cream!

Serves 1 | **330 calories** | **Cold Soakable**

BEFORE THE TRAIL

⅛ cup (2 tablespoons) dehydrated strawberries

½ cup old-fashioned oats (not instant)

2 tablespoons coconut milk powder

1 tablespoon chia seeds

1½ teaspoons brown sugar, or to taste

ON THE TRAIL

1 cup water

BEFORE THE TRAIL

1. Place the strawberries in a small, light bag (e.g., a fold-over sandwich bag) to keep them separate from the other dry ingredients, and seal or tie shut.
2. Place the oats, coconut milk powder, chia seeds, and brown sugar, along with the sealed bag of strawberries, in a larger ziplock bag, and seal the bag.

ON THE TRAIL

1. Bring the water to a boil over high heat.
2. Reduce the heat to low, and stir in the strawberries and oat mixture.
3. Remove from the heat, cover, and let sit for 5 minutes, until all of the water is absorbed. Stir and enjoy.

STRAWBERRIES & CREAM OVERNIGHT OATS

To cold soak this recipe, before bed, place the strawberries and oat mixture in a sealable container and add the water. Seal the container, and shake or mix well. Store in an animal-safe way, and soak overnight. In the morning, stir and enjoy.

HOMEMADE GRANOLA

Granola with oat milk is one of our favorite backpacking breakfasts because it requires minimal effort on trail. It is also super tasty and filling.

Serves 1 | **380 calories**

BEFORE THE TRAIL

1½ tablespoons oat milk powder

⅔ cup Homemade Granola (see below)

ON THE TRAIL

½ cup water

BEFORE THE TRAIL

1. Place the oat milk powder in a small, light bag (e.g., a fold-over sandwich bag), and seal or tie shut.
2. Place the granola and the sealed bag of oat milk powder in a larger ziplock bag and seal the bag.

ON THE TRAIL

1. Add the water and oat milk powder to your pot or bowl, and mix vigorously until smooth.
2. Add the granola. Stir and enjoy.

HOMEMADE GRANOLA

Makes about eleven ⅔-cup servings

4 cups old-fashioned oats (not instant)

1 cup raw cashews or nuts of choice, slightly broken up by hand or chopped

1 cup raw sunflower seeds

1 teaspoon ground cinnamon, optional

⅓ cup maple syrup

⅓ cup canola oil

1. Preheat the oven to 325°F. Line a baking sheet with parchment paper.
2. Combine the oats, cashews, sunflower seeds, and cinnamon, if using, in a large bowl.
3. Whisk together the maple syrup and canola oil in a small bowl.
4. Pour the syrup-oil mixture over the dry mixture, and mix with a spoon.
5. Transfer the granola to the baking sheet, and spread into a thin, even layer.
6. Bake for 30 to 35 minutes, until lightly toasted.
7. Remove from the oven, then let cool on the pan for at least 30 minutes to solidify.
8. When completely cool, store or package for the trail.

snow peak

snow peak

TOFU SCRAMBLE

Sometimes it's nice to start the day with a hot, savory scramble rather than sweet oats. Eat this tofu wrapped in a tortilla for a simple breakfast burrito.

Serves 1 | **260 calories** | **Cold Soakable**

BEFORE THE TRAIL

½ cup dehydrated tofu crumbles (see page 202)

¼ cup cooked and dehydrated rice (see page 203)

¼ cup dehydrated mushrooms, peppers, and onions (see page 196)

1 tablespoon nutritional yeast

½ teaspoon garlic powder

¼ teaspoon ground turmeric

¼ teaspoon table salt

⅛ teaspoon black pepper

ON THE TRAIL

⅔ cup water

BEFORE THE TRAIL

1. Combine the tofu, rice, mushrooms, peppers, onions, nutritional yeast, garlic powder, turmeric, salt, and pepper in a large ziplock bag, and seal the bag.

ON THE TRAIL

1. Combine the water and tofu mixture in a pot. Cover, and bring to a boil over high heat.
2. Reduce the heat to low and simmer, covered, for 1 minute, uncovering to stir occasionally. It will still look watery and uncooked after 1 minute.
3. Remove from the heat, and let sit, covered, until all of the water is absorbed, 10 minutes. Stir and enjoy.

COLD-SOAKED TOFU SCRAMBLE

To cold soak this recipe, before bed, place all ingredients in a sealable container and add the water. Seal the container, and shake or mix well. Store in an animal-safe way, and soak overnight. In the morning, stir and enjoy.

OVERNIGHT COCONUT CHIA PUDDING

Chia seeds have the surprising ability to gelatinize when soaked, turning coconut milk into pudding. This recipe makes it possible to enjoy a texture on the trail that we usually associate with non-trail foods. Depending on our mood and what's in season while we're prepping this, we use a variety of dried or dehydrated fruits to make this recipe unique each time we make it.

Serves 1 | **370 calories** | **Cold Soakable**

BEFORE THE TRAIL

⅛ cup (2 tablespoons) dehydrated fruit (see Tip)

¼ cup chia seeds

3 tablespoons coconut milk powder

1½ teaspoons brown sugar

ON THE TRAIL

1 cup water

BEFORE THE TRAIL

1. Place the fruit in a small, light bag (e.g., a fold-over sandwich bag) to keep it separate from the other ingredients, and seal or tie shut.
2. Place the chia seeds, coconut milk powder, and brown sugar, along with the sealed bag of fruit, in a larger ziplock bag, and seal the bag.

ON THE TRAIL

1. Before bed, place the chia seed mixture in a sealable container and add the water. Seal the container, and shake or mix to break up any clumps in the coconut milk powder. Store in an animal-safe way, and soak overnight.
2. In the morning, stir and enjoy.

TIP

Chop larger pieces of fruit, such as dehydrated mangoes, into ½-inch pieces. Small fruits, like dehydrated blueberries, can be left whole.

COLD-SOAKED RICE & BEANS

This is one of our go-to lunches on trail. These rice and beans are simple to make, yet so satisfying! We sometimes carry individual-sized hot sauce pouches for a topping. Serve on a tortilla for an extra-large meal.

Serves 1 | **440 calories** | **Cold Soakable**

BEFORE THE TRAIL

⅔ cup cooked and dehydrated basmati rice (see page 203)

⅓ cup dehydrated canned pinto or black beans (see page 200)

⅓ cup dehydrated bell peppers, onions, and corn (see page 196)

2 teaspoons taco seasoning

¼ teaspoon table salt

ON THE TRAIL

1 cup water

BEFORE THE TRAIL

1. Combine the rice, beans, bell peppers, onions, corn, taco seasoning, and salt in a large ziplock bag, and seal the bag.

ON THE TRAIL

1. One or more hours before lunch, place the rice mixture in a sealable container and add the water. Seal the container, and shake or mix well. Soak for at least 1 hour while you hike.
2. At lunchtime, stir and enjoy.

HOT RICE AND BEANS

Bring the water and the rice mixture to a boil over high heat, reduce the heat to low, and boil for 1 minute. Remove from the heat, cover, and let sit for 10 minutes. Stir and enjoy.

COLD-SOAKED TOMATO & NUT COUSCOUS

Cold-soaked couscous is easy to make on trail because small-grain couscous doesn't need to be cooked and dehydrated; it is cold soakable as purchased. After jazzing it up with a protein, veggies, and spices, it is a tasty and filling trail meal.

Serves 1 | **485 calories** | **Cold Soakable**

BEFORE THE TRAIL

- ⅓ cup small-grain couscous (see Note)
- ¼ cup pine nuts (see Note)
- ⅛ cup (2 tablespoons) dehydrated grape tomatoes or store-bought sun-dried tomatoes
- 1 tablespoon nutritional yeast
- 1 teaspoon dried parsley
- ½ teaspoon dried thyme
- ¼ teaspoon lemon pepper
- ¼ teaspoon table salt

ON THE TRAIL

- ⅔ cup water

BEFORE THE TRAIL

1. Combine the couscous, pine nuts, tomatoes, nutritional yeast, parsley, thyme, lemon pepper, and salt in a large ziplock bag, and seal the bag.

ON THE TRAIL

1. One or more hours before lunch, place the couscous mixture in a sealable container and add the water. Seal the container, and shake or mix well. Soak for at least 1 hour while you hike.
2. At lunchtime, stir and enjoy.

HOT TOMATO & NUT COUSCOUS

Add the couscous mixture and water to a pot, and bring to a boil over high heat. Remove from the heat, cover, and let sit for 10 minutes. Stir and enjoy.

NOTE

Be sure to use small-grain couscous because the large-grain variety does not cold soak well. Also, pine nuts may go rancid more quickly than the other ingredients in our recipes. If you intend to store this for several months or more, consider using a different nut or seed.

NEVER EATING COUSCOUS AGAIN AFTER THE PACIFIC CREST TRAIL

Before setting out on the PCT, we spent 2 months in a cabin on a frozen lake in Northern Wisconsin dehydrating food. We assembled about 150 days' worth of breakfasts, lunches, dinners, and snacks that we planned to have Tim's mom mail to us along the hike route. We made a large variety of super-tasty homemade dehydrated dinners, but we ran out of time to dehydrate our lunches. So we decided to buy lots of prepacked Near East couscous and some Knorr rice side packets, which we added dehydrated beans to. There was not nearly enough variety in these lunches. At the beginning, it was fine, but as the trail went on, I dreaded pulling another bag of couscous out of our backpacks. I got so sick of eating cold, dry, chemical-tasting couscous that I didn't eat couscous for years after we finished the hike. Even now, I rarely eat it. (But don't worry, this homemade couscous is great—just don't eat it every day!) For our subsequent thruhikes, we only dehydrated and mailed dinners. We realized we could buy breakfasts, lunches, and snacks easily enough in stores along the trail, which allowed us to mix things up based on our changing cravings and hunger levels.

—Renee

COLD-SOAKED SHEPHERD'S PIE

This is a fun meal to eat on the trail, with a savory layer of stewed lentils on the bottom and a comforting layer of mashed potatoes on the top.

Serves 1 | **315 calories** | **Cold Soakable**

BEFORE THE TRAIL

⅔ cup dehydrated Shepherd's Pie Filling (see below)

½ cup plain instant potatoes

1 tablespoon nutritional yeast

¼ teaspoon vegetable bouillon

⅛ teaspoon ground nutmeg

ON THE TRAIL

1⅓ cups water

BEFORE THE TRAIL

1. Cook and dehydrate the shepherd's pie filling.
2. Place the dehydrated shepherd's pie filling in a small, light bag (e.g., a fold-over sandwich bag).
3. Place the potatoes, nutritional yeast, bouillon, and nutmeg in a larger ziplock bag, and shake it a bit to mix. Add the sealed small bag of shepherd's pie filling to the larger bag, and seal the bag.

ON THE TRAIL

1. One or more hours before lunch, place the dehydrated shepherd's pie filling in a sealable container.
2. Add the potato mixture on top of the shepherd's pie filling.
3. Slowly add the water, trying not to disturb the two layers. Seal the container, and soak for at least an hour while you hike. Enjoy.

SHEPHERD'S PIE FILLING

Makes about five ⅔-cup dehydrated servings

1 cup green lentils

4 cups water, plus more for sautéing

1 medium onion, chopped

2 large carrots, chopped

2 large celery sticks, chopped

One 15-ounce can tomato sauce

5 garlic cloves, minced

2 tablespoons soy sauce

1 teaspoon dried thyme

½ teaspoon dried rosemary

COOK THE SHEPHERD'S PIE FILLING

1. Add the lentils and 4 cups water to a pot, and bring to a boil over high heat. Cook until soft, about 15 minutes (or according to the package instructions). Drain.
2. Sauté the onion, carrots, and celery in a large cast-iron or nonstick pan over medium heat, using a little water instead of oil, until soft, 7 to 10 minutes (see Note on page 243).
3. Add the lentils, tomato sauce, garlic, soy sauce, thyme, and rosemary, and stir to combine. Continue to heat until hot, 3 to 5 minutes. Let cool before dehydrating.

DEHYDRATE THE SHEPHERD'S PIE FILLING

1. Spread the cooked shepherd's pie filling onto mesh dehydrator trays in thin, even layers.
2. Dehydrate at 135°F until completely dry and brittle, at least 8 hours.

HOT SHEPHERD'S PIE

Place the shepherd's pie filling and 1 cup water in a pot, and bring to a boil over the highest heat, stirring occasionally. Reduce the heat to the lowest setting. Add the instant potatoes on top of the shepherd's pie filling. Slowly add the remaining ⅓ cup water, distributing it over as much of the potatoes as possible. Boil for 1 more minute. Remove from the heat, cover, and let sit for 10 minutes. Enjoy.

snow peak

HOMEMADE RAMEN

Ramen is a great trail food—salty and easy. We sometimes buy pre-flavored ramen packets from the store and cold soak them as a snack on the trail. But our homemade version with veggies and protein is so much tastier and more nutritious. You can buy unflavored ramen noodle cakes at Asian grocery stores in bulk. We like to cook this ramen for dinner or cold soak it for lunch.

Serves 1 | **330 calories** | **Cold Soakable**

BEFORE THE TRAIL

1 ramen noodle cake (about 2 ounces)

⅓ cup dehydrated tofu cubes (see page 202)

⅓ cup dehydrated vegetables, such as chile peppers, green onions, garlic, and cabbage (see page 196)

1½ teaspoons vegetable bouillon

ON THE TRAIL

1½ cups water (see Note)

BEFORE THE TRAIL

1. Combine the ramen, tofu, vegetables, and bouillon in a ziplock bag, and seal the bag.

ON THE TRAIL

1. Combine the water and ramen mixture in a pot, and bring to a boil over high heat, stirring occasionally.
2. Reduce the heat to low. Cover, and simmer for 1 minute, uncovering to stir occasionally.
3. Remove from the heat and let sit, covered, for 10 minutes. Stir and enjoy.

NOTE

You can use more or less water, depending on how soupy you want your ramen to be.

COLD-SOAKED RAMEN

Place the ramen, tofu, vegetables, and bouillon in a sealable container and add the water. Seal the container, and shake or mix. Soak for about an hour (depending on how soft you want your noodles) while you hike. Stir and enjoy.

SPAGHETTI RAMEN

If you are looking for a simple, cold-soakable, tomato-based pasta dish, you can't go wrong with this recipe. If you are looking for a creamier tomato-based pasta dish that requires cooking, check out our Creamy Tomato Rotini (page 253). You can buy unflavored ramen noodle cakes in bulk at Asian grocery stores.

Serves 1 | **480 calories** | **Cold Soakable**

BEFORE THE TRAIL

1 ramen noodle cake (about 2 ounces)

⅓ cup dehydrated canned black or kidney beans (see page 200)

⅓ cup dehydrated veggies (such as mushrooms, onions, bell peppers, and garlic; see page 196)

15 grams dehydrated tomato sauce (about ⅓ cup folded/loosely packed; see page 204)

1 teaspoon Italian seasoning

1 teaspoon sugar

¼ teaspoon table salt

ON THE TRAIL

1½ cups water

BEFORE THE TRAIL

1. Combine the ramen, beans, mushrooms, onions, bell peppers, garlic, tomato sauce, Italian seasoning, sugar, and salt in a ziplock bag, and seal the bag.

ON THE TRAIL

1. Set the sheet of tomato sauce aside. Combine the water and remaining ramen mixture in a pot. Tear the tomato sauce into small pieces and add to the pot. Cover, and bring to a boil over high heat, uncovering to stir occasionally.
2. Remove from the heat, and let sit, covered, until all of the water is absorbed, 10 minutes. Stir and enjoy.

COLD-SOAKED SPAGHETTI RAMEN

Tear the tomato sauce into small pieces. Place all of the ingredients in a sealable container and add the water. Seal the container, and shake or mix well. Soak for about an hour (depending on how soft you want your noodles) while you hike.

COCONUT CURRY NOODLES

We have taken this thick curry with us on all of our long adventures. The crunchy cauliflower is a favorite veggie in this recipe.

Serves 1 **555 calories**

BEFORE THE TRAIL

2 tablespoons coconut milk powder

1½ teaspoons curry powder

½ teaspoon paprika

¼ teaspoon ground ginger

3 ounces udon or rice noodle sticks (with a 6- or 7-minute cook time; see Tip)

⅓ cup dehydrated tofu cubes (see page 202)

⅓ cup dehydrated veggies (such as cauliflower, julienned carrots, zucchini, and mushrooms; see page 196)

¼ teaspoon table salt, or to taste

ON THE TRAIL

1½ cups water

BEFORE THE TRAIL

1. Place the coconut milk powder, curry powder, paprika, and ginger in a small, light bag (e.g., a fold-over sandwich bag), and seal or tie shut.
2. Place the udon noodles, tofu, cauliflower, carrots, zucchini, and mushrooms, and salt, along with sealed bag of powders, in a larger ziplock bag, and seal the bag.

ON THE TRAIL

1. Set the small bag aside. Combine the water and the contents of the large bag in a pot. Cover, and bring to a boil over high heat, stirring occasionally.
2. Reduce the heat to low, and simmer, covered, for 2 minutes, uncovering to stir occasionally. (It will still look watery and uncooked.)
3. Remove from the heat, and add the contents of the small bag. Stir, cover, and let sit until all of the water is absorbed, 10 minutes. Stir and enjoy.

TIP

Using noodles with a 6- or 7-minute cook time ensures that they will cook at the same rate as the rest of the meal rehydrates. Different brands make noodles that take very different amounts of time to cook. There is a little bit of wiggle room, but noodles that cook much faster than 6 minutes will end up mushy, and those that take much longer than 7 minutes will be crunchy.

CURRY RICE

This was one of the first dehydrated recipes we ever made, and it is still in our rotation more than 10 years later! When we are going for Persian-inspired flavors, we use raisins and cashews. When we want a more ultralight version, we use beans in place of the cashews and leave out the raisins.

Serves 1 | **560 calories** | **Cold Soakable**

BEFORE THE TRAIL

2 tablespoons raisins

⅔ cup cooked and dehydrated basmati rice (see page 203)

⅓ cup raw cashews

⅓ cup dehydrated zucchini, mushrooms, and julienned carrots (see page 196)

2 teaspoons curry powder

1 teaspoon vegetable bouillon

½ teaspoon garlic powder

¼ teaspoon ground turmeric

ON THE TRAIL

1 cup water

BEFORE THE TRAIL

1. Place the raisins in a small, light bag (e.g., a fold-over sandwich bag) to keep them separate from the other dry ingredients, and seal or tie shut.
2. Place the rice, cashews, zucchini, mushrooms, carrots, curry powder, bouillon, garlic powder, and turmeric, along with the small bag of raisins, in a larger ziplock bag.

ON THE TRAIL

1. Set the raisins aside. Combine the water and the remaining rice mixture in a pot. Cover, and bring to a boil over high heat.
2. Reduce the heat to low, and simmer, covered, for 1 minute. (It will still look watery and uncooked.) Stir minimally to avoid breaking the rice.
3. Remove from the heat. Add the raisins, stir, cover, and let sit until all of the water is absorbed, 10 minutes. Enjoy.

COLD-SOAKED CURRY RICE

Place the rice mixture in a sealable container and add the water. Seal the container, and shake or mix. Soak for at least an hour while you hike.

snow peak

DAL WITH RICE

This Indian-inspired dal, spinach, and rice dish is full of protein, fiber, and carbs. Serve with naan for an extra-large meal.

Serves 1 | **400 calories** | **Cold Soakable**

BEFORE THE TRAIL

⅔ cup dehydrated Dal (see page 243)

⅔ cup cooked and dehydrated basmati rice (see page 203)

ON THE TRAIL

1 cup water

BEFORE THE TRAIL

1. Cook and dehydrate the dal.
2. Combine the dehydrated rice and dal in a ziplock bag.

ON THE TRAIL

1. Combine the water, dal, and rice in a pot. Cover, and bring to a boil over high heat.
2. Reduce the heat to low, and simmer, covered, for 1 minute. (It will still look watery and uncooked.) Stir minimally to avoid breaking the rice.
3. Remove from the heat, and let sit, covered, until all of the water is absorbed, 10 minutes. Enjoy.

COLD-SOAKED DAL WITH RICE

Place the dal and rice in a sealable container and add the water. Seal the container, and shake or mix. Soak for at least an hour while you hike.

DAL

Makes about four ⅔-cup dehydrated servings

- 1 medium onion, diced
- 3 cups water, plus more for sautéing
- 1 large tomato, diced
- 1 chile pepper, diced
- 5 garlic cloves, minced
- 2 teaspoons ground cumin
- 2 teaspoons table salt
- ½ teaspoon ground coriander
- ½ teaspoon ground turmeric
- 1 cup red lentils
- 4 ounces frozen, chopped spinach, thawed
- Juice of ½ lemon

COOK THE DAL

1. Sauté the onions in a little water (see Note) in a medium pan over medium heat until soft, 5 to 10 minutes.
2. Add the tomatoes, and cook until they start to disintegrate, about 5 minutes.
3. Add the chile pepper and garlic, and sauté until the garlic is fragrant, about 2 minutes.
4. Add the cumin, salt, coriander, and turmeric, and stir until incorporated.
5. Add the lentils and remaining 3 cups water. Cover, and bring to a boil. Reduce the heat to low, and simmer, stirring occasionally, until all the water is fully absorbed, 15 to 20 minutes.
6. Mix in the spinach and lemon juice.
7. Let cool before dehydrating.

DEHYDRATE THE DAL

1. Spread the cooked dal onto dehydrator sheets in thin, even layers.
2. Dehydrate at 135°F until completely dry and brittle, at least 8 hours.

NOTE

Oil and fat shorten the shelf life of dehydrated food so we avoid it when we can. Water works just as well in this recipe.

RISOTTO RICE

Makes about seven ⅔-cup dehydrated servings

- 2 cups Arborio, carnaroli, short-grain, or medium-grain rice
- 1¾ cups water
- 1¾ cups white wine

COOK THE RISOTTO RICE

1. Cook the rice according to package directions, in the water and wine.
2. Let cool before dehydrating.

DEHYDRATE THE RISOTTO RICE

1. Spread the cooked rice onto dehydrator sheets in thin, even layers.
2. Dehydrate at 135°F until completely dry and crispy, at least 8 hours.

MUSHROOM RISOTTO

We lived in Germany for several years and were surprised by how much our European friends love risotto, so we decided to make a trail version! This rich, creamy mushroom risotto hits the spot, and the wine adds a unique flavor on trail. Jonas (trail name Parmesan), our friend from Germany, approves!

Serves 1 | **420 calories** | **Cold Soakable**

BEFORE THE TRAIL:

⅔ cup cooked and dehydrated Risotto Rice (see page 244)

⅓ cup dehydrated canned white beans (see page 200)

⅓ cup dehydrated mushrooms (see page 196)

1 teaspoon vegetable bouillon

1 teaspoon nutritional yeast

½ teaspoon garlic powder

½ teaspoon dried oregano

¼ teaspoon dried parsley

⅛ teaspoon black pepper

ON THE TRAIL:

1 cup water

BEFORE THE TRAIL

1. Prepare and dehydrate the risotto rice.
2. Combine the rice, beans, mushrooms, bouillon, nutritional yeast, garlic powder, oregano, parsley, and pepper in a ziplock bag, and seal the bag.

ON THE TRAIL

1. Combine the water and rice mixture in a pot. Cover, and bring to a boil over high heat.
2. Reduce the heat to low and simmer, covered, for 1 minute. (It will still look watery and uncooked.)
3. Remove from the heat, and let sit, covered, until all of the water is absorbed, 10 minutes. Stir and enjoy.

COLD-SOAKED MUSHROOM RISOTTO

Place the dry ingredients in a sealable container and add the water. Seal the container, and shake or mix. Soak for at least an hour while you hike.

SWEET PEPPER MEXICAN RICE

Colorful bell peppers add a crunchy texture and sweet flavor to this savory Mexican-style rice and pinto bean dish.

Serves 1 | **455 calories** | **Cold Soakable**

BEFORE THE TRAIL

⅔ cup dehydrated Mexican Rice (see page 247)

⅓ cup dehydrated pinto beans (see page 200)

⅓ cup dehydrated sweet red, yellow, and orange bell peppers (see page 196)

ON THE TRAIL

1 cup water

BEFORE THE TRAIL

1. Cook and dehydrate the Mexican rice.
2. Combine the rice, beans, and peppers in a ziplock bag, and seal the bag.

ON THE TRAIL

1. Combine the water and rice mixture in a pot. Cover, and bring to a boil over high heat.
2. Reduce the heat to low, and simmer, covered, for 1 minute. (It will still look watery and uncooked.) Stir minimally to avoid breaking the rice.
3. Remove from the heat, and let sit, covered, until all of the water is absorbed, 10 minutes. Stir and enjoy.

COLD-SOAKED SWEET PEPPER MEXICAN RICE

Place the rice mixture in a sealable container and add the water. Seal the container, and shake or mix well. Soak for at least an hour while you hike.

MEXICAN RICE

Makes about five ⅔-cup dehydrated servings

1 medium onion, diced

2½ cups water, plus more for sautéing

Dash of table salt

3 garlic cloves, minced

1½ cups basmati rice

1 cup tomato sauce (from an 8-ounce can)

2 tablespoons dried parsley

2½ teaspoons vegetable bouillon

COOK THE MEXICAN RICE

1. Sauté the onion in a little water in a large nonstick or cast-iron pan over medium-high heat (see Note on page 243). Add the salt, and cook until soft, 5 to 10 minutes.
2. Add the garlic, and sauté for another 30 seconds.
3. Add the rice, and cook until slightly brown, about 3 minutes.
4. Add the remaining 2½ cups water, the tomato sauce, parsley, and bouillon. Bring to a boil, cover, reduce the heat to medium-low, and cook until all of the water is absorbed, about 20 minutes. (Or transfer to a rice cooker if you have one and cook until the rice is cooked through.)
5. Turn off the heat. Wait about 10 minutes and then fluff and mix gently to avoid breaking the rice.
6. Let cool completely before dehydrating.

DEHYDRATE THE MEXICAN RICE

1. Spread the cooked Mexican rice onto mesh dehydrator trays in thin, even layers.
2. Dehydrate at 135°F, breaking up the clumps a few times, until completely dry and crispy, at least 5 hours.

CHILI

Makes about ten ⅔-cup dehydrated servings

- 1 onion, chopped
- 1 carrot, chopped (peeled if desired)
- 2 celery stalks, sliced
- 2 bell peppers (any color), ribs and seeds removed, and chopped
- 1 small jalapeño
- 4 garlic cloves, minced
- 1 tablespoon chili powder
- 2 teaspoons ground cumin
- 1½ teaspoons dried oregano
- 4 cups water, plus more for sautéing
- One 15-ounce can diced or chopped tomatoes
- One 8-ounce can tomato sauce
- One 15.5-ounce can kidney beans, drained and rinsed
- One 15.5-ounce can black beans, drained and rinsed
- One 15.5-ounce can white beans, drained and rinsed
- 5 teaspoons vegetable bouillon
- 1 cup bulgur
- Juice of 1 lime
- ⅓ cup soy sauce

COOK THE CHILI

1. Sauté the onion, carrot, celery, bell peppers, and jalapeño in a little water (see Note on page 243) in a large pot over medium-high heat until they soften a bit, 7 to 10 minutes.
2. Add the garlic, and sauté for another minute.
3. Add the chili powder, cumin, and oregano, and mix until the vegetables are coated.
4. Add the remaining 4 cups water, the diced tomatoes, tomato sauce, kidney beans, black beans, white beans, and bouillon. Bring to a boil.
5. Reduce the heat to low, cover, and simmer for 25 minutes.
6. Add the bulgur.
7. Reduce the heat to the lowest setting that will maintain a simmer, and cook, uncovered, for another 25 minutes, stirring occasionally to prevent the bulgur from settling and burning on the bottom of the pot (see Tip).
8. Remove from the heat, add the lime juice and soy sauce, and stir to incorporate. Let cool completely before dehydrating. (You can place it in the refrigerator for a day or two before dehydrating; it will thicken, and the flavor will become richer with time.)

TIP

Pay attention to the consistency as the chili boils—it will thicken as the bulgur cooks, but if it gets too thick, it will burn on the bottom of the pot. If this starts to happen, add a little more water or stop the cooking early.

DEHYDRATE THE CHILI

1. Pour the cooked chili onto solid dehydrator trays in thin, even layers.
2. Dehydrate at 135°F, flipping halfway through, until completely dry and crispy, at least 8 hours.

CHILI MAC

A hearty bowl of chili and macaroni noodles is a great way to end a day of hiking. Soy sauce and lime are the secret ingredients in our favorite chili, along with bulgur, which provides a wonderful texture that is somewhat comparable to a ground beef–based chili. If you prefer, you can dehydrate your own favorite chili recipe. A low-fat chili, like the one we share below (inspired by our favorite chili recipe from *The Whole Foods Market Cookbook: A Guide to Natural Foods with 350 Recipes*)**, will last longer than a fattier chili because fatty food spoils more quickly. A snack-sized bag of Fritos makes a great topping.**

Serves 1 | **485 calories**

BEFORE THE TRAIL

⅔ cup dehydrated Chili (see page 248)

½ cup small elbow macaroni (with a 6- or 7-minute cook time; see Tip on page 239)

ON THE TRAIL

1½ cups water

BEFORE THE TRAIL

1. Cook and dehydrate the chili.
2. Combine the macaroni and dehydrated chili in a ziplock bag, and seal the bag.

ON THE TRAIL

1. Combine the macaroni, chili, and water in a pot. Cover, and bring to a boil over high heat.
2. Reduce the heat to low, and simmer, covered, for 2 minutes, uncovering to stir occasionally. (It will still look watery and uncooked.)
3. Remove from the heat, and let sit, covered, until all of the water is absorbed, 10 minutes. Stir and enjoy.

PEANUT BUTTER PASTA

This creamy pasta dish is so satisfying after a long day of hiking! It is truly one of our favorite dinners on trail. The thick, slightly sweet coconut milk and peanut butter sauce perfectly balances the kick of the cayenne.

Serves 1 | **705 calories**

BEFORE THE TRAIL

2 tablespoons peanut butter powder

1½ teaspoons coconut milk powder

⅛ teaspoon cayenne, or to taste

½ cup small elbow macaroni (with a 6- or 7-minute cook time; see Tip on page 239)

⅓ cup dry roasted, unsalted peanuts

⅓ cup dehydrated veggies (such as broccoli, julienned carrots, and corn; see page 196)

¼ teaspoon table salt

ON THE TRAIL

1¼ cups water

BEFORE THE TRAIL

1. Place the peanut butter powder, coconut milk powder, and cayenne in a small, light bag (e.g., a fold-over sandwich bag), and seal or tie shut.
2. Place the macaroni, peanuts, broccoli, carrots, corn, and salt, along with the small bag of powders, in a larger ziplock bag, and seal the bag.

ON THE TRAIL

1. Set the small bag aside. Combine the macaroni mixture and the water in a pot. Cover, and bring to a boil over high heat, stirring occasionally.
2. Reduce the heat to low, and simmer, covered, for 2 minutes, uncovering to stir occasionally. (It will still look watery and uncooked.)
3. Remove from the heat, and add the contents of the small bag. Stir, cover, and let sit until all of the water is absorbed, 10 minutes. Stir and enjoy.

CREAMY TOMATO ROTINI

Who doesn't love a comforting bowl of pasta at the end of the day? This rotini features a creamy tomato sauce loaded with veggies and beans.

Serves 1 | **490 calories**

BEFORE THE TRAIL

1½ teaspoons nutritional yeast

1½ teaspoons oat milk powder

1 teaspoon Italian seasoning

1 teaspoon sugar

⅔ cup rotini (with a 6- or 7-minute cook time; see Tip on page 239)

⅓ cup dehydrated canned kidney beans (see page 200)

¼ teaspoon table salt

⅓ cup dehydrated veggies (such as onions, mushrooms, zucchini, and broccoli; see page 196)

15 grams dehydrated tomato sauce (about ⅓ cup folded/loosely packed; see page 204)

ON THE TRAIL

1⅓ cups water

BEFORE THE TRAIL

1. Place the nutritional yeast, oat milk powder, Italian seasoning, and sugar in a small, light bag (e.g., a fold-over sandwich bag), and seal or tie shut.
2. Put the rotini, beans, salt, onions, mushrooms, zucchini, broccoli, and tomato sauce, along with the sealed bag of powders, in a larger ziplock bag, and seal the bag.

ON THE TRAIL

1. Set the small bag and the tomato sauce aside. Add the remaining contents of the large bag and the water to a pot. Tear the tomato sauce into small pieces, and add it to the pot. Cover, and bring to a boil over high heat.
2. Reduce the heat to low, and simmer, covered, for 2 minutes, uncovering to stir occasionally to ensure the sauce doesn't burn. (It will still look watery and uncooked.)
3. Remove from the heat, and add the contents of the small bag. Stir, cover, and let sit until all of the water is completely absorbed, 10 minutes. Stir and enjoy.

CREAMY SHELLS IN WHITE SAUCE

Who would have thought you could make a rich white sauce on the trail with just a few nondairy powders? This thick, creamy pasta is full of noodles swimming in a rich sauce. It won't leave you craving town food. (At least, not too much ...)

Serves 1 **660 calories**

BEFORE THE TRAIL

3 tablespoons oat milk powder

1 tablespoon nutritional yeast

1 tablespoon all-purpose flour

½ cup (2 ounces) small pasta shells (with a 6- or 7-minute cook time; see Tip on page 239)

⅓ cup dehydrated canned white beans (see page 200)

⅓ cup dehydrated zucchini, corn, onions, and mushrooms (see page 196)

1 teaspoon vegetable bouillon

½ teaspoon dried parsley

⅛ teaspoon cayenne, optional, but yummy if you like a kick

ON THE TRAIL

1⅓ cups water

BEFORE THE TRAIL

1. Place the oat milk powder, nutritional yeast, and flour in a small, light bag (e.g., a fold-over sandwich bag), and seal or tie shut.
2. Place the pasta, beans, zucchini, corn, onions, mushrooms, bouillon, parsley, and cayenne, if using, along with the small bag of powders, in a larger ziplock bag, and seal the bag.

ON THE TRAIL

1. Set the small bag aside. Combine the water and pasta mixture in a pot. Cover, and bring to a boil over high heat, stirring occasionally.
2. Reduce the heat to low, and simmer, covered, for 2 minutes. (It will still look watery and uncooked.)
3. Remove from the heat, add the contents of the small bag, and mix thoroughly. Cover, and let sit until all of the water is absorbed, 10 minutes. Stir and enjoy.

LAST-MINUTE "RAMEN BOMB"

As great as it is to have wholesome dehydrated meals on the trail, sometimes the opportunity for an adventure comes up at the last minute without the lead time necessary for proper meal prep. Rather than spending a bunch of money on name-brand backpacking food, it is easy to throw together a "ramen bomb," which is a cheap, filling staple item for many long-distance backpackers thruhiking the country's national scenic trails. Our favorite brand of ramen to use is Indomie because it comes with multiple oil and sauce packets!

Serves 2 | **525 calories** | **Cold Soakable**

BEFORE THE TRAIL

¼ cup fried onion topping, optional

One 3-ounce package ramen, including the spice packet (your favorite store-bought flavor)

½ cup instant potatoes (your favorite store-bought flavor)

¼ cup sunflower seeds or other seeds or nuts

2 tablespoons (⅛ cup) sun-dried tomatoes or 1 packet dehydrated "soup vegetables" (see Tip), optional

ON THE TRAIL

1½ cups water

BEFORE THE TRAIL

1. Place the fried onions, if using, in a small, light bag (e.g., a fold-over sandwich bag), and seal or tie shut.
2. Unpackage the ramen, and set aside the spice packet.
3. Place the ramen noodles, instant potatoes, sunflower seeds, and sun-dried tomatoes, if using, along with the sealed bag of fried onions and the ramen spice packet, in a larger ziplock bag, and seal the bag.

ON THE TRAIL

1. Set the small bag of onions aside, if using.
2. Combine the water, ramen spice packet, and ramen noodle mixture in a pot, breaking up the noodles up a bit. Cover, and bring to a boil over high heat, stirring occasionally.
3. Remove from the heat, and let sit, covered, until all of the water is absorbed, 10 minutes.
4. Stir, and top with the fried onions, if using. Enjoy.

TIP

Packets of dehydrated veggies, sometimes labeled as soup vegetables, can be found in some grocery stores or online.

COLD-SOAKED LAST-MINUTE RAMEN BOMB

Place all of the ingredients, except the fried onions, in a sealable container and add the water. Seal the container and shake or mix well. Soak for 45 to 60 minutes while you hike. If using, add fried onions right before eating.

APPLE-PEAR CRISP

We love celebrating special occasions like birthdays on the trail with special treats. This fruity crisp takes some work, but it's worth it.

Serves 1 | **330 calories**

BEFORE THE TRAIL

⅔ cup dehydrated Apple-Pear Filling (see below)

⅓ cup Homemade Granola (page 226)

ON THE TRAIL

⅓ cup water

BEFORE THE TRAIL

1. Cook and dehydrate the apple-pear filling.
2. Place the granola in a small, light bag (e.g., a fold-over sandwich bag), and seal or tie shut.
3. Place the apple-pear filling, along with the small bag of granola, in a larger ziplock bag, and seal the bag.

ON THE TRAIL

1. Set the small bag aside. Combine the water and the apple-pear filling in a pot. Cover, and bring to a boil over high heat.
2. Reduce the heat to low, and simmer for 2 minutes, stirring constantly. (It will still look watery and uncooked.)
3. Remove from the heat, cover, and let sit until all of the water is absorbed, 10 minutes.
4. Stir, and top with granola. Enjoy.

APPLE-PEAR FILLING

Makes about six ⅔-cup dehydrated servings

½ cup all-purpose flour

½ cup brown sugar, packed

2 teaspoons ground cinnamon

¼ teaspoon ground nutmeg

2 medium apples, sliced into ⅓-inch pieces (about 3 cups)

2 large pears, sliced into ⅓-inch pieces (about 3 cups)

Juice of ½ lemon

COOK THE APPLE-PEAR FILLING

1. Preheat the oven to 350°F.
2. Mix the flour, brown sugar, cinnamon, and nutmeg in a medium bowl.
3. Mix the apples, pears, and lemon juice in a large bowl. Add the dry ingredients and mix well.
4. Transfer the mixture to a 9×13-inch glass baking pan, and bake for about 1 hour or until soft.
5. Remove from the oven, and let cool completely before dehydrating.

DEHYDRATE THE APPLE-PEAR FILLING

1. Spread the cooked apple-pear filling onto mesh dehydrator trays in thin, even layers.
2. Dehydrate at 135°F until dry and leathery, at least 8 hours.

TIM'S BIRTHDAY SNICKERS ON THE JOHN MUIR TRAIL

Renee's perspective: We celebrated Tim's 28th birthday on the John Muir Trail. As we were planning for our 2-week hike, I wondered how to make Tim's birthday special. Presents are a challenge when you have to carry everything on your back for days. But backpackers are always dreaming of food, so a Snickers candy bar seemed like the perfect gift, paired with a crossword puzzle. I hid the Snickers bar in one of our food bags. Somehow, when it came time to split up the food to put in our packs, the Snickers ended up in Tim's bag. I felt a bit bad he was carrying the extra weight, but he definitely enjoyed it on his birthday and even gave me a few bites.

Tim's perspective: September 1 is a good date for a birthday. On all of our major trips, I've been lucky enough to celebrate my birthday on the trail. When we hiked the John Muir Trail, my birthday fell toward the end of our trip. We had planned ahead by dehydrating birthday lasagna. (I ate lasagna on my birthday every year growing up, so we figured out how to make a trail version for this trip.) I figured that because we were in the wilderness, Renee wouldn't be able to plan any other surprises, and I was 100 percent okay with that—being in the remote High Sierras was exciting enough! However, when I woke up on September 1, Renee pulled out a birthday crossword puzzle that she had made herself, along with a king-size birthday Snickers bar! The crossword puzzle was perfect—it was virtually weightless, specially made for me, and gave us something fun to do for the day. The Snickers bar was amazing, but while enjoying it I got to thinking ... *Who had carried this gigantic bar for so many days?* Turns out, I had! Renee had hidden the bar inside another food bag that ended up in my backpack. To this day I appreciate the Snickers, but the treat would have been even sweeter if Renee had been the one who carried it!

EASY BEAN DIP WITH CHIPS

Granola bars, nuts, and dehydrated fruit are our go-to snacks while hiking, but it can be fun to mix it up with some bean dip. This is super tasty hot or cold.

Serves 1 | **305 calories** | **Cold Soakable**

BEFORE THE TRAIL

⅓ cup dehydrated Bean Dip (see below)

1 snack-sized bag tortilla chips or Fritos scoops

ON THE TRAIL

⅓ cup water

BEFORE THE TRAIL

1. Prepare and dehydrate the bean dip.
2. Place the bean dip in a ziplock bag, and seal the bag. Keep the bag of chips separate.

ON THE TRAIL

1. One or more hours before eating, place the bean dip in a sealable container and add the water. Seal the container, and shake or mix well. Soak for at least an hour while you hike.
2. Stir to fully mash up the beans, and enjoy with the chips.

BEAN DIP

Makes about five ⅓-cup dehydrated servings

One 16-ounce can fat-free refried beans

One 16-ounce can salsa

1. Mix the refried beans and salsa in a medium bowl.
2. Pour the bean mixture onto flexible plastic dehydrator trays, and spread thinly.
3. Dehydrate at 135°F until completely dry and brittle, about 8 hours.

Cauliflower
Zucchini
Mushrooms
Carrots

THRUHIKERS' TIPS

RECIPES

- Adjust the salt recommendations in the recipes to match your tastes. More salt may be desired on longer or harder hikes.
- In recipes that call for vegetable bouillon, you can adjust the recipe to match the water ratio on your bouillon package. Some bouillons call for 1 teaspoon per 1 cup of water, for example, while others call for 1 teaspoon per 2 cups. Our recipes are calibrated for 1 teaspoon bouillon per 1 cup water.
- We've found that old-fashioned oats keep us full longer than instant oats because old-fashioned oats are less processed.
- In rice-based recipes, dehydrated rice can be substituted with store-bought instant rice, both of which can be cold soaked. Rice dehydrated at home has more flavor and better texture than instant rice.
- Our pasta-based recipes are not cold soakable because the pasta is not precooked.
- For all of the pasta recipes in this book, using noodles that call for a 6- or 7-minute boil time is much more important than the type of noodle. This ensures that they'll cook and absorb water at the same rate as the rest of the meal.
- Choose no- or very low-fat foods to avoid spoiling. (Fats spoil faster than other ingredients.)
- For recipes that include powders or semimoist ingredients like raisins, seal the powder or semimoist food in a small bag and add it to the larger bag with the rest of the ingredients.
- Label bags with the recipe name, amount of water required, and boil time to make cooking on the trail as easy as possible.
- For recipes like chili that require you to cook a large quantity at home before dehydrating, you can make a batch, eat it for dinner at home, and only dehydrate a portion of it for the trail. Or if you have leftover dehydrated food, you can take it to work for lunch if you don't have another backpacking trip scheduled.

CONCLUSION

Now that you've learned about life on the trail, it's time to get out there and make your own memories! If you would like to follow along with our adventures, check out our website at thruhikers.co, or find us on social media: @thruhikers.

BACKPACKING & THRUHIKING LINGO

BASE WEIGHT: The weight of a backpack, excluding consumables such as food and water. Because consumables change during a trip, base weight is a good metric to use to assess how heavy your gear is.

BONK: Running out of energy during exercise by depleting your body's stored fuel. When this happens, you will suddenly feel heavy and slow and you may become sleepy. Prevent bonking by eating more before it happens, and cure it by eating more while bonked.

CAMEL UP: Drinking extra water at water sources to hydrate before a dry stretch of the trail.

CLIMBING: Walking up a steep slope or mountain.

CONTINUOUS FOOTPATH: Long-distance hikes usually involve hitchhiking off trail and into town to resupply and/or sections of trail that are closed due to forest fires. Hikers who achieve a continuous footpath connect every step of a trail, from terminus to terminus, allowing for these blockages along the way. If they hitchhike to resupply, the hiker will return to the exact spot where they left the trail before continuing onward, and if a section of the trail is closed, the hiker will walk a detour around it rather than skipping the section altogether.

COWBOY CAMPING: Camping under the stars with no tent, tarp, or any shelter at all.

FLIP-FLOP: Hiking part of a trail continuously and then leaving the trail, traveling to another point on it, and hiking back to where you left. This type of hike is common when difficult weather conditions, such as late-season snow, make part of a trail difficult but conditions are expected to improve over time.

HIKER BOX: A box where hikers leave gear and supplies they don't need for other hikers to take if they do need it. You can often find these at resupply stops frequented by hikers, such as post offices in trailside towns. Common finds include books, dehydrated food a hiker lost their appetite for, and barely worn shoes that didn't fit right.

HIKER HUNGER: Hiking burns a lot of calories and, therefore, requires A LOT of food. But in the effort to minimize pack weight, there is never enough. Hiker hunger is when a hiker wants to eat anything and everything in sight.

HIKER MIDNIGHT: 9 PM.

LEAVE NO TRACE: A set of principles for minimizing your impact and keeping an area beautiful for others in the future.

NERO: A day hiking "near zero" miles, often paired with a resupply by hiking a few miles into town and then resting, or resting in town and then hiking a few miles out.

NOBO: Northbound.

POST-TRAIL DEPRESSION: Feeling sad after a thruhike and finding it hard to return to daily life.

RESUPPLY: Stopping in a town to get food, gear, or other supplies for the next stretch of trail.

SECTION HIKE: Walking a portion of a long trail but not the whole thing.

SOBO: Southbound.

SOCIAL TRAIL: Unofficial paths created by hikers, often to avoid obstacles such as downed trees obstructing the official trail.

THRUHIKING: Hiking an entire trail from beginning to end. Usually associated with long-distance trails of 100 miles or more.

TRAIL ANGEL: A person who assists hikers on their way. Assistance can include giving hikers a ride into or out of town to resupply, letting hikers use their laundry or showers, and more.

TRAIL MAGIC: A gift left for hikers on a trail, such as a cooler of beer or soda.

TRAIL NAME: A nickname used by a hiker on a trail. Often, but not always, trail names are given by other hikers based on a unique characteristic or funny story.

TRAMILY: A "trail family," or group of people hiking together on a trail, especially a long-distance trail.

TRIPLE CROWN: The three most famous long-distance trails in the United States: the Appalachian Trail (AT), the Pacific Crest Trail (PCT), and the Continental Divide Trail (CDT).

YELLOW BLAZING: Hitchhiking or driving instead of hiking portions of a trail.

ZERO: A day without hiking, usually spent in town resting and recovering during a long trip.

INDEX

D

E

F

G

H

I

J

Q

R

S

T

U

V

W

Y

Z

ACKNOWLEDGMENTS

Thank you to our families, friends, colleagues, and students for believing in, supporting, and putting up with all of our crazy adventures, including this book. A special thanks to Janet Beissinger, Tim's mom, for taking Tim camping when he was young, for giving Renee the book that introduced her to thruhiking, and for reading this manuscript and providing valuable input to improve it.

Thank you to the whole DK team, including Becky, Christy, Georgette, and Johnna. Thanks to our recipe tester, Trish Sebben Malone, photographer, Nader Khouri, and food stylist, Jillian Knox. Thank you to our illustrator, Kendra "Skunkbear" Allenby, whom we met on the Continental Divide Trail while we were all thruhiking it in 2021. A special thanks to our editor, Olivia Peluso, for working on this book with us from beginning to end!

ABOUT THE AUTHORS

Renee Miller and Tim Beissinger, @thruhikers, are outdoor adventurers who love to travel by foot, canoe, bike, ski, or any other form of nonmotorized transport. They thruhiked from Mexico to Canada twice on US National Scenic Trails—the 2,650-mile Pacific Crest Trail in 2018 and the 3,100-mile Continental Divide Trail in 2021. They thruhiked/thru-canoed the Pacific Northwest Circuit—a route they developed—in 2022. It covered 2,700 miles, including the Pacific Northwest Trail and the full length of the Columbia River.

Renee and Tim have backpacked all over the United States and Germany, including 1,000 miles on Germany's named trails, and bike toured in Europe and South America. They also enjoy running, biking, and swimming and have competed in many running and triathlon races, including Ironman.

Renee and Tim also love to cook and eat, especially outside. They have dehydrated and mailed more than a year's worth of backcountry meals that they pick up and eat while out adventuring.

When they are not on a trip, Renee works as an engineer and Tim as a scientist.

They can be found on social media (@thruhikers) and on their website (thruhikers.co).

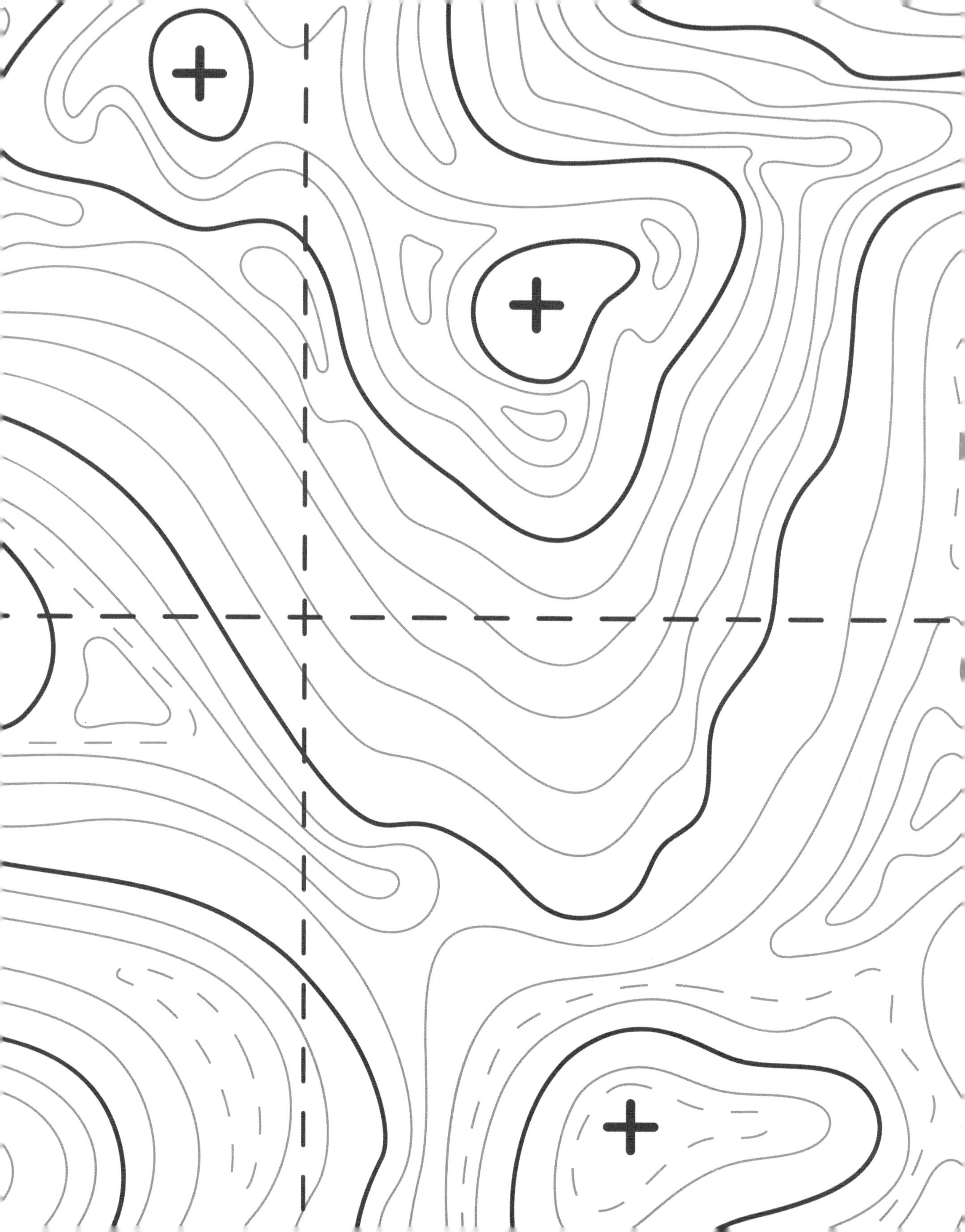